T4-AEB-037

A SHORT HISTORY OF GREECE

A SHORT HISTORY OF
GREECE

FROM EARLY TIMES TO 1964

BY

W. A. HEURTLEY, H. C. DARBY
C. W. CRAWLEY AND
C. M. WOODHOUSE

CAMBRIDGE
AT THE UNIVERSITY PRESS
1965

PUBLISHED BY
THE SYNDICS OF THE CAMBRIDGE UNIVERSITY PRESS

Bentley House, 200 Euston Road, London, N.W. 1
American Branch: 32 East 57th Street, New York 22, N.Y.
West African Office: P.O. Box 33, Ibadan, Nigeria

©
CAMBRIDGE UNIVERSITY PRESS
1965

Printed in Great Britain by
Willmer Brothers & Haram Ltd., Birkenhead

CONTENTS

LIST OF MAPS AND DIAGRAMS   *page* vii

PUBLISHER'S NOTE   viii

I ANCIENT GREECE
by W. A. HEURTLEY

1	Prehistoric Greece	1
2	The Rise of the Greek City States	7
3	Classical Greece	15
4	Macedonian and Hellenistic Greece	25
5	Roman Greece	30

II MEDIEVAL AND TURKISH GREECE
by H. C. DARBY

1	Byzantine Greece	35
2	Frankish and Venetian Greece	52
3	Byzantine Civilization, by S. J. PAPASTAVROU and W. H. PLOMMER	72
4	Turkish Greece	77

III MODERN GREECE, 1821–1939
by C. W. CRAWLEY

1	The War of Independence, 1821–32	91
2	The Reign of Otho I, 1833–62	98
3	The Reign of George I, 1863–1913	101
4	The Crisis of 1912–23	109
5	Domestic Affairs, 1923–40	124
6	Foreign Affairs, 1923–40	130
7	Modern Greek Literature by S. J. PAPASTAVROU	135

CONTENTS

IV MODERN GREECE, 1939–64
by C. M. WOODHOUSE

1	Relations with the Fascist Powers	138
2	The Enemy Occupation	143
3	Post-war Troubles	151
4	The Beginning of Reconstruction	161
5	The Cyprus Dispute	165
6	The Return to Normality	174

BIBLIOGRAPHICAL NOTE 184

INDEX 189

LIST OF MAPS AND DIAGRAMS

1	Prehistoric Greece	page 2
2	Greek Settlements in the Mediterranean, c. 550 B.C.	10
3	Architectural orders—Doric, Ionic and Corinthian	14
4	Greece in 431 B.C.	17
5	Reconstruction and plan of the Acropolis	20
6	Athens	22
7	The empire of Alexander, 323 B.C.	26
8	The Byzantine Empire, A.D. 962–1190	37
9	The Balkan Peninsula about A.D. 800	42
10	The Balkan Peninsula, A.D. 910–1265	44
11	The Balkan Peninsula, 1340–55	45
12	The distribution of the Vlachs in the Balkans	47
13	Greece in 1214	54
14	Greece in 1265	55
15	Greece about 1355	57
16	Greece in 1388	60
17	Venetian possessions in the Greek lands	67
18	Genoese possessions in the Greek lands	70
19	Greece in 1440	78
20	The growth of Greece, 1832–1922	98
21	The Balkans in 1878	104
22	Rectification of the Turco-Greek frontier, 1897	106
23	The Balkans, 1912–13	112
24	The Macedonian Front, 1918	116
25	The languages of Greece and adjoining areas	118
26	Major ethnic groups in Macedonia, 1912 and 1926	122
27	The Occupation of Greece, 1941	144
28	Modern Greece	162

PUBLISHER'S NOTE

Most of the material and all the maps in this book were originally published by the Naval Intelligence Division of the Admiralty as part of a Handbook on Greece, in three volumes, for service use. By arrangement with the Controller of Her Majesty's Stationery Office, the original owner of the copyright, the historical sections are now reissued in this shorter form. The original contributors were C. W. Crawley, Professor H. C. Darby and the late W. A. Heurtley. A chapter on the history of Greece since 1939 has been added by the Hon. C. M. Woodhouse, M.P. The publishers gratefully acknowledge the help of Professor N. G. L. Hammond, Professor R. Jenkins, Mr S. J. Papastavrou, Dr W. H. Plommer and Mr F. H. Stubbings.

Complete consistency in the transliteration of Greek proper names is impossible. Where there is an anglicized version it has been used, otherwise the Greek spelling has been followed as far as possible.

Three companion volumes have already been published: *A Short History of Germany, 1815–1945*, by E. J. Passant, with contributions by C. J. Child, W. O. Henderson, and Donald Watt; *A Short History of France*, by H. Butterfield, D. W. Brogan, H. C. Darby, and J. Hampden Jackson, with contributions by Sir Ernest Barker, A. Ewert, and I. L. Foster; and *A Short History of Italy*, by the late C. M. Ady and the late A. J. Whyte, revised and edited by H. Hearder and D. P. Waley.

CHAPTER I

ANCIENT GREECE

1. PREHISTORIC GREECE

GREEK history, narrowly speaking, begins about 800 B.C., but Greek origins go back for more than two thousand years before that date. Civilizations had succeeded one another and had left material remains. Though it is not possible to speak of a historical background to those remains, it is possible, by piecing together the evidence of archaeology, mythology, tradition and legend, to gain a more or less coherent picture, at least in outline, of the general course of events. For the earlier phases, the principal evidence is, for obvious reasons, supplied by archaeological excavation, but the interpretation of this evidence is naturally somewhat speculative.

THE BEGINNINGS, BEFORE 3000 B.C.

The earliest inhabitants of Greece of whom we have any knowledge were in a pre-metal stage of civilization. Their settlements, most numerous in the plains of Thessaly, which suited their agricultural economy, are now known to date in some cases as far back as the 5th or 6th millennium B.C. Their tools and weapons were of stone, and their pottery, both plain and painted, was of exceptionally fine quality. A similar culture is represented in central Greece at least as far south as Corinth; and Crete too had an equal early neolithic civilization, best known from the central site of Cnossus, but this seems to have had but little contact with the mainland. The origins of these cultures are still obscure, though evidence of affinities with Asia Minor is accumulating.

In a second phase of this pre-metal age, settlement in central Greece and the Peloponnese seems denser than before. Many old sites remained occupied, but, at some, changes in pottery and new house-types suggest the arrival of a new people; and the occurrence of a few fortified settlements illustrates for the

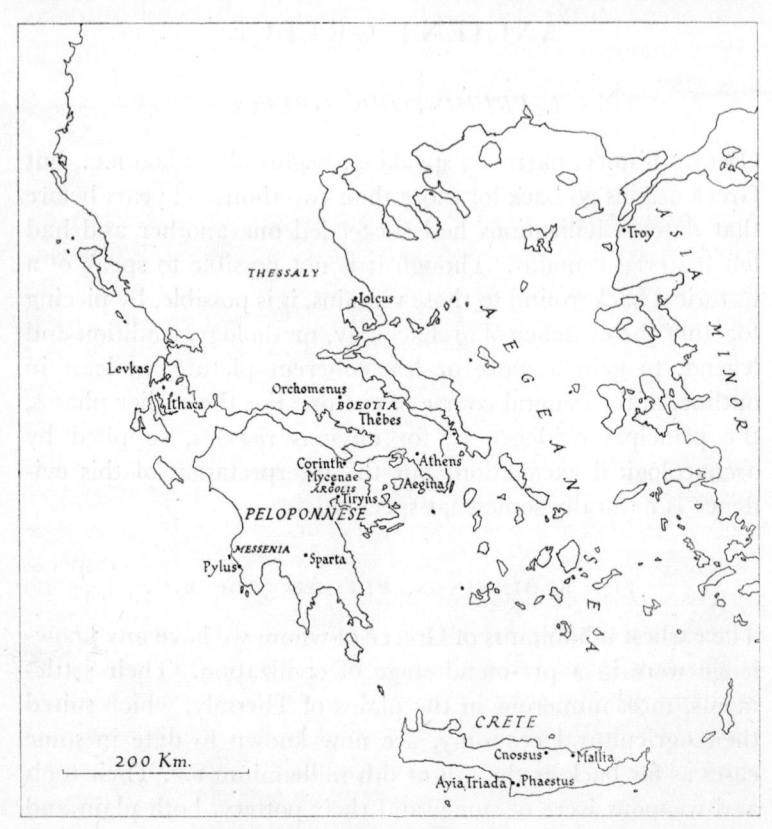

Fig. 1. Prehistoric Greece

first time a recurring feature in Greece's history: the possibility of conquest and government by relatively small bodies of well-organized invaders.

THE MINOAN AND HELLADIC CIVILIZATIONS, 3000–1100 B.C.

The use of metal (first copper, then bronze), already long

familiar in the East, had been spreading westwards and had reached the coast of Asia Minor. From here it was carried, early in the third millennium B.C., by what seems to have been a mass migration of people to Greece, overland through Macedonia into Thessaly, and by sea via the islands to central and southern Greece and Crete.

The Minoan Civilization

This third civilization carried with it the seeds of development, which reached their full flowering in Crete. The geographical position of the island favoured intercourse with Egypt and the East, and, owing to this intercourse and to their own natural talents, the Cretans made a rapid advance in knowledge and skill. In their spacious palaces, designed for comfort and convenience, life seems to have been easy and serene. The arts flourished, especially those of the lapidary, the goldsmith, the worker in ivory, the fresco painter and the vase painter; and such a degree of excellence was reached in these arts that Cretan civilization can be compared with, and in some respects surpasses, that of Egypt or Sumeria. The centre of all this splendour was the great palace of Cnossus; other palaces were at Phaestus, Ayia Triada, and Mallia. That the Cretans were familiar with the art of writing is proved by the hundreds of clay tablets, inscribed first with pictographs which may represent words and later with linear signs which represent syllables. This 'Linear B' script has been found only at Cnossus, and on the mainland at Pylus and Mycenae. The earlier 'Linear A' script occurs only in Crete.

The Minoan civilization, so called after the legendary king Minos, seems to have been based on sea-power and on seaborne trade; and evidence has been found of Minoan contacts not only with Greece, Syria and Egypt but with lands as far distant as Sicily and Spain. Perhaps it was the sense of security given them by their navy which allowed the islanders to leave unfortified their palaces and the towns which clustered around them. Consequently, when invasion came, after more than a thousand years of peaceful development, it found them unprepared.

The Helladic Civilization

On the mainland, development was much less rapid. The immigrants of the early third millennium B.C. settled in the neighbourhood of Corinth, in Argolis, and on the island of Aegina. From here, perhaps, they spread northwards into Boeotia and the Sperchios valley and southwards as far as Messenia, and, eventually, westwards to Ithaca and Levkas in the Ionian islands. Their standard of living was not high; and their settlements were small, not more than villages, and only rarely fortified. Their potters produced vases of extraordinarily fine quality, but undecorated: simple gold ornaments have been found in their tombs.

Middle Helladic

About 2000 B.C. signs of upheaval appear on the mainland. At some sites, marks of a general conflagration, houses of a new type built on the debris of the earlier, new styles of pottery, and different burial customs, indicate a change of population. Converging lines of evidence make it likely that this upheaval was caused by the entry into central and southern Greece of the first Greek-speaking people, sometimes called Achaeans, perhaps as part of a westward movement through Asia Minor. The new civilization, now known as Middle Helladic, which was to prevail for four hundred years, may have been materially poorer than that which it displaced; but its pottery, especially its plain wares, suggests an austere and controlled vigour.

The Mycenaean Civilization

The contact of this civilization with that of Crete produced great changes, and, from about 1600 B.C. onwards, palaces very like the Minoan were being built for the nobles of the mainland; Minoan artists were decorating them and Minoan craftsmen were supplying objects of luxury. Thus arose the civilization known as Mycenaean, in which Minoan imagination was yoked to Helladic restraint and order. The fusion is illustrated by the difference between the palaces of the mainland and those of Crete itself. The Minoan palace is a medley of rooms and corridors which seems to have grown rather than to have been planned. The Mycenaean palace, on the other hand, gives the impression of having been planned in relation to the *megaron* or hall, in which stood the hearth; the hall was approached by a series of vestibules, broad stairways and ramps leading directly from the main gateway in the circuit wall. The reason for this arrangement was perhaps religious, the hearth having a sacred and symbolic character, and being the focus of the life of the palace. Mycenaean palaces too, in contrast to Minoan, were strongly fortified, the seats of a quasi-feudal aristocracy, perhaps newly arrived and themselves creating the demand for Minoan fashions. The first of these overlords at Mycenae, the chief centre, were buried in the rectangular Shaft Graves, but this type of royal burial was soon replaced throughout southern and central Greece by the 'beehive' tombs, the most distinctive architectural monuments of the Mycenaeans. The profusion of gold vessels and ornaments in the Shaft Graves suggests a somewhat barbaric taste, but mainland craftsmen learned rapidly from their Minoan masters, and within 200 years of the first contacts with Crete there is little to distinguish the two cultures, with some hints of a mainland reaction upon Cnossus itself. Indeed the occurrence of Linear B script on the mainland, and the decipherment, in 1952 by Michael Ventris, of the Linear B texts of both areas as an early form of Greek, make it almost certain that by the 15th century B.C. Mycenaeans had conquered Cnossus; but whether it became subordinate to Mycenae or was ruled by some independent prince we cannot tell. Either way, the two centres seem to have become rivals, perhaps as competitors for east Mediterranean trade; and when *c.* 1400 B.C. we find the Minoan palaces sacked, never fully to recover, this can hardly be attributed to any power but one from the mainland. For henceforth the Mycenaeans were dominant in the Aegean and expanded their overseas activity throughout the east Mediterranean, notably in Cyprus, important for its copper mines. For nearly two hundred years more the mainland palace sites at Mycenae, Tiryns, and Pylus, with other minor centres, continued to prosper, though not, we may deduce, without internal rivalries, early in the course of which Orchomenos and Thebes in central Greece had been eclipsed by Mycenae and the Peloponnese.

The Trojan War

About 1200 B.C. an expedition in which most of the Mycenaean nobility took part was launched. Ostensibly it sought to avenge the abduction of Helen, the wife of Menelaus, king of Sparta, by Alexander (Paris) of Troy, but in reality it aimed at obtaining control of the commercial advantages which Troy at the entrance to the Dardanelles commanded as mistress of the shortest crossing for trade between Europe and Asia. Here was the key to the rich Black Sea trade. The expedition achieved its immediate object, the capture of Troy, and left a profound impression on Greek folk memory; but, ultimately, it turned out to be a disaster, for the Mycenaean power never recovered from the exhaustion which the protracted campaign had involved.

THE DORIAN INVASIONS, 1100–800 B.C.

Almost as great an impression was left by another event or series of events, which occurred within the 'third generation' after the Trojan war, and which completed the disintegration of the Mycenaean power. This event was the 'coming of the

Dorians'. The Dorian invasion formed part of wider movements which were taking place beyond the northern frontiers of Greece, and which had the effect of shifting southwards Greek tribes already established in northern Greece, who, in their turn, displaced others. Aided by weapons of iron, the Dorians pushed through to the Peloponnese, dispossessed the Mycenaeans, destroyed their strongholds, and drove them overseas or into the mountains. This movement was long drawn-out, and the unsettled conditions of the time were unfavourable to civilization.

The art of the 'Dark Ages', as this period has not inappropriately been named, is known chiefly from the gigantic painted vases which have been found associated with tombs or sanctuaries. On the mainland of Greece, the last phase of Minoan-Mycenaean vase-painting lingered sufficiently long for some of its elements to be incorporated in the new style which succeeded it. The vase-painters' repertoire now consisted almost exclusively of rectilinear designs, which, in Attica, came to be symmetrically disposed with mathematical precision over the whole surface of the vase. Votive offerings made of bronze, which often take the form of figurines of men or animals, have been found in sanctuaries, notably at Olympia. The art of this period is known under the generic name of 'Geometric'.

2. THE RISE OF THE GREEK CITY STATES

THE GROWTH OF THE CITY STATE, AFTER 800 B.C.

The years following the arrival of the Dorians, from 800 B.C. onwards, were marked by recovery after invasion and by the rise of the city state. The beginnings of this characteristic Greek institution date from the later days of Mycenaean rule, when, mainly for reasons of security, the inhabitants of a district moved from their scattered villages and took up their abode beneath the walls of the neighbouring castle. Thus, in

Attica, these villages or groups of villages were originally independent, and it was only when the lords of the Acropolis had obtained a certain pre-eminence that the villages surrendered their independence and merged their governments in a single government with its centre at Athens. By this arrangement, Athens became the head of a united state, which included all Attica, and of which all the inhabitants of Attica became citizens. The political rights of citizenship could be exercised at any time by going to Athens, and the duty of the state to protect its citizens in time of danger was recognized by allowing them to shelter within the walls. The other city states developed on more or less similar lines, but the villages of Boeotia were never welded into complete unity with the leading city of Thebes; and in the Peloponnese the city of Sparta always remained dominant in relation to the other settlements, whose inhabitants had no political rights in the Spartan state.

The years following the formation of the city state formed essentially a period of experiment in methods of government. Athens, for instance, soon passed from monarchy to oligarchy; next, an attempt to establish a 'tyranny' (the Greek term for the unconstitutional rule of an individual) in 630 B.C. failed; then the rich industrialist, Solon, was given dictatorial power to introduce constitutional and social reforms on democratic lines (594 B.C.); from 561 to 528 B.C. the 'tyrant' Peisistratus was in power, a period incidentally of great building and artistic activity; finally in 507 B.C., the reforms of Cleisthenes introduced a genuinely democratic constitution, in which the Assembly of citizens had sovereign power. The other states, after somewhat similar experiments, arrived at some kind of democratic government, with the exception of Sparta, which retained its peculiar dual kingship and constitution based on a rigid military code, attributed to the semi-legendary law-giver Lycurgus.

Despite their democratic character, slavery was a common institution in the Greek city states, especially in the fifth and fourth centuries B.C. It was justified by the Greeks on the grounds of necessity; without it, citizens would be unable to devote their time to serving the state. The slaves were mostly Thracians, Scythians and Asiatics, and only rarely Greeks. For the most part they were either purchased or captured in war or piracy. They were employed in domestic work, in agriculture, in industry (conditions in the silver mines of Laurium were very bad), and in public service as roadmen, clerks and policemen. There have been very varied estimates about the number of slaves in Greece, and it has even been said that the slave population of fifth-century Athens outnumbered the freemen.

All the city states had this in common, that in relation to their neighbours they were sovereign and independent. Between them, boundaries were fixed, war or peace declared, ambassadors exchanged, treaties and alliances made. All the apparatus, in fact, which has been employed throughout history by large countries or empires in their mutual relations, is here seen in full employment by tiny states, most of them smaller than an English county. The process of world history, exhibited in microcosm, gives a peculiar value to Greek history.

It has been said with truth that there is no history of ancient Greece, only a history of separate Greek states. But despite this political dismemberment and despite their local antagonisms, the Greeks were spiritually one. The rise of the great sanctuaries at Delphi and Olympia, the institution of periodic festivals and games, the peculiar position of the Delphic oracle described as the 'common hearth of Greece'—all these stand for the Greek consciousness of a common heritage, and for a strong sense of unity.

GREEK COLONIZATION, 770–550 B.C.

Commercial enterprise went hand in hand with political experiment. This commercial development was earliest and greatest not in mainland Greece, but among the Ionian cities of western Asia Minor, peopled, so tradition ran, by Greeks from Attica in the days of the Dorian invasions. These cities were aided in their early development by contacts with the rich inland state of Lydia. The leading city, Miletus, opened up the Black Sea trade. Phocea and Samos similarly opened up trade with the western Mediterranean. A great movement of colonization was thus inaugurated between 770 and 550 B.C. (Fig. 2).

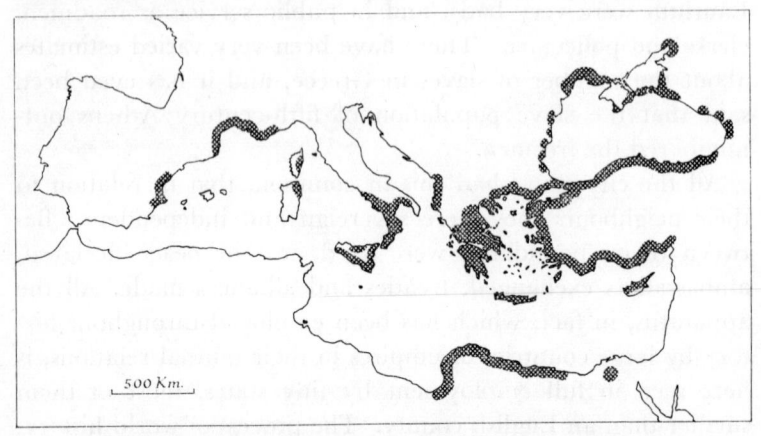

Fig. 2. Greek settlements in the Mediterranean, *c.* 550 B.C.
Based on W. R. Shepherd, *Historical Atlas*, p. 12 (London, 1930).
Note the absence of Greek settlements in north-west Africa and south-east Spain—areas occupied by the Carthaginians.

Commerce, however, was not the only motive for founding colonies. Discontented with conditions at home, especially in those states where a defective land system made it difficult for many to get a living, or impelled merely by a spirit of adventure, groups of citizens set sail to try their fortunes overseas. Once founded, these colonies remained politically independent but in as close touch with their mother cities as circumstances permitted; they sent representatives to the Pan-Hellenic games, and never lost consciousness of being Hellenic cities and outposts of civilization among barbarians. Some of these cities have vanished, but many have survived; Syracuse, Taranto and Istanbul, for example, were originally Greek colonies.

As their trade expanded, Greek merchants were brought into relations with Phoenician merchants of the Syrian coast-towns,

THE RISE OF THE GREEK CITY STATES

who had for some centuries monopolized the trade of the Mediterranean, and who already had trading stations in Greece, on the coast of Asia Minor, in Sicily and North Africa and beyond. The result of Greek competition was to deprive these Phoenicians of their Aegean and of some of their Sicilian markets, and to confine them to the eastern and western corners of the Mediterranean and the African coast.

Trade was revolutionized in the late seventh century by the invention of coinage, values having previously been estimated in heads of cattle. This invention was due to the Lydians of Asia Minor, and was adopted from them by their neighbours, the Ionian Greeks, from whom it passed to the other city states.

THE RISE OF HELLENIC CIVILIZATION

The early importance of Ionian Greece on the western shores of Asia Minor was evident not only in colonizing activity but also in artistic development. It was here, too, that the beginnings of Greek literature and philosophy were to be found. Some have called this early development 'the springtime of Greece'; others have named it 'Greece before Greece'; and it has also been said that 'Greece was educated by Ionia'. This early development was at one time obscure, but it is now evident that the inland state of Lydia in Asia Minor played an important role in the evolution of the Ionian cities.

Vase painting

In the Ionian cities, in Cyprus and in Crete, the Minoan-Mycenaean civilization had not come so near to vanishing point as on the mainland; and now, quickened by contact with the civilizations of Egypt and the East, metal-working, vase-painting and other arts revived. From Cyprus and Crete the products of these schools soon found their way to the mainland where similar local schools experimented with the new elements, each in its own way. 'Geometric' art was revolutionized. For about a century and a half, that is from about 700 to 550 B.C., Corinthian vases dominated the market, and were exported in large quantities to Sicily and Italy, but around 550 the monopoly had passed to Athens, on account of the superiority of her potters and painters, and the great period of Attic vase painting now began. Many of the pictures painted, or rather sketched, on these vases are masterpieces, and exhibit the finest qualities of Greek art. The cutting of dies in the mints of many of the Greek city states also gave Greek craftsmen an opportunity for the exercise of their amazing skill and sense of beauty in the production of coins.

Sculpture

Among the earliest subjects of Greek sculpture, standing figures, male and nude, are very frequent. They have been found at various sanctuaries on the mainland and in some of the islands, and were dedications, set up in the precincts of temples, according to Greek religious custom. Terra-cotta prototypes of these figures, dating from about 700 B.C., have been located in Crete, where, indeed, Greek tradition itself placed the origin of Greek sculpture. The life-size figures of this type, in stone and later in marble, in the rest of Greece and the islands, belong mostly to the sixth century and are the products of local schools, but many show strong Ionian influences.

Architectural sculpture during this period is represented in the Acropolis Museum by some remarkable sculptured groups from the pediments (gables) of temples or shrines on the Acropolis destroyed by the Persians. These figures are of coarse local stone and, except for the flesh parts, are painted in bright colours. Sculpture in relief was also popular, either in the form of architectural ornament or of tombstones. Finds in bronze and ivory also show considerable technical development.

Architecture

In this period was fixed the type of the Greek temple, based on the Mycenaean *megaron*, to which, in course of time, more and more columns were added. The closed central part (*sikos*) was divided into a vestibule, a hall (*naos*) in which was the statue of the god, and a room at the back (*opisthodomos*) reserved for the temple treasure or votive offerings. A row of columns ran round the *sikos*. The altar at which offerings were made stood outside the temple in the open air. The temple and its altar stood in a walled enclosure (*ieron*), which might include other temples with their altars, small shrines and votive statues, as at Delphi, for instance, or Olympia. Architecturally, Greek temples are of three 'orders', the Doric, the Ionic and the Corinthian, readily distinguished by differences in their columns (Fig. 3).

Literature

In this period, too, Greek literature, philosophy and science had their beginnings, and these, as in the case of the visual arts, must be looked for outside Greece. Homer, the earliest Greek poet and perhaps the greatest, is believed to have composed the *Iliad* in Ionia, and a later poet composed the *Odyssey*, attributed also to Homer. These epics reflect contemporary civilization to some degree, but they are concerned with events which had occurred some four centuries earlier—the Trojan war and its aftermath. The mature perfection of their technique, and their elaborate rules and conventions, presuppose a school of epic poetry with a long tradition behind it. This school may, conceivably, have had its origin in the lays sung by minstrels at the courts of Achaean nobles. The first authors of the rare fragments of lyric poetry which have survived and which show no less distinction in this more intimate class of poetry were also the eastern Greeks of Asia Minor. Thales, the first of the long line of brilliant Greek thinkers, who sought to solve the problem of the universe, was a Greek of Miletus. Other Ionian thinkers were Anaximander, Pythagoras and Hecataeus.

A CORNICE
B FRIEZE
C ARCHITRAVE
D CAPITAL
E SHAFT
F STYLOBATE
G BASE

DORIC IONIC CORINTHIAN

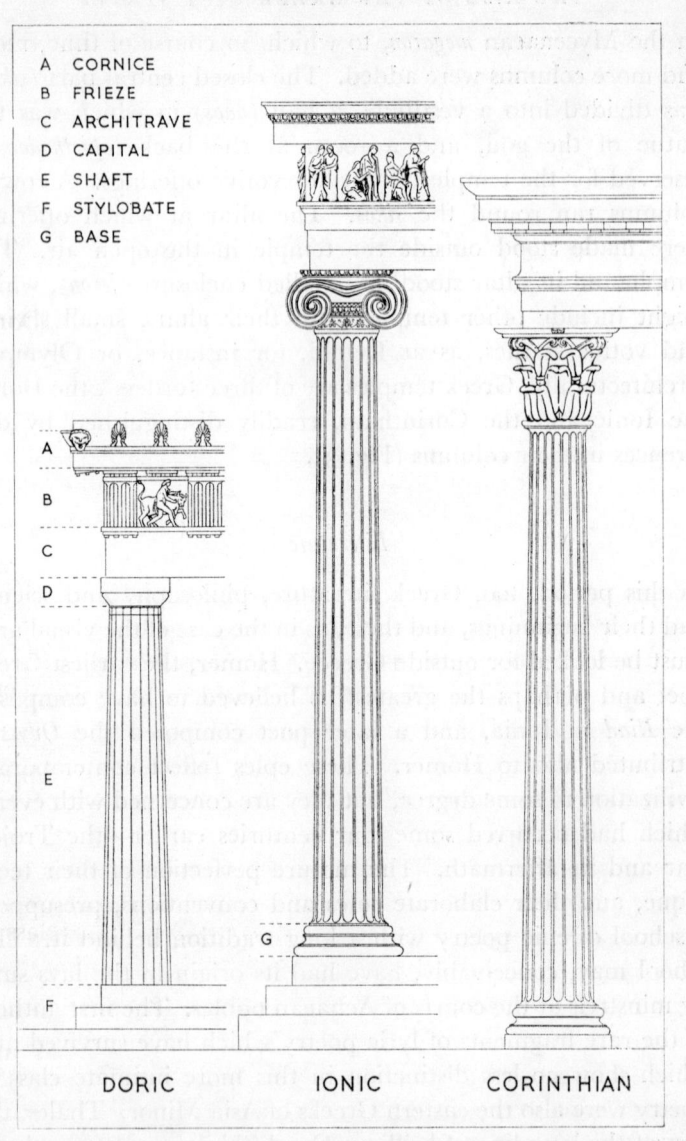

Fig. 3. Architectural orders—Doric, Ionic and Corinthian
Doric, based on the Parthenon, Athens; Ionic, from the Erechtheum, Athens; Corinthian, from the Temple of Olympian Zeus, Athens.
Only a general impression of the chief characteristics of the three orders can be given on such small-scale drawings.

14

3. CLASSICAL GREECE

THE PERSIAN WARS

Towards the end of the sixth century B.C. there came an event which was to have a profound influence on Greek history. In order to understand this, it is necessary to consider the historical events which had formed a background to the high civilization of Ionia on the western shores of Asia Minor. The relations between the Greek settlements there and their inland neighbours had been fairly good, at least until the seventh century, when they fell under the control of the inland state of Lydia. The Lydians, in turn, were defeated by the expanding state of Persia in 546 B.C., and the Greek cities of Ionia automatically became part of the vast Persian empire, now stretching to the borders of India. But in 499 B.C., these Greek cities revolted, and it was this revolt which was to have far-reaching effects on their fellow-Greeks in the west, for Athens had assisted the Ionian Greeks, and Darius, the Persian king, determined to punish the insignificant little city which had defied him. He sent a fleet of transports to the coast of Attica (490 B.C.); the troops disembarked in the bay of Marathon and were attacked by a small force of Athenians who had marched out from Athens. After a short engagement, the Persians were routed and hastily re-embarked for home. Ten years later, Xerxes, the successor of Darius, dispatched another expedition. The army came by land through Macedonia, and the fleet sailed along the coast. The army was halted at the pass of Thermopylae by a small force of Spartans, whose heroic resistance was, however, soon overcome, and the Persians pressed on to Attica. They took Athens and destroyed all the buildings on the Acropolis. The Greek fleet, however, more than half of which was Athenian, defeated the Persian fleet in the Bay of Salamis. In the following year the Persian army, which had withdrawn to an entrenched camp on the north slope of Mt Cithaeron near the town of Plataea, was routed by a confederate Greek army. Salamis and Plataea were decisive, and the Persian menace was thus effectively removed.

By this time, the pattern of Greece as it was to be during the next three centuries had taken shape. The five city states, Athens, Sparta, Thebes, Argos and Corinth, had each acquired that individuality with which they were henceforth to be associated in later times. The subsequent history of Greece until the time of the Roman conquest was to be, in a great measure, the history of the interrelations of these five city states.

Curiously enough, the Cretans, who had played such a great part in the prehistoric period, scarcely appeared in the affairs of classical Greece. Thus they took no part either in the Persian or in the Peloponnesian wars, nor in any of the conflicts of the Hellenistic period. The internal history of Crete during these years, as Polybius (202–120 B.C.) has told us, was one long series of bitter civil wars. The leading cities involved were Cnossus, Gortyn and Cydonia, though, in alliance with these, there were many other independent cities.

THE ATHENIAN EMPIRE AND THE PELOPONNESIAN WAR

The prestige acquired by Athens, from her share in the defeat of the Persians, enabled her to found a maritime confederacy with its headquarters and treasury in the island of Delos, and later to transform the confederacy into an empire based largely on tribute (Fig. 4). The treasury was shortly afterwards removed to Athens 'for security' (454 B.C.), and some of the money was used to pay for the ambitious building programme of the statesman Pericles, now leader of the Athenian democracy. This high-handed action on the part of Athens provoked hostility throughout Greece, and many of the city states prepared to range themselves on the side of Sparta, between whom and Athens, it was clear, rival interests and 'ideology' would inevitably lead to a collision.

In 431 B.C. the Peloponnesian war broke out, a war in which most of the city states took part. The conflict has become more famous than perhaps its importance and the numbers engaged

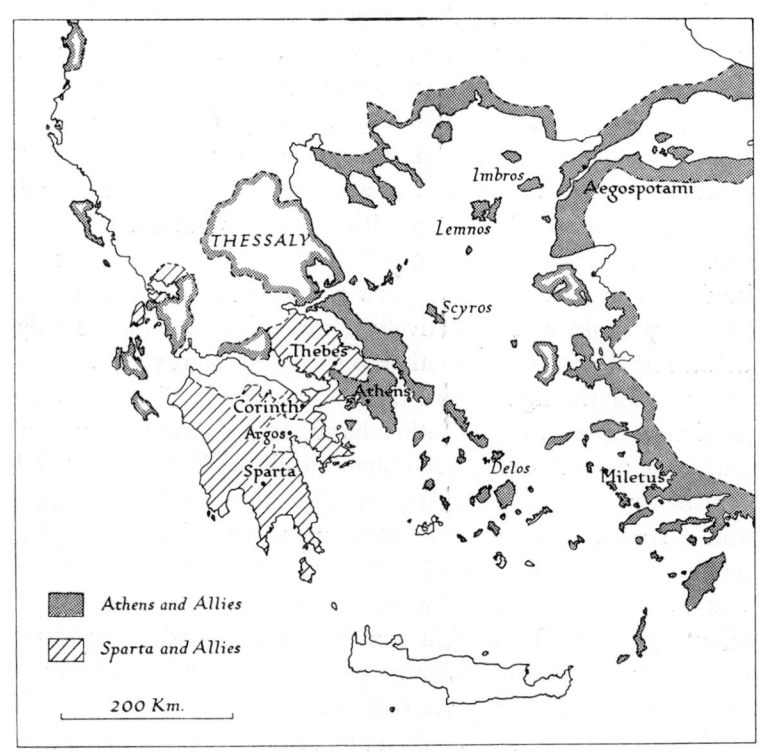

Fig. 4. Greece in 431 B.C.

Based on: (1) J. B. Bury, *A History of Greece*, p. 396 (London, 1924); (2) W. R. Shepherd, *Historical Atlas*, p. 17 (London, 1930).
The areas of the non-tributary allies of Athens (e.g. Thessaly) are not completely shaded.

in it would seem to justify, because detailed description of it has been left by a historian of genius, Thucydides, himself a contemporary and a participant. Moreover, the war is of peculiar interest to a student of sea-power, because, as well as exemplifying a struggle between rival political ideologies, it is a fine example on a small scale of how a war waged between a maritime and a continental power tends to be conducted.

Pericles himself had a clear vision of the strategy involved. To the Athenians he said: 'The visible field of action has two parts, land and sea. In the whole of one of these you are completely supreme. . . . Your naval resources are such that your vessels may go where they please.' Of the Spartans he wrote: 'In a single battle the Peloponnesians and their allies may be able to defy all Hellas, but they are incapacitated from carrying on a war against a power different in character from their own. . . . Familiarity with the sea they will not find an easy acquisition.' As a maritime power with only a small army, Athens was obliged to avoid large-scale engagements on land, and to seek out those parts of the theatre of war where her navy could most effectively damage Spartan interests by detaching Spartan allies either by force or persuasion. This accounts for the fighting off the western coasts of Greece and in Sicily. Sparta, on the other hand, as a continental power with only a weak navy, was obliged to direct her blows at the continental possessions of Athens. Thus the invasion of Attica and destruction of the crops right up to the walls of Athens formed the routine part of each year's campaign, and there was much fighting in Thrace, where Athens had powerful tributary allies. It is little wonder therefore that, with the opponents fighting in different spheres, the struggle dragged on for years in an indecisive fashion.

The weakness of the Athenian position was that she depended for her food supply on imported corn, and should her 'life-line' be cut, she would be faced with starvation. The main source of her corn supply was south Russia, and Athenian interest in the route to the Black Sea was correspondingly great; the islands of Scyros, Lemnos and Imbros marked the way. Whenever the Athenian Assembly met, the agenda always contained the item 'Respecting corn'. Thus ten times a year attention was officially drawn to this vital question. At length in 405 B.C. Athenian power was crushed at its weakest spot. The

Athenian navy was caught by surprise and destroyed at Aegospotami in the Hellespont itself. The Spartans had succeeded in fitting out an adequate fleet with the aid of Persia, and it was by sheer good fortune that they had in Lysander an exceptionally competent admiral. In the following year, Athens was blockaded and forced by famine to surrender. Treachery also contributed to the Athenian downfall, and this is not surprising, for there were in almost every city state discontented factions, prepared to assist the common enemy if, by so doing, they could destroy their political rivals or upset the existing constitution.

Despite Spartan predominance, Athens later succeeded, amidst the complicated rivalries of the Greek city states, in recovering something of her lost empire. It is interesting to note which three islands she bargained for and obtained— Scyros, Lemnos and Imbros. At last by the Peace of Callias in 371 B.C. the two states agreed to recognize each other's predominance: that of Athens on sea and that of Sparta on land. During the struggle, Corinth, at first dreading the development of Athenian trade, had been on the side of Sparta; but after 395 B.C. the domineering attitude of Sparta forced her into alliance with Athens.

But already new forces were rising in the Greek world. Thebes became prominent for a time, but by now the political life of Greece was in great confusion. The mutual rivalries of the city states were intense, and within each city the rivalry of parties was so great that it often endangered the life of the state. Into this confusion the new power of Macedonia was soon to arrive.

THE CIVILIZATION OF THE FIFTH AND FOURTH CENTURIES B.C.

Much more important than the political history of Greece was the Greek contribution to the art and thought of later times. The intense life of the small communities of the Greek city

ANCIENT GREECE

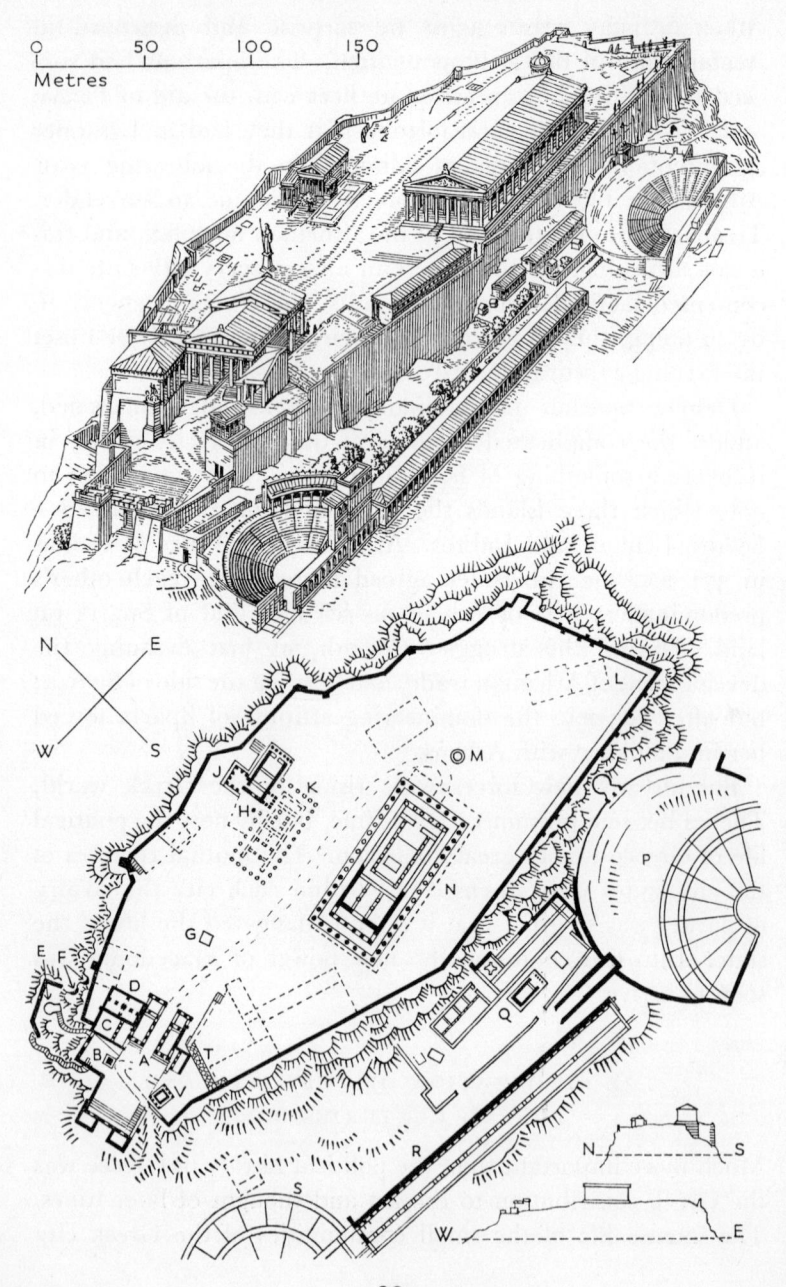

CLASSICAL GREECE

states brought artistic achievement to its highest point. The architecture of fifth-century Athens reached a splendour unknown in Europe up till then and perhaps unsurpassed since; and in this glorious setting the writers and thinkers of the city produced works that have become the inspiration of later times.

Architecture

The great period of classical Greece, the fifth and fourth centuries B.C., was one of great building activity. During these years the Greek temple reached and passed its zenith. In the fifth century the Parthenon, the Erechtheum, and the Theseum were built at Athens; the great temple of Zeus at Olympia; the temples at Bassae, Sunium, and Aegina; and the round temple at Delphi. To the fourth century B.C. belong the temple at Tegea, and the new temple of Apollo at Delphi. Of secular buildings, the Propylaea on the Acropolis were built in the fifth century, and the monument of Lysicrates in the fourth. To the fourth century also belong many of the theatres, of which that of Epidaurus is the most noteworthy, and many of the secular buildings attached to the great sanctuaries, as, for instance, the Leonidaeum at Olympia, and the Gymnasium at Epidaurus. Some of the finest examples of fortifications, too, were built in the fourth century—at Eleutherae, Messene and elsewhere.

Fig. 5. Reconstruction and plan of the Acropolis

Based on drawings from (1) H. Luckenbach, *Kunst und Geschichte*, pp. 41–2 (Munich and Berlin, 1920); (2) Sir Banister Fletcher, *History of Architecture*, p. 77 (London, 1896, 10th ed. 1938).

A   Propylaea
B   Pedestal of Agrippa
C   Pinacotheca
D   Roman cistern
E   Clepsydra
F   Caves of Apollo and Pan
G   Statue of Athena Promachus
H   Sacred Olive tree
J   Erechtheum
K   Old Temple of Athens
L   Platform for votive statues
M   Roman temple
N   Parthenon
P   Theatre of Dionysus
Q   Aesculapium
R   Stoa of Eumenes
S   Odeum of Herodes Atticus
T   Mycenaean wall
V   Temple of Athena of Victory

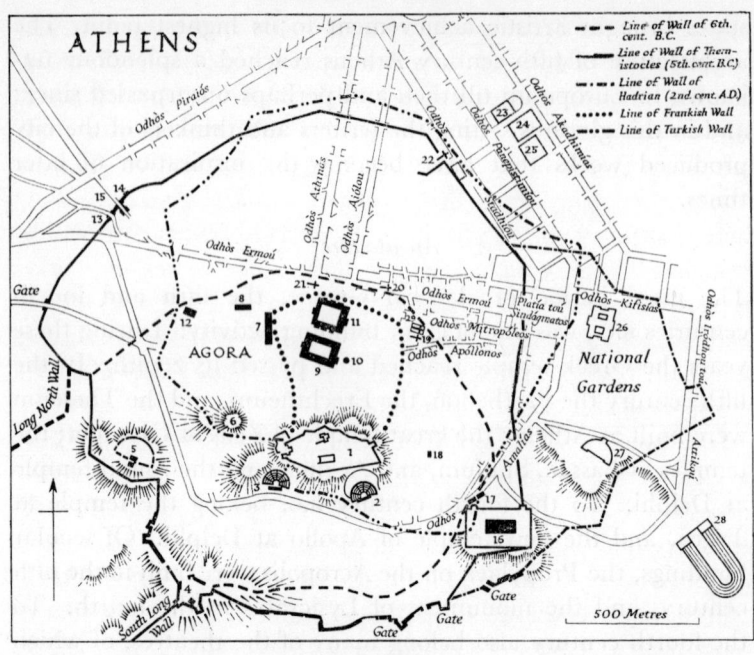

Fig. 6. Athens

Based on plans in *Les Guides Bleus—Grèce*, pp. 11 and 20 (Paris, 1935).

Classical Monuments: 1, Acropolis; 2, Theatre of Dionysus; 3, Odeum of Herodes Atticus; 4, Tomb of Philopappos; 5, Pnyx; 6, Areopagus; 7, Portico of Attalus; 8, Portico of the Giants; 9, Roman Market; 10, Tower of the Winds; 11, Library of Hadrian; 12, Theseum Temple of Hephaestus; 13, The Sacred Gate; 14, The Dipylon Gate; 15, Cemetery; 16, Temple of Olympian Zeus; 17, Arch of Hadrian; 18, Monument of Lysicrates. *Byzantine Churches:* 19, The Old Cathedral (Ayios Elevtherios); 20, Church of Kapnikarea; 21, Church of Our Lady of the Great Monastery; 22, Church of Saint Theodore. *Modern Buildings:* 23, University Library; 24, University; 25, Academy; 26, Royal Palace; 27, Zappion; 28, Stadium; 29, New Cathedral.

Sculpture

Outstanding examples of architectural sculpture of the fifth century are the pediment groups from the temples of Aegina, Olympia and the Parthenon. Separated from each other in point of time by intervals of about twenty years, they illustrate stages in the process by which Greek sculptors were ridding themselves of certain conventions and coming to see 'things as they are'. The Parthenon groups have been acclaimed as the noblest achievement of Greek sculpture and their place is assured, but some modern critics prefer the Olympian. Among the famous statues of the fifth century were the colossal gold and ivory figures of Athena in the Parthenon, and of Zeus at Olympia, both works of the Athenian sculptor Phidias. What these were like can only be conjectured from small-scale copies or representations on coins. But large-scale copies of works by two other renowned sculptors, Myron and Polycletus, are familiar in European collections, e.g. the Discus-thrower (Discobolus) of Myron, and the Athlete with a spear (Doryphorus) of Polycletus.

Fourth-century architectural sculpture is well represented in the National Museum at Athens by fragments from the pediment sculptures of the Temple of Athena at Tegea, and from the Temple of Asclepius at Epidaurus. The former are probably by Scopas, the architect of the temple. Other great sculptors of the period were Praxiteles and Lysippus who made many bronze statues of athletes.

Literature

The great period of Greek architecture and sculpture was also the great period of Greek literature and thought. The works of Homer had become known in mainland Greece in the course of the sixth century, and their influence had been immediate and decisive. But before that a school of epic poetry had existed on the mainland, though its origins are obscure. The Boeotian, Hesiod, had used the same metre as Homer but without Homer's mastery. His theme, too, was not war and adventure, but husbandry and the sorrows of the peasant. The influence of Homer is plain, however, in the great lyric odes of Pindar (*c.* 522–450 B.C.), composed in honour of victories in the Olympic and other games, and intended to be recited in the cities from which the victors came.

Attic drama had its remote origins in the religious songs and dances performed at the temples of gods or the tombs of heroes, and this religious character was never lost; so that when these primitive songs and dances had developed into plays, performed in theatres before large audiences, the plots were still concerned with the gods and heroes of mythology, and, as such, were familiar to the audience. Interest was thus not so much in the plot as in the author's handling of it. The plays were produced in daylight, without elaborate costumes or scenery, before highly critical and intelligent spectators. The great age of Greek tragedy was the fifth century, and the three great tragedians, Aeschylus, Sophocles and Euripides, had no successors. Aristophanes, the greatest of the comic dramatists, belongs also to this age.

Prose of the fifth century is represented by Herodotus and Thucydides. Both were historians, the former a naïve but entertaining collector of information, in which fact and fable were indiscriminately mixed; the latter endowed with a critical sense, a philosophic outlook, great powers of description, and a fine style. When it is realized that this kind of descriptive writing was in its infancy, that no official reports were available, and that his material had to be laboriously collected by word of mouth, Thucydides' *History of the Peloponnesian War* must be regarded as a work of genius.

Literary activity of the fourth century reflects the contemporary spirit of inquiry in numerous works of philosophy and science, and in technical treatises. Oratory was brought to a fine art, and speeches for delivery either in the Assembly or in the law courts were prepared with the same elaborate care as poems. Many of the speeches of Demosthenes, the protagonist of Greek independence against the kings of Macedonia, have been preserved and have the permanent value of great literature.

In this age of inquiry the same religious and social problems which vex the modern mind were being discussed with the utmost freedom. Freedom was, however, held to have gone too far in the case of Socrates, whose perpetual questioning of everything in heaven and on earth was considered by the orthodox to be sapping the foundations of the state. He was tried and condemned to death in 399 B.C. His work was continued by his disciples who never forgave democracy for the treatment of their master, so that the ideal constitution envisaged by the greatest of them, the philosopher Plato, was almost an absolutism on the Spartan model. Aristotle, the other great figure in Greek philosophy, was born in 384 B.C. After having been tutor to Alexander the Great, he settled in Athens in 335 B.C. where he founded the Lyceum, which soon supplanted Plato's institution, the Academy. His works on the science of ethics, politics and metaphysics place him among the greatest thinkers of all time.

4. MACEDONIAN AND HELLENISTIC GREECE

THE EMPIRE OF ALEXANDER THE GREAT

Macedonia had hitherto played but a small part in Greek affairs. It had lagged behind the development of southern Greece, but, amidst the confused conditions in the middle of the fourth century, the rising state of Philip of Macedon (359–336 B.C.) had decided advantages. It was unexhausted by long wars and it possessed natural resources, in cereals, gold and timber, greater than those of any of the city states to the south. Under Philip the northern area was consolidated into a strong unit that extended into Thessaly, and the confused politics and divisions of the south provided ample opportunity for interference. At length, at the battle of Chaeronea (338 B.C.), Philip defeated an army of Athenians, Thebans and others, induced to join together by the new threat of this northern power. It was hatred of Philip that inspired the famous 'Philippics' of Demosthenes. But in the following year all the Greek states, with the exception of Sparta, had answered an invitation to send representatives to a Pan-Hellenic Congress under Philip's presidency at Corinth. In 336 B.C. Philip was assassinated, and his son Alexander succeeded him. It was this Alexander who was to become 'the Great' by turning against Asia and conquering what seemed almost the whole world, or at any rate that part of it which mattered.

That the Greeks should attempt an attack on the vast Persian empire and succeed might seem an almost impossible feat, unless the state of the Greek world and of the Persian empire is remembered. Among the Greeks the idea of an attack on Persia had long been current. During the fourth century there had grown up the idea that any dominant power

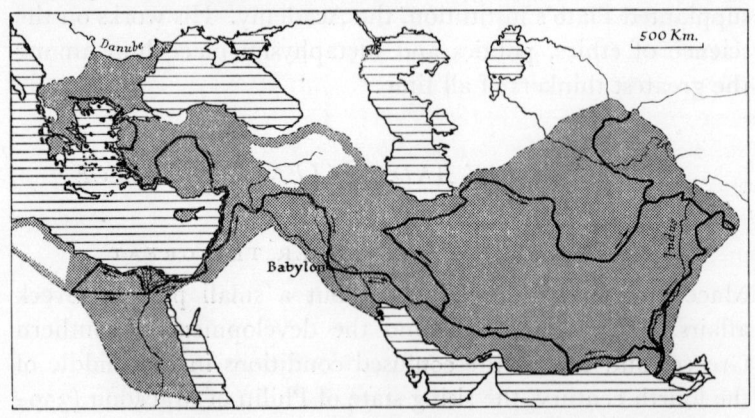

Fig. 7. The empire of Alexander, 323 B.C.
Based on W. R. Shepherd, *Historical Atlas*, pp. 18–19 (London, 1930).
The route of Alexander's march is indicated by a heavy line.

in Hellas would be obliged by self-interest and by racial duty to turn its arms against Asia, to rescue the Ionian Greeks of Asia Minor, and to conquer an empire. Many Greek writers had dwelt upon the theme. Then, in the second place, the condition of the Persian empire invited an aggressor. The king, no longer powerful, was by now little more than a titular lord over ever-rebelling provinces. Treachery or lack of resources had brought one rebel after another to disaster, but an empire whose high officers dared such adventures was clearly nearing its death. The Persians, too, had become involved more than once in the politics of the Aegean world, and there had been a number of invasions of Asia Minor by Spartan forces. Philip of Macedon had been planning an invasion, and had announced his design at the Congress of Corinth in 337 B.C. His son Alexander now inherited the idea and, two years after the death of his father, he crossed into Asia Minor with a force of about 35,000 infantry and 4,500 cavalry.

The account of the victorious march of Alexander to Egypt and right across Persia over the Khyber Pass to India itself reads like a legend (Fig. 7). In the midst of his work of organization, and while planning new conquests, he contracted a fever and died at Babylon in 323 B.C. The great empire he had created broke up with his death, but his work was far from being transitory in character. He had carried the seeds of Greek culture to the East. The Greek language and Greek ideas were spread right over the Near East, and became an important factor in the political and religious history of these lands. As for Alexander himself, his name passed into the legendary cycles of medieval Europe.

POLITICAL HISTORY AFTER THE DEATH OF ALEXANDER, 323–146 B.C.

Several states arose upon the ruins of Alexander's empire. The Ptolemies ruled in Egypt; the Seleucids in Syria and for a time in Persia itself. Various smaller states arose in Asia Minor. In Greece itself, Macedonia remained a powerful kingdom in the north, but was not again to dominate the world; while in the south, the Greek city states acquired varying degrees of freedom.

These years were characterized by the formation of coalitions or 'leagues' among the Greek states, of which the purpose was to offer a united front against the interference of Macedonia. This united front was seldom achieved, and the leagues even took to fighting one another. In the course of the rather confused history of the period, Athens was twice occupied by Macedonian troops, once in the year after Alexander's death and again in 262 B.C. when she took the wrong side in one of the numerous disputes for the Macedonian throne. An outstanding event of this period was the appearance before Delphi of a band of Gauls, a detachment from the main body which was on the move towards Asia Minor. They were thrown back by the Aetolians, now the official guardians of the sanctuary. The Aetolian cities, hitherto some of the most backward and least heard-of in Greece, had formed themselves into a league after the death of Alexander, and were prominent in Greek affairs throughout the third century. In 220 B.C. they went to war with the Achaean League, a coalition founded forty years earlier, which had defended Greece against Macedonia, but which was now supported by Macedonia against the Aetolians. By this time, however, events in the west were casting their shadow over Greece, and the war was brought to an end in 217 B.C.

During the Second Punic War between Rome and Carthage, Philip V of Macedonia allied himself with Hannibal (215 B.C.), and, to offset this, the Romans secured the alliance of the Aetolians and Spartans. The Romans, who had, some years before, been thanked by the Aetolians and Achaean leagues for clearing the Illyrian Sea of pirates, thus acquired a firmer footing in Greece. In the second of the three Macedonian Wars which followed, Philip was defeated (197 B.C.), and the victorious Roman consul Flamininus in a moving scene at the Isthmian Games of 196 B.C. declared Rome the 'protector of Greek freedom'.

The third Macedonian War ended in the defeat of Philip's son and successor, Perseus, at the battle of Pydna (168 B.C.) and the dissolution of the Macedonian empire. Anti-Roman elements continued to be active both in Macedonia and Greece, so that in 148 B.C. the Romans made Macedonia a Roman province, and Sparta, Rome's ally, gave the Romans a pretext for suppressing the Achaean League and adding Greece to her empire as a dependency of Macedonia (146 B.C.). Crete, however, was not subdued until 67 B.C. and only then after a campaign of three years.

HELLENISTIC CIVILIZATION

Architecture

Greek building activity in this period was largely in the lands to which Hellenism had spread, following the wake of Alexander's conquests. In Egypt, Syria and Asia Minor, Greek architects were busy laying out new cities and erecting secular and religious buildings which Greek sculptors were embellishing. The most impressive monuments of the Hellenistic Age, as this period is called, is the great altar of Zeus at Pergamum in Asia Minor, adorned with sculpture in the rather florid style characteristic of the Pergamene school. In Greece itself, a number of monumental secular buildings were erected, such as the Portico of Attalus and the 'Tower of the Winds' at Athens and the Portico of Echo and the Palaestra at Olympia. At Delos, too, there are many buildings of this period, and domestic architecture is represented there as nowhere else. The finest mosaic of the period is that recently discovered in the 'Roman Villa' at Corinth. Fortifications continued to be built, and the hills of Aetolia are still crowned with walls, towers and gates recalling the days of the Aetolian League. At Oeniadae, in Acarnania, the remarkable harbour-works, still to be seen, were constructed by Philip V of Macedonia in 219 B.C.

Sculpture

The sculpture of the Hellenistic Age exhibits the characteristics of an art that has passed its best period, but is, nevertheless, full of life and vigour, and there was no falling off in technical skill. The chief schools of sculpture were those of Pergamum, Rhodes and Ephesus; in Greece itself, little was produced. Well-known works of this period are the Aphrodite of Melos, the Apollo Belvedere (known only from copies), the Dying

Gaul, and the 'Victory', all of Samothrace. Portraits were extremely popular and there was a great demand for busts of famous persons, living and dead, to adorn public buildings, libraries and the like.

Literature

The schools of philosophy at Athens remained open, but intellectual pre-eminence passed to Alexandria. Here, though the creative genius which had characterized Attic writers of the fifth and fourth centuries was spent, the Attic literary tradition was carried on by scholars and men of learning attracted by the great library. Historians, grammarians, commentators and scientists predominated, and even poetry acquired a flavour of learning. Epicurus (341–270 B.C.) taught at Athens during the earlier part of the period. Poets also cultivated an artificial but often charming simplicity, and the pastoral idylls of Theocritus and many epigrams (a form of poetry which became popular at this time) are among the most beautiful things in Greek literature. Epic poetry, also, was revived with some success.

5. ROMAN GREECE

GRAECO-ROMAN POLITICAL AND ECONOMIC DEVELOPMENT

As part of the Roman state, Greece entered upon a period of peace such as she had not before known in her history. The Romans treated the Greeks in a generous manner, and the *Pax Romana* was regarded by most Greeks as a relief from the confusion of the Hellenistic period. As the contemporary historian Polybius wrote, 'If we had not perished quickly, we should not have been saved'. The Achaean League was dissolved and, fearing a competitor, the Romans destroyed the city of Corinth. For administrative purposes, the Greek states were subordinated to the Roman province of Macedonia, but Athens and Sparta were given special privileges. The quiet of the new Roman province was disturbed, however, when in 88 B.C. Athens and some other cities unwisely allied themselves with Mithridates, king of Pontus in Asia Minor, who was in conflict with Rome. For her share in the war, Athens was sacked by the Roman general Sulla, and the walls of the Piraeus were levelled.

During the last decades of the Roman republic (up to 27 B.C.), Greece was scarcely affected by the wider events of Roman policy, yet two civil wars were fought out on Greek soil or in Greek waters, and many Greeks took sides in the conflicts. The struggle between Caesar and Pompey was decided at Pharsalus in Thessaly in 48 B.C., and although the Greeks had supplied Pompey with a fleet, the victorious Caesar treated them leniently; individual cities, however, received severe punishment. Greece also became involved in the struggle between Mark Antony and Octavian until the great naval victory of Actium (31 B.C.) in which Octavian was triumphant. The geographer Strabo, who was in Greece two years later, has left a melancholy account of the effects of civil war upon the countryside; large tracts of country remained desolate and many notable cities stood in ruins.

Under the Roman emperors, from Augustus (Octavian) onwards, Greece was specially favoured. Augustus himself separated Greece from Macedonia and formed it into the separate province of Achaea with its capital at Corinth which had been refounded in 44 B.C. Nero thought a Greek audience was 'the only one worthy of himself and his accomplishments'. The results of the liberality of Hadrian are still to be seen at Athens (see p. 33). Marcus Aurelius, too, found time to visit Athens where he established a university in A.D. 176. Large numbers of Romans were attracted to the country—to visit its sanctuaries, to admire its artistic treasures, and to study at Athens. In return, Greek culture was having considerable influence upon Roman thought and writing; indeed many Romans were complaining that Rome itself was becoming 'a Greek city'. Captive Greece was taking her barbarian captors captive. But already a new ingredient was being added to the combined civilizations of Greece and Rome, for about the year A.D. 54 St Paul had visited Athens and Corinth. It was at Corinth that the two Epistles to the Thessalonians were written. Subsequently, the Epistles to the Corinthians show something of the life of the most flourishing city of Roman Greece. Some believed, but for long the new faith made little progress, and the beginnings of the Christian Church were small.

A picture of the Greek countryside under the Roman empire is given in the famous 'Description of Greece' written by Pausanias about the years A.D. 160–80. Compared with Strabo's time, the land was much more prosperous, but a lot of it was still in a desolate state, and the economic life of the country was not as flourishing as its intellectual and social pre-eminence might imply. It is true that new luxury industries (marble, textiles, table delicacies) were springing up to meet the needs of Rome, but the only cities with a really flourishing trade were Corinth and Patras.

The Roman peace was broken in A.D. 175 by the Costoboci, a northern tribe who raided into central Greece. They were defeated by the local militia, and retired beyond the Roman frontier. This was the first hint of northern interference that was to prove so important a factor in later Greek history. A more serious invasion was that of the Goths. They appeared on the frontier about A.D. 250, and the Emperor Valerian caused the walls of Athens to be rebuilt and other fortifications to be put across the Isthmus. But these precautions did not save Athens, for the Goths captured and pillaged the city in A.D. 267. Ultimately they were repulsed and retired beyond the Danube, and Greece was spared another Gothic invasion for over a century (see p. 37).

GRAECO-ROMAN CIVILIZATION

Architecture

The Graeco-Roman style which now came into being was fundamentally Greek, but a certain loss of fineness may have been due to the Roman element or to an inherent tendency already perceptible in Hellenistic work. However that may be, the principal cities and sanctuaries of Greece now received magnificent additions in the way of monuments and public buildings in this style. Such are almost all the buildings of Corinth. The damage and loss inflicted by Mummius, Sulla and Nero were to some extent offset by the enlightened liberality of the Emperor Hadrian (A.D. 117–38), who showed his deep interest in Greece by repairing and adding to old buildings, and erecting new ones. He completed the magnificent temple of Zeus at Athens, built the library, and also the arch known by his name; and, in more questionable taste, he erected many statues of himself at Olympia and other places. Another individual who has left memorials of his liberality was Herodes Atticus, a rich citizen of Marathon (A.D. 101–177). At Athens he built the Odeum, still named after him; at Corinth he enlarged and beautified the Peirene fountain and built the Odeum; at Olympia he built an aqueduct to take water into the sacred enclosure. At Olympia, too, a palace and a triumphal arch were built by the Emperor Nero.

Sculpture

After the sack of Corinth, hundreds of works of Greek art, especially statues, were shipped to Rome; Sulla and the Emperor Nero carried off more. When the demand for originals could no longer be satisfied, Greek sculptors produced copies to take their place, and it is from these copies that our conception of much of Greek sculpture is formed. Greek sculptors also made portrait busts for Roman families. The extreme realism of these portraits was no doubt demanded by Roman patrons, who wanted a portrait to be before all things a likeness, but it had been anticipated in portraits of the Hellenistic Age.

Literature

Greek had now become a cosmopolitan language; educated Romans made a point of learning it, and Greek slaves, imported to Rome, introduced a knowledge of it into Roman families. Thus it came to have a profound influence upon Latin literature. The numerous treatises on scientific subjects, medicine, philosophy and the like, which Greek scholars continued to produce, created a vocabulary of abstract terms which became international and are still in use. The two outstanding historians of the period were Polybius (202–120 B.C.), whose *History* was originally designed to record the dramatic rise of Roman supremacy in the Mediterranean, and Plutarch (A.D. 46–120), famous for his *Lives*. Christianity directed Greek thought into new channels, and, in the language of the Greek philosophers, theologians found ready to hand an instrument well adapted to express the fine distinctions which the definition of Christian doctrine required.

CHAPTER II

MEDIEVAL AND TURKISH GREECE

1. BYZANTINE GREECE

THE EASTERN ROMAN EMPIRE

THE Roman emperors had for some time felt the need of a new administrative centre when in A.D. 285 the empire was divided into two by Diocletian—an eastern and a western half. Diocletian took up his residence in the east, at Nicomedia near the Sea of Marmora, where he could keep in close touch with the critical frontiers on the Danube and the Tigris, and where oriental ideas of sovereignty could be developed unhampered by the republican traditions of Rome itself. Early in the next century, Constantine reunited the two halves, but fixed the capital in the east, and between 328 and 330 he enlarged the old town of Byzantium to form the city of 'New Rome which is Constantinople'. Soon the whole empire was divided again, and what had started as an administrative partition became after 395 a more fundamental separation.

The fates of the two empires in east and west respectively were very different. Whereas the western empire collapsed under the strain of the Barbarian invasions, the Roman empire in the east continued for centuries as a permanent factor amidst the changing political geography of Europe and the Near East. The wealth of the eastern provinces, the strategic position of the capital, and the intelligent policy of successive emperors, explain this contrast between east and west, and account for the survival of the eastern provinces as an imperial entity.

The eastern or Byzantine empire was thus a continuous development of the Roman empire, and was characterized by the fusion of two traditions—Greek and Roman. In language, literature and theology, Greek influence was paramount. In law, diplomacy and military tradition, the Roman tradition was important.

The administrative reorganization of Diocletian and Constantine was but part of wider changes that were transforming the old pagan empire of Rome into the medieval Christian empire called Byzantine. The religious attitude of Constantine had been as momentous as his imperial policy. Christianity now became the recognized religion of the empire. Soon, the minor bishopric of Byzantium became the patriarchate of Constantinople, and a Council in 381 gave it first place in the Eastern Church, directly after the see of Rome. It had to face the opposition of the older patriarchates of Antioch, Alexandria and Jerusalem until these were engulfed in the advancing tide of Islam during the seventh century. There remained the problem of relations with Rome, and, after a chequered history, varied by schisms and heresies, the final break came in 1054, when the two great leaders of the Christian Church put each other under a ban.

The separation of the eastern and western empires had meant that Greek interests were henceforward identified with those of the Byzantine emperors. This was in some senses a gain, in others a loss. On the one hand, Greek became the language of the court, and Greek culture became an important element in Byzantine civilization. On the other hand, the imperial city grew at the expense of Greece; Constantinople, rather than Athens, became the important factor in Greek life, and Greece became increasingly provincial. The Greeks themselves now became known not as 'Hellenes' but as 'Romaioi'. It was Justinian too, who, in 529, virtually abolished the University of Athens, the stronghold of pagan philosophy. Christianity was now spread throughout the whole of Greece, save in the mountain regions of Laconia, which did not become Christian until well into the ninth century.

THE DANUBE FRONTIER

The Byzantine emperors had continually to face two groups of frontier problems, to the east and north respectively (Fig. 8). The former were concerned with the attacks of the Moslems upon the Asiatic provinces of the empire; but it was not until the rise of the Ottoman Turks in the fourteenth century that the Greek lands themselves were threatened by this eastern peril. The other frontier problems were caused by the restless tribes beyond the Danube, and Greece was affected by these from an early date.

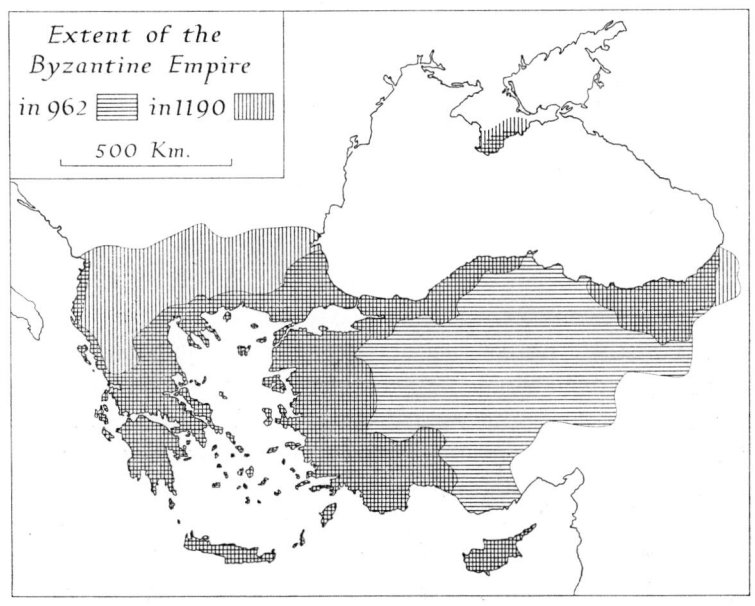

Fig. 8. The Byzantine Empire, A.D. 962–1190
Based on R. L. Poole, *Historical Atlas of Modern Europe*, plates 5 and 6 (Oxford, 1902).
This shows the reaction of the Byzantine frontiers to attacks from Europe and Asia. The strength of the empire lay in its seaward margins. Compare, for example, with Fig. 10.

This Danube frontier was an old problem that had frequently confronted the Roman emperors. In the third century some Goths had raided as far as Athens (see p. 32). These newcomers proved to be but a vanguard. Towards the end of the fourth century, the Visigoths (the western branch of the Goths), fearing the Huns of the steppelands behind them, had defeated the imperial generals, and had poured into peninsular Greece (378-95). But their destiny lay in the west, and, before the end of the century, they had moved northwards, and so into Italy; by 412 they had reached Spain. The Huns themselves raided the empire up to the neighbourhood of Constantinople itself more than once in the 440's, and Ostrogoths also threatened the city more than once in the 480's before they left for Italy in 488. But neither in the fourth nor fifth centuries was there any large-scale settlement of northerners on the lands of the empire.

These raids of Goths and Huns were only a prelude to far greater movements of peoples from beyond the river. Indeed, one of the most important factors in the history of Greece from the sixth to the twelfth century was the complete breakdown of the Danube frontier. The ethnography of the northerners that came swarming southwards is not always clear. The Byzantine chroniclers speak of Slavs, Antae (also Slavs), Bulgars, Huns (by whom they may have meant Bulgars), Avars, Cumans and Patzinaks; the vague names of 'Getae' and 'Scythians' are also mentioned. Of these, the two peoples that had direct effect upon the fortunes of medieval Greece were the Slavs and the Bulgars.

THE SLAVS

Of all the northerners the Slavs were the most important to Greece. Expanding from their homeland in the Pripet marshes, the Slavs reached the lands immediately to the north of the Danube by, at latest, the third century, but there is no sure evidence that they had penetrated (at any rate in considerable numbers) southwards into the peninsula before the end of the fifth century. Early in the sixth century their raids became frequent, and Macedonia, Thessaly and Epirus were repeatedly devastated; and with the reign of Justinian (527-65), conditions along the Danube deteriorated. Despite the fierce resistance put up by the imperial troops, hordes of Slavs and

Bulgars crossed the river almost every year to raid and loot. In 540, they raided Greece as far south as the Isthmus of Corinth, and Justinian was forced to organize defensive measures on a large scale. Large numbers of new forts were set up and old ones were strengthened. From the river Sava to the Black Sea some eighty castles were built or restored, and behind these some hundreds of fortified positions provided a 'defence in depth'. Despite these efforts, the raids continued. It is unlikely that they led to permanent settlements on any large scale, but their influence upon the countryside was very marked. The historian Procopius, who lived during the first half of the sixth century, compared the ravaged lands of Greece to the 'Scythian deserts', and he described how the inhabitants fled into the mountains and the forests for safety.

In the latter part of the sixth century, after the death of Justinian, the Slav raids grew in intensity, and about the year 580 an army of some 100,000 'Slavonians' poured into Thrace and Illyricum. A contemporary chronicler, John of Ephesus, tells of the horror that now fell upon the countryside and it is from this time that we must date the arrival of Slav settlers in considerable numbers into Greece. Raiding had passed definitely into settlement. To the north, the lands of what is now Yugoslavia were likewise open to the penetration of other Slav peoples (Slovenes, Croats and Serbs) during the first half of the seventh century.

The widespread incursions of the Slavs were reinforced by those of the Avars, a nomad group prominent in the northern lands during the sixth and early seventh centuries. Moreover, in the early years of the seventh century, the main effort of the Byzantine empire was engaged in a struggle with the Persians, and the European provinces were thus left exposed. The Byzantine diplomats spoke of lands occupied by the Slavs in Thrace, Macedonia and Greece as grants made through the generosity of the emperor; the frontier might therefore be placed either at the Danube or at no great distance from the Aegean Sea according to the imperial or the Slav point of view.

Some dates stand out. In 597, and again in 609, Salonica, protected by its strong walls and by its Saint Demetrius, had managed to withstand the assault of the surrounding Slav tribes in Macedonia. In 623, Slavs were raiding Crete. In 626, a united horde of Avars, Slavs and Bulgars were besieging Constantinople, not for the first time, but they failed to take the city. The Avar power ceased to be important after about 630, but Slav pressure southwards continued. Thus in 674 a body of Slavs seized the opportunity of an Arab siege of Constantinople to settle in the rich plain of Thessaly, where the place-name of Velestínon still recalls the name of one of their tribes (the Velegezêtes).

It is difficult to form a clear picture of the extent of Slav settlement in Greece during these years, and the subject has aroused much controversy. A contemporary encyclopedist, Isidore of Seville (*d.* 639), summed up the situation by saying that 'the Slavs took Greece from the Romans', but it is certain that the large towns, at any rate, did not fall to the Slavs. Athens was still in Greek hands, nor, wrote J. B. Bury, 'had the country yet become Slavised, as it is said to have become in the following century'.[1] There is little evidence about the relations of the immigrant Slavs and the Greeks at this time, but it seems likely that the newcomers were easily converted to Christianity and that they lived more or less under the suzerainty of the Byzantine emperor.

It is not surprising that, in view of these incursions, the command of the imperial army in Greece was an important office. The system of themes, or districts under military organization (*thema*=regiment), that had been found necessary to meet the Persian and Arab wars of the seventh century, was now extended under the Emperor Leo III (717–40) from Asia to Europe. The number of themes varied, but by the tenth century they comprised about thirty, of which eight covered what is now Greece and the Aegean islands.

---

[1] J. B. Bury, *A History of the Later Roman Empire, A.D. 395 to 800*, vol. II, p. 280 (London, 1889).

It was during the eighth century that Slav influence became greatest in Greece. In 746 a great plague breaking out in the Near East reached Monemvasia in the Peloponnese, and, from there, spread over the whole empire. The population of Greece suffered heavily, and was then further reduced by the migration of many skilled workmen to Constantinople; whole families left both the mainland and the islands. Empty districts were thus left free to be colonized by the Slavs who now pressed southwards in greater numbers than ever. In the words of the imperial historian, Constantine Porphyrogenitus, 'all the open country was Slavonized and became barbarous, when the plague was devouring the whole world'. According to W. Miller,[1] this is the real explanation of the Slav colonization of Greece. Whatever be the truth, the Slavs had by now certainly spread widely over the Greek lands. So widespread were their settlements that in the eighth century the southern Balkan lands and mainland Greece were known as 'Sclavinia' (Fig. 9).

The central government at Constantinople, alarmed at this influx, dispatched the general Staurakios to deal with the newcomers, and they were reduced and forced to pay tribute (783). But early in the following century, when the imperial forces were being threatened by Saracens and Bulgars, the Slavs of the Peloponnese rose in revolt, and, conspiring with the Saracens, they attacked the fortress of Patras (807). But the siege was raised, and, after some time, the rebellion was put down. There was a fresh rising in the Peloponnese in the year 841–2, which was again suppressed, and military colonists were established here as in northern Greece. Special terms were made with two Slav tribes in the south near Mount Taygetos— the Milings and the Ezerites, who agreed to pay tribute. These two tribes were in rebellion again in the middle of the tenth century, and, although they were once more reduced to obedience, it is apparent that they still retained a large measure of independence.

The military reduction of the Slavs prepared the way for

[1] *Essays on the Latin Orient*, p. 39 (Cambridge, 1921).

their assimilation, and in this work the Church played a great part. With the foundation of monasteries and churches went on the active work of assimilation. The Orthodox religion and the Greek language regained the ground they had lost, and by the tenth century many people of Slav descent were occupying

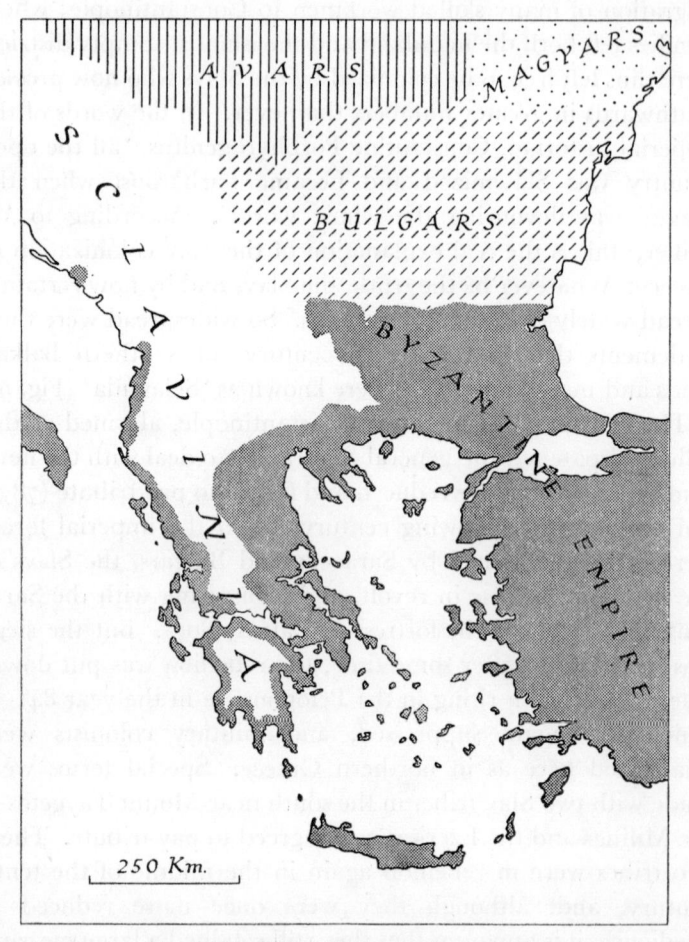

Fig. 9. The Balkan Peninsula about A.D. 800

Based on R. L. Poole, *Historical Atlas of Modern Europe*, plate 4 (Oxford, 1902).
This map shows dominant political groupings rather than ethnic distributions; thus Slavs were also to be found in the areas marked as 'Avars' and 'Bulgars'. For the Byzantine frontier against the Slavs, see p. 39.

high positions in the empire. But even in the thirteenth century, some Slav tribes still lived apart from the Greeks and maintained their old customs in the mountainous districts of Elis and Arcadia. The Milings remained separate longest, possibly even until the eve of the Ottoman conquest.

The Slavs have left evidence of their settlement in the numerous Slavonic place-names that are to be found in Greece today. Over much of the Peloponnese a Slavonic place-name can be found every three or four miles.

THE BULGARS

The Bulgars, like the Huns and the Avars before them, were peoples from the Asiatic steppes who during the sixth century were to be found in the country north of the Black Sea. Their early history in Europe is obscure, but it seems fairly certain that they took part in some of the attacks of the Slavs and the Avars against Salonica and Constantinople during the sixth and seventh centuries. Towards the end of the seventh century, the main body moved southwards and, in 679, established themselves between the Danube and the Balkan Mountains. The river definitely ceased to mark the northern frontier of the Byzantine empire.

South of the Danube, the newcomers found the land already peopled with Slavs, and the new state that came into being was the result of fusion between Bulgars and Slavs. The two centuries that followed 679 were marked by intermittent warfare with the Byzantine emperors. In order to check the growth of the Slav and Bulgar population in Thrace and Macedonia, the emperors established Syrian and Armenian colonists there in the eighth and ninth centuries. Later emperors followed the same policy, and from the eleventh to the thirteenth century colonies of Uzes, Patzinaks and Cumans from the lands to the north of the Black Sea were introduced.

Although continually raiding the empire, the Bulgars were culturally its children, and in 865 they officially adopted the

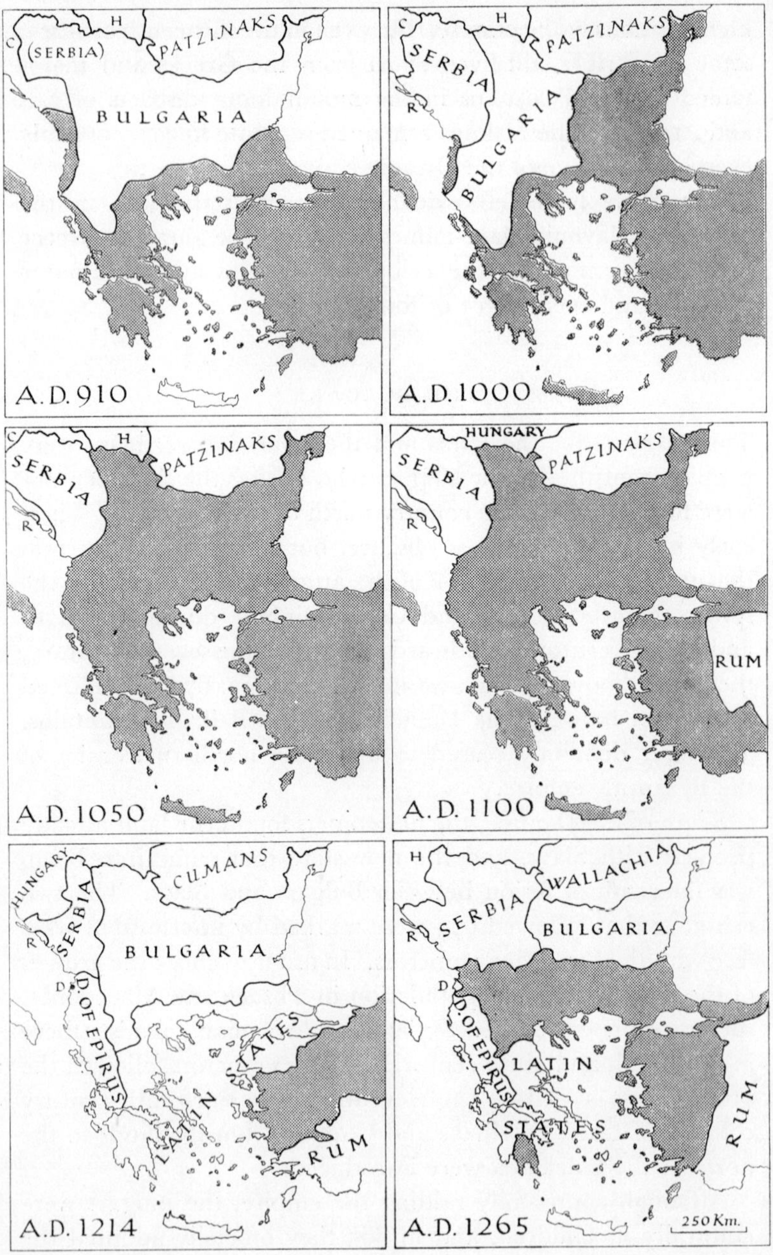
C
H
(SERBIA)
PATZINAKS
BULGARIA
A.D. 910
C
H
PATZINAKS
SERBIA
R
BULGARIA
A.D. 1000
C
H
PATZINAKS
SERBIA
R
A.D. 1050
HUNGARY
PATZINAKS
SERBIA
R
RUM
A.D. 1100
HUNGARY
CUMANS
SERBIA
R
BULGARIA
D.
D. OF EPIRUS
LATIN STATES
RUM
A.D. 1214
H
WALLACHIA
SERBIA
R
BULGARIA
D
D. OF EPIRUS
LATIN
STATES
RUM
A.D. 1265
250 Km.

Greek form of Christianity. Under Simeon the Great (893–927) the Bulgar state greatly extended its frontiers westward over the Slavs of Serbia and southward into northern Greece (Fig. 10). In Macedonia and in Epirus, the empire was able to keep only the coastlands, and Bulgar raids penetrated even as far south as the Isthmus. The new Bulgarian realm soon broke into two owing to revolt in the western Serb provinces. In 972, eastern Bulgaria came to an end, and by 1018 the now independent western unit had also been recovered by the empire. From 1018 to 1186, the Bulgars ceased to form a separate state. The second Bulgarian empire, which came into existence as the result of revolt of Bulgars and Vlachs, once more included a part of northern Greece within its territory, but it lasted only for a short time (1186–1258), and was ultimately succeeded by Serb domination in the Balkan peninsula (Fig. 11).

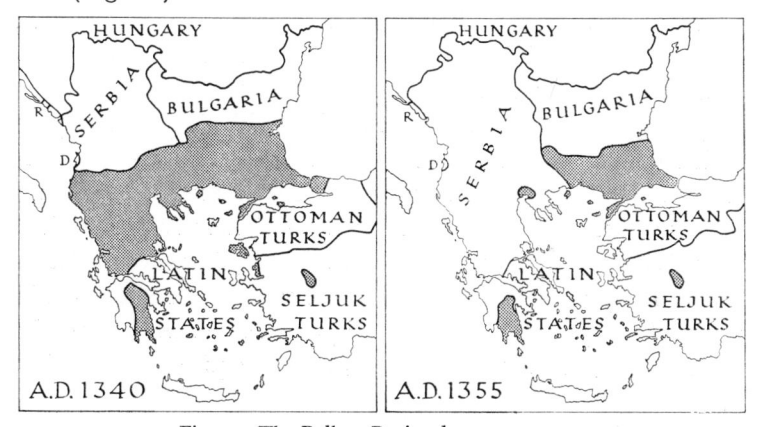

Fig. 11. The Balkan Peninsula, A.D. 1340–55

Based on: (1) E. A. Freeman, *Atlas to the Historical Geography of Europe*, maps 40 and 41 (London, 1903); (2) W. R. Shepherd, *Historical Atlas*, p. 89 (London, 1930). The area included in the Byzantine empire is stippled. D=Durazzo; R=Ragusa.

Fig. 10. The Balkan Peninsula, A.D. 910–1265

Based on: (1) E. A. Freeman, *Atlas to the Historical Geography of Europe*, maps 34–37 (London, 1903); (2) W. Miller, *The Latins in the Levant*, p. 81 (London, 1908); (3) W. R. Shepherd, *Historical Atlas*, pp. 59, 67, 89 (London, 1930).
The area included in the Byzantine empire is stippled. C=Croatia; D=Durazzo; H=Hungary; R=Ragusa.

Although Macedonia and the lands around had passed from Bulgar control, Bulgars continued to be an important element in the population of the area. Unlike the Slavs of peninsular Greece, the Bulgars and Slavs of these areas were not assimilated by the Greeks, and they remained distinct groups. Linguistically separate from the Greeks, they were to form a complicating factor in the 'Macedonian problem' of later times.

THE VLACHS

Apart from the Slavs and the Bulgars, another non-Greek people emerge in the history of medieval Greece. Their language is a dialect of Romanian and is therefore derived from Latin; and it is generally admitted that they are descended from Roman colonists and Latinized provincials in the areas north and south of the Danube.[1] Their existence may be inferred from records as early as the sixth century in date, but the first definite mention of them was not until the year 976. During the next two centuries, reference to them became frequent, but they were intermingled with other peoples in such a way that it is difficult to form any clear idea of their distribution. Several districts were called after them; thus 'Great Vlachia' was the name given to Thessaly, and 'Little Vlachia' to Acarnania and Aetolia, while there were Vlachs also in Bulgaria and to the north. These last were involved in the revolt against the Byzantine empire which led to the establishment of the second Bulgarian empire in 1186 (see p. 45).

In the eleventh-century *Strategicon* by Cecaumenos, there is a description of the Vlachs around Trikkala and Larissa, in Thessaly. Their mode of living then seems to have been very similar to that of recent times; from April to September they lived

[1] The Vlachs, or Wallachs, called themselves *Romans*; the name 'Vlach' was applied to them by their neighbours; its origin is identical with the English 'Wealh' or 'Welsh' (i.e. stranger), and represents a Slavonic adoption of a general term applied by Teutonic peoples to Roman provincials in the fourth and fifth centuries.

with their flocks in the mountains, and descended to the plains only in winter. There is also reference, in the same account, to the appointment of a Byzantine official to administer the Vlachs. Towards the end of the eleventh century, these southern Vlachs were mentioned by the Byzantine historian Anna Comnena, who referred to nomadic folk 'commonly called Vlachs' in the mountainous region of Thessaly. About

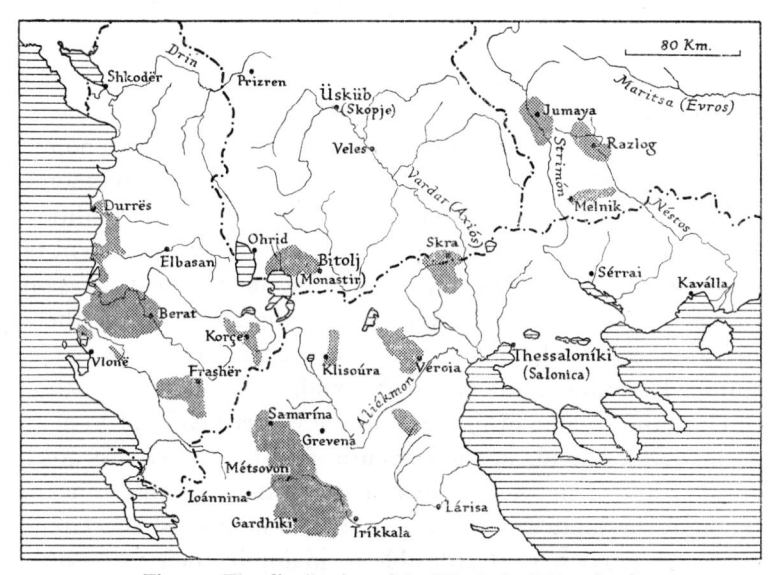

Fig. 12. The distribution of the Vlachs in Balkan lands
Based on A. J. B. Wace and M. S. Thompson, *The Nomads of the Balkans*, p. 206 (London, 1914).
Different authorities give varying ideas about the exact distribution of the Vlachs; this map, for example, differs in detail from the distribution of Vlachs as given on Fig. 25.

the year 1170, Benjamin of Tudela described them thus: 'Here are the confines of Wallachia, a country of which the inhabitants are called Vlachi. They are as nimble as deer and descend from their mountains into the plains of Greece committing robberies and taking booty. Nobody ventures to make war on them, nor can any king bring them to submission.' At the division of the Byzantine empire in 1204, Great Vlachia was included in the kingdom of Salonica under Boniface, but it soon reappeared as an independent principality under its old name (see p. 58).

THE ECONOMIC DEVELOPMENT OF BYZANTINE GREECE

If it is difficult to obtain any detailed evidence about the coming of Slavs and Bulgars into the Greek lands, it is even more difficult to form a clear picture of the domestic history of Greece in the Byzantine empire from the death of Justinian in 565 to the fall of Constantinople in 1204. Certain facts, however, stand out: something can be said about the economic condition of the area, and especially about its commerce; some evidence is also available about the internal political condition of the Greek themes during the twelfth century; the advent of western armies into Greece, culminating in the great invasion of 1204, is comparatively well documented; and, lastly, there are archaeological remains which speak for themselves of the former Byzantine influence in the land.

Until the coming of the ships of the western cities of Venice, Genoa and Amalfi, in the eleventh century, the Greeks were to a great extent the carriers of the eastern Mediterranean. Though the land was filled with Slav immigrants, the Greek cities of the coast were still able to maintain their mercantile connexions. A great movement of exchange centred on Constantinople itself, and in the ninth and tenth centuries Byzantine trade was at its height. It is true that the advance of Islam had restricted trade in the eastern Mediterranean, but the Black Sea trade was important; amber, furs and metals came from Russia and the northern shores of Asia Minor. Greek ships also carried much of the trade between Constantinople and the west, but the Italian merchant fleets gradually shut out the Greeks from western waters. The Italian cities, at first the rivals, were soon the superiors of the Greeks in wealth and industry, and they came ultimately to dominate the carrying trade of the Aegean.

One great hindrance to Aegean shipping was piracy. In 826 or 827, some Saracens, who had migrated from Spain to Alexandria, fell upon Crete, at that time recovering from an earthquake, and conquered it. Their control was marked by religious toleration which reconciled the inhabitants to their rule; and in the years that followed, Christians helped to man the ships of the Moslem corsairs who menaced the coasts and islands of the Aegean. Cretan pirates became the terror of the eastern seas, and Crete grew into a great centre for traffic in slaves. At last, after many attempts, the island was restored to Christian rule in 961. Some of the Moslems left; others sank into serfdom. As in the Peloponnese, the missionary followed the soldier, and many Greek and Armenian Christians were attracted here. The Christian recovery of the island was in the main successful, though not a few Moslems kept their religion. But the recovery of Crete did not mean the abolition of piracy in the Aegean. The chronicle ascribed to the English Benedict of Peterborough states that in 1191 piracy was still rife; some of the Aegean islands were uninhabited for fear of the pirates; in other islands, they themselves lived. Despite their depredations, however, commercial activity, though interrupted, never broke down, and indeed, with the coming of the Italian cities, it greatly increased.

An important item in Greek trade was silk. About the year 550 two Persian monks had smuggled some eggs of the silkworm into the Byzantine empire, and from these precious eggs were derived all the varieties of silk-worm that stocked the western world for over a thousand years. The silks of the Byzantine empire became famous throughout medieval Europe, and the cities of central and southern Greece shared greatly in this prosperity. Thebes in particular became an important centre. No silk is now made at Thebes and there are no mulberry trees there, but the plain around the town is still known as 'Morokampos' from the mulberry trees which once gave the town its prosperity.

Though the carrying trade was passing into the ships of the

west, the Greek cities did not lose their prosperity. Some indication of conditions in Greece in the twelfth century is furnished by the large number of Jewish communities in the area. Benjamin of Tudela, writing about 1160, provided a list of the Jewish communities. The great city of Thebes had about 2,000 Jews who were 'the most skilled artificers in silk and purple cloth throughout Greece'. Salonica, 'a very large city' on the Via Egnatia from Durazzo to Constantinople, had about 500 Jews; Armylo (Almirós), another 'large city', had 400; Corinth had 300; Egripo (Khalkís) was 'a large city upon the sea-coast where merchants come from every quarter', and it had about 200 Jews. There were also many smaller Jewish communities.

THE POLITICAL CONDITION OF GREECE IN A.D. 1200

Though the economic circumstances of the Greek cities in the twelfth century seem to have been moderately prosperous, the political condition of Greece was far from happy. The financial oppression of the Byzantine government was heavy, and money that should have been spent on the defence of the country went instead to support the ostentation of the imperial capital. Byzantine officials regarded the country, in the words of a contemporary, as an 'utter hole', to be exploited as much as possible; the imperial governors received no salaries, but made their office self-supporting. Besides this, the Greek population had to endure the exactions of native tyrants. Under the Comneni dynasty of the twelfth century, feudalism had made considerable progress. Large tracts of land were under the control of families whose quarrels disturbed the life of the country. The historian Niketas speaks of these notables (*archontes*) as 'inflamed by ambition against their own fatherland, slavish men, spoiled by luxury, who made themselves tyrants, instead of fighting the Latins'.

Beset by imperial exactions, disturbed by internal feuds, raided by pirates, occupied in part by Vlachs, threatened by the rising second empire of Bulgaria, it is little wonder that the condition of Greece seemed ripe for western interference. The raids of western princes in the twelfth century and the ever-growing strength of the western cities (especially of Venice) in the Aegean Sea, formed but a prelude to the great disaster that fell upon the Byzantine world in 1204.

WESTERN INTERFERENCE UP TO 1204

The Norman conquerors of southern Italy, seeking to match the exploits of William the Conqueror in England, seized a pretext to invade the Byzantine provinces that lay so near across the narrow Straits of Otranto. Between 1081 and 1084, they occupied Corfu, took Durazzo, and penetrated as far as Larissa in Thessaly. They retired only to return again in 1106, but without success. For forty years Greece was left alone, until the expedition of Roger of Sicily in 1146. In that year, a landing was made at Itea on the north of the Gulf of Corinth, and the Normans marched to Thebes. The city was looted and many of its silk weavers were sent back to Sicily. From Thebes the invaders marched to Corinth, plundered it, and then sailed home with their booty. In the years that followed, the Normans became increasingly involved in the domestic intrigues of the empire, and after 40 years a Norman army once again marched across Greek soil (1185). Starting from Durazzo, it made for Salonica, and a fleet was sent by sea to help in the siege of the city. After successfully looting it, the Normans were defeated and returned home.

Faced with the Norman peril in the eleventh century, the emperor had sought aid from Venice whose wealthy merchants were now trading in eastern waters. The price of assistance was free trade throughout the empire, and a charter of 1082 laid the sure foundation for Venetian supremacy in the commerce of the Aegean and the Black Seas. 'On that day', says one historian, 'began the world commerce of Venice.'[1] The Venetians were soon everywhere. Their very success, however,

[1] C. Diehl, *Une république patricienne: Venise*, p. 33 (Paris, 1915).

aroused distrust, and, to counteract Venetian influence, succeeding emperors granted commercial privileges to Pisa, Genoa and Amalfi. During the twelfth century the empire and Venice were sometimes at war and sometimes acting together, according to the exigencies of the moment; but all the while the antagonism between the two powers was developing. It was this antagonism together with Norman raids of the twelfth century that provided the background for the spectacular events of 1204 which inaugurated a new period in the history of Greece.

2. FRANKISH AND VENETIAN GREECE

THE FOURTH CRUSADE

From the end of 1199 onwards, a fourth crusade was preached in France and Germany. Its leading members were French feudal lords like Baldwin of Flanders; its goal was Jerusalem; and its immediate strategic objective was the heart of Moslem power in Egypt. The Venetians agreed to provide transport, and, by August 1202, the army was assembled at Venice, but the crusaders then found it impossible to pay the sum agreed upon. The Venetians therefore proposed that payment be postponed in return for help against the Adriatic city of Zara which had been occupied by the Hungarians. In spite of papal protests against this attack on a Christian city, the crusading fleet sailed in November 1202, and Zara was successfully taken. But this diversion to Zara was only a preliminary to a much greater diversion. For a long time, many in the west had looked with hatred towards the Byzantine empire, and, during the preparations of 1200–2, the crusading plan had become involved in a series of complicated motives which led the crusaders ultimately not against the infidel but to Constantinople. Venice in particular had everything to gain by an attack on its great commercial rival in the east. The details of this great diversion are obscure and have been the subject of controversy, but the result is clear enough. In June 1203, the crusading fleet appeared outside the harbour of Constantinople, and the crusaders were very soon in possession of the city. Involved in disputes about the imperial throne, they decided to divide the empire amongst themselves. A new emperor was to be elected with control over one-quarter of the empire. The remaining three-quarters were to be divided, one-half to the Venetians and one-half to the crusaders. The year 1204 is one of the great landmarks in European history.

Count Baldwin of Flanders was elected emperor to rule over a restricted Latin empire that included the territory on either side of the Sea of Marmora together with some nearby islands. Venetian nobles occupied many other islands, and Venice assumed direct sovereignty over a number of other areas. Rewards for the Frankish adventurers were found on the mainland of Greece. Representatives of the old Byzantine emperors remained only in three areas—in the territory around Nicaea in Asia Minor, in Epirus, and in Trebizond on the Black Sea coast. Although the Latin empire at Constantinople lasted only for 57 years, some of the Venetian and Frankish states continued for two or three hundred years. From 1204 onwards until the coming of the Turk, the history of the Greek lands lost its unity and became the story not of one but of many separate states. The units that thus arose in the Greek world fall conveniently into the following groups, each of which must be considered separately (Fig. 13):

- (1) The Latin empire of Romania, 1204–61.
- (2) The Greek empire of Nicaea, 1204–1453.
- (3) The Latin kingdom of Salonica, 1204–23.
- (4) The duchy of Athens, 1205–1460.
- (5) The principality of Achaia, 1205–1432.
- (6) The duchy of the Archipelago, 1207–1566.
- (7) The county palatine of Cephalonia, 1194–1483.
- (8) The despotat of Epirus, 1204–1336.
- (9) Scattered Venetian possessions, various dates from 1204 to 1715 in the Aegean and to 1797 in the Ionian Islands.

(10) Scattered Genoese possessions, various dates from 1261 to 1566.

(11) The Knights of Rhodes, 1309–1522.

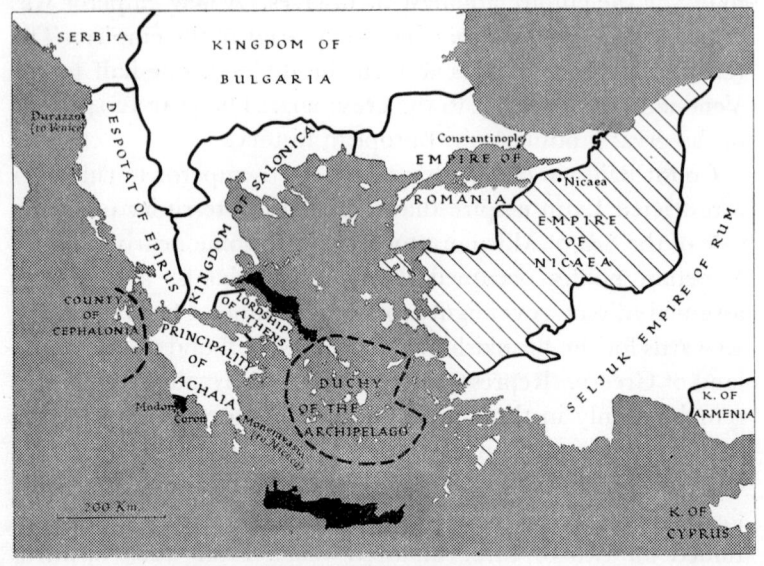

Fig. 13. Greece in 1214

Based on: (1) *The Cambridge Medieval History*, vol. 4, map 43 (Cambridge, 1923); (2) W. Miller, *The Latins in the Levant*, p. 81 (London, 1908).

Venetian possessions are shown in black. The empire of Trebizond lay along the south-eastern shores of the Black Sea—off this map.

THE LATIN EMPIRE OF ROMANIA, 1204–61

The Latin empire, lying athwart the Sea of Marmora, soon began to shrink both in Thrace and in Asia Minor. In Thrace, it had to face the attacks of the Bulgars, and in Asia Minor it had a rival in the Greek empire of Nicaea which still maintained the Byzantine tradition. Only the rivalries of the states around kept it alive for as long as 57 years, and it fell to the Nicaean Greeks in 1261. The last of the emperors to reign, like the first, was named Baldwin. He fled to the west where the empty title of 'Latin Emperor' continued until the death of its last holder in 1383.

THE GREEK EMPIRE OF NICAEA, 1204-1453

The Latin empire of Constantinople was never able to make much progress in Asia Minor. There, in the prosperous city of Nicaea, Theodore Lascaris, the son-in-law of a former Byzantine emperor, established a court that soon became the centre of a small but reviving Greek empire. Under Theodore and his successors, the new empire was organized efficiently and its frontiers were extended in Asia Minor and over the islands of Lesbos, Chios, Samos and Icaria. Soon, it recovered ground in Europe, and the Maritsa became its northern boundary against Bulgaria. In 1246, much of the Epirot empire of Salonica was annexed and the Byzantine frontier was carried to the Adriatic itself (Fig. 14).

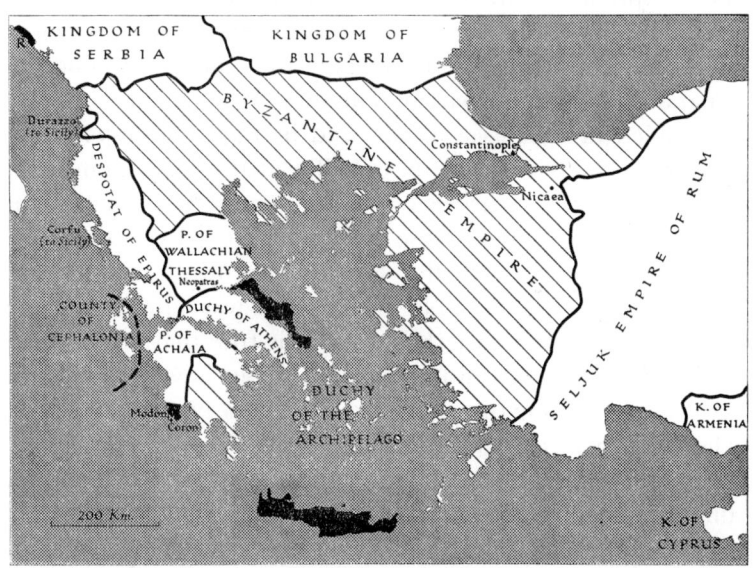

Fig. 14. Greece in 1265
Based on W. R. Shepherd, *Historical Atlas*, p. 89 (London, 1930).
Venetian possessions are shown in black; R=Ragusa.

The Lascarid dynasty was replaced by the noble family of Palaeologus in 1259, but this involved no change of external policy, and at last, in 1261, Constantinople itself was captured. It was the culmination of a steady progress since 1204. Now, after an interval of 57 years, the empire of Nicaea became merged in that of Constantinople. The revival had not recovered the whole of Byzantine territory, but at any rate it had got back the heart and centre of the empire, together with a substantial extent of territory.

The revived Byzantine empire was to last another two hundred years, and its European must be distinguished from its Asiatic history. In the Peloponnese, in 1262, it recovered Monemvasia together with Mistra and Maina (see p. 62), and during the fourteenth century this southern base became a most important element in the empire (Fig. 16). By 1432, the whole Peloponnese had been restored to Byzantine rule, with the exception of some coastal stations held by Venice (see p. 63). The story of Byzantine recovery in northern Greece was different. For a time the frontiers of the empire continued to expand. The greater part of Thessaly (Wallachian Thessaly) was added in 1318 (see p. 58), and in 1336 the despotate of Epirus itself was won (see p. 66). But at this very moment of success, the great resurgence of Serbia under Stephen Dushan wrested a great part of these possessions from Byzantine rule. Stephen's empire stretched to the Gulf of Corinth, and all that remained to Constantinople in the north was Thrace and the district around Salonica (Fig. 15). It is true that the Serbian state soon broke up into fragments; these, however, did not return to Byzantine rule, but passed to a new power, the Turks, who were soon to engulf the whole Aegean world.

In Asia Minor, the Byzantine empire had started to shrink almost as soon as its centre had been transferred from Nicaea to Constantinople. Various Turkish powers encroached on imperial territory until only a narrow strip remained along the Sea of Marmora. With the rise of one of these powers, the Ottoman Turks, the loss was accelerated, and, by the middle of the fourteenth century, only a few isolated Byzantine points were left in Asia Minor. But the Ottomans did not restrict their activities to Asia. By 1356 they had landed in Europe, and in 1361 they transferred their capital to Adrianople. What Stephen Dushan had torn from Byzantine territory, the Ottomans were now to inherit—and more. By the two battles of the Maritsa (1371) and Kossovo (1389), the power of the Bulgarians and the Serbians was broken, and their territories passed into Turkish hands; by 1390, the Turks had reached the Danube. In 1393, they conquered Thessaly and Neopatras. At the end of the century, the Byzantine empire consisted only of Salonica, the Peloponnese and Constantinople. In 1453, the great city itself fell. What the Fourth Crusade had started in 1204, the Ottomans now completed, and by 1461 they were masters of almost all mainland Greece. The islands of the Aegean, however, held out for over another century, and not until the duchy of the Archipelago fell in 1566 was Ottoman supremacy as complete in the islands as on the mainland (see p. 64).

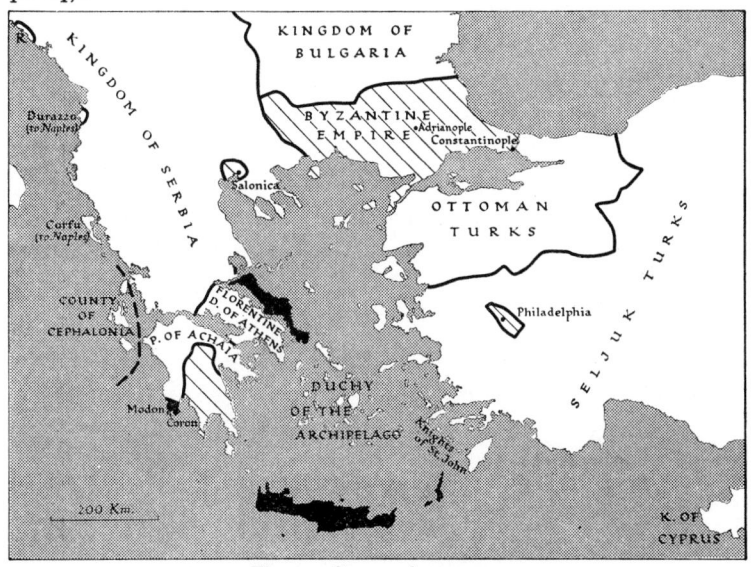

Fig. 15. Greece about 1355
Based on W. R. Shepherd, *Historical Atlas*, p. 89 (London, 1930).
Venetian possessions are shown in black; R=Ragusa. The island of Santa Maura (Levkás) was not united to the county of Cephalonia until 1362.

THE LATIN KINGDOM OF SALONICA, 1204-23

The leader of the crusaders, Boniface of Montferrat, obtained, as his share of the spoil, the title of king and a grant of land including Macedonia, Thessaly and much of central Greece. He set out in the autumn of 1204 to take possession of his kingdom and to parcel it out among his barons. Thus Larissa became the fief of a Lombard noble; Velestino passed into the hands of a Rhenish count; the commanding position of Boudonitza, near the pass of Thermopylae, was assigned to the Pallavicini family from near Parma, and their ruined castle still looks down on the countryside around. The new kingdom was not destined to last very long. The reluctance of the king to acknowledge the overlordship of the emperor of Romania was a source of weakness; and the attacks of the Bulgars formed another weakness. In 1223 the kingdom was occupied by the despot of Epirus, and it remained under Epirot control until the reviving Greek empire of Nicaea annexed the greater part of it in 1246 (see p. 55).

A branch of the Epirot dynasty continued, however, to rule in Thessaly, for one of its members had married the heiress of the hereditary chieftain of the Wallachians (see p. 66). This principality, sometimes independent, and sometimes in alliance with one of the surrounding states, was known variously as 'Great Wallachia' or the 'Duchy of Neopatras' (Fig. 14). When the line of the Wallachian princes became extinct in 1318, their territories were divided. The greater part of the rich Thessalian plain was annexed by the Byzantine empire. The southern area, including the city of Neopatras itself, in the valley of the Spercheus, was conquered by the Catalan Company, then dominating Athens, and this enlarged state became known as the 'duchies of Neopatras and Athens' (see p. 59).

THE DUCHY OF ATHENS, 1205-1460

One of the associates of Boniface was a Burgundian noble named

Othon de la Roche who, in 1205, received the territories of Athens and Thebes in the south of the kingdom of Salonica. This unit in central Greece maintained its identity long after the Latin kingdom of Boniface had disappeared, and it became one of the most permanent of the Frankish states in Greece. At first its ruler was known merely as 'Sire' or 'Megaskyr' (Great Lord), but from the middle of the thirteenth century onwards he became the 'duke' of Athens. After twenty years' rule, Othon, with his wife and his two sons, left Greece for ever to return to his native land (1225), and he bequeathed his domain of Thebes and Athens to his nephew Guy who carried on his work. Under the tolerant Frankish régime, the silk manufacture of Thebes once again prospered; Athens, too was prosperous. 'The splendour of the Theban Court and the excellent French spoken at Athens struck visitors from the West.'[1]

But at the beginning of the fourteenth century this prosperous Frankish rule was cut short from an unexpected quarter. A band of Catalan mercenaries, after fighting in Sicily and in Asia Minor, was employed by the duke of Athens against the neighbouring principality of Neopatras, but they soon proved dangerous allies. Disputes about payment culminated in the overthrow of the Franks. On a fatal day in the spring of 1311 the Catalans were outstandingly victorious on the plain of Boeotia, and only a few Frankish knights survived the battle; the widows of the fallen provided wives for the newcomers. The Catalan mercenaries, surprised by their own sweeping victory, which so struck the imagination of their contemporaries, sought a ruler outside their own ranks, and turned to their former employer, Frederick II of Sicily. Thus it was that for over half a century the duchy of Athens was ruled in name by absentee dukes of the Sicilian House, while the real power was wielded by vicar-generals appointed to represent them. To the north, the Catalans conquered the southern part of the Wallachian duchy of Neopatras, including the city of Neo-

[1] W. Miller, *The Latin Orient*, p. 29 (London, 1920).

patras itself (1318), and the double title of 'dukes of Athens and Neopatras' was borne by the kings of Aragon, the successors of the Sicilian rulers, long after the Catalan duchy had disappeared.

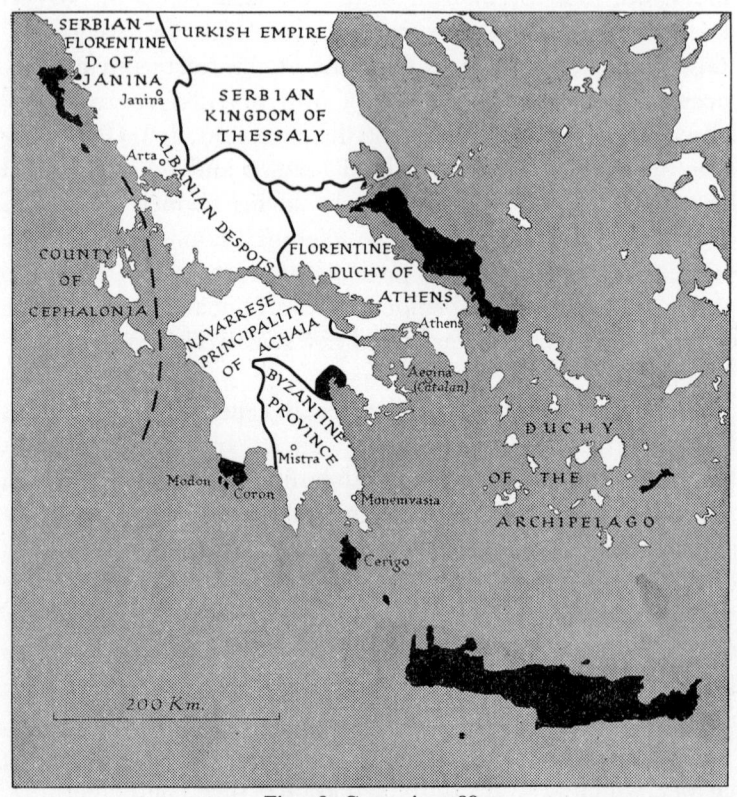

Fig. 16. Greece in 1388

Based on W. Miller, *The Latins in the Levant*, p. 332 (London, 1908).

Venetian possessions are shown in black. The southern portion of the despotat of Epirus was now under the control of an Albanian chieftain (Ghin Boua Spata) at Arta; the northern portion, centred on Janina, had been held by a Serbian chieftain (Thomas Preliubovitch), but he died in 1385 and his widow married Esau Buondelmonti, a Florentine noble.

The sons of the mercenaries did not possess the fighting qualities of their fathers; and in 1388 Athens was occupied by a Florentine family of bankers named Acciajuoli who were prominent in the affairs of the Peloponnese to the south. Thus began the third chapter in the history of the medieval duchy of Athens (Fig. 16). The Catalans vanished from the scene almost as completely as the Franks before them, and the next half-century saw many Florentine families in the area. But the independence of the duchy was difficult to maintain before the rising tide of Turkish successes. In June 1456 the Turks occupied Athens, and Thebes fell four years later. From 1460 onwards, central Greece remained Turkish, apart from two brief intervals when the Venetians occupied Athens (1466 and 1687-8).

By the time of the arrival of the Turks, a new element had been added to the population of Attica and Boeotia. Towards the end of the Catalan regime the area had been disturbed by civil war, and, to repair the ravages, Albanian settlers were invited to colonize the waste lands (c. 1380). After the occupation of Epirus by the Tocco family in 1418, still more Albanians came in under the Florentine dukes. The settlement had permanent results. From these colonists of the fourteenth and fifteenth centuries are descended many of the Albanians of Attica and Boeotia who still speak Albanian as well as Greek.

THE PRINCIPALITY OF ACHAIA, 1205-1432

Just before the conquest of Constantinople, Geoffrey de Villehardouin, nephew and namesake of the historian of the conquest, was driven by bad weather into the port of Modon in the Peloponnese. While he was staying there and becoming involved in the local quarrels, the great drama of the break-up of the Byzantine empire was taking place. In the winter of 1204, Boniface was taking possession of his kingdom of Salonica, and Geoffrey accordingly made his way to the headquarters of Boniface. There he outlined to an old friend from Champagne, William of Champlitte, a scheme for the conquest of the Peloponnese, promising to acknowledge William as his overlord. The two men, with only a few hundred soldiers, won almost the whole of the peninsula in a single battle. The newly won land was partitioned into twelve baronies among their followers, the ruins of whose baronial castles can still be seen standing in strong positions. William, recalled by affairs in France, died on his way home, and Geoffrey then became 'prince of Achaia' in his stead.

There were two areas which Villehardouin was unable to acquire. One was the territory around the Venetian ports of Modon and Coron, guarding the sea route to the east; occupied in 1206, they remained in Venetian possession until 1500. The other was the southern rock of Monemvasia, 'the Gibraltar of Greece', under the flag of the Byzantine state of Nicaea; this, however, was conquered in 1246, but only with the aid of Venetian galleys, and only after a siege of three years. Then, in the south, the fortress of Mistra was built to overawe the Slavs of Taygetos and the restless people of Maina. But Monemvasia was not kept for long. The third of the Villehardouins, William, became involved in disputes between the despotate of Epirus and the reviving empire of Nicaea; captured by the Nicaean Greeks, he was restored to freedom only in return for the fortresses of Monemvasia, Mistra and Old Maina (1262). It was the gain of this southern territory that paved the way for the ultimate restoration of Byzantine authority in the Peloponnese (Fig. 14).

William de Villehardouin left no male heir, and the marriage of his daughter Isabella to the son of Charles I of Naples united the fortunes of the principality with those of the Angevin power at Naples. After William's death in 1278, the principality was ruled by deputies appointed from Naples, for Isabella, though young, was already a widow. She next married Florent of Hainaut, a young Flemish nobleman who thus became prince of Achaia, and, after this, many Flemings appeared in Greece. Widowed for a second time, Isabella married a prince of the House of Savoy, and the Flemings were replaced by Piedmontese. The newcomers were so unpopular, however, that Isabella and her husband left Greece for ever, and the government lapsed to the Angevin power at Naples. A disputed succession followed, and the barren title of 'prince of Achaia' continued to pass from one absentee to another.

This unsatisfactory state of affairs continued during the fourteenth century, until a band of mercenaries did for Achaia what the Catalans had done for Athens in 1311. The origin of the Navarrese Company is obscure. They had been employed by the king of Navarre in his struggle with Charles V of France; and, seeking adventures farther afield, became involved in the complications of the succession to Achaia. They soon occupied much of the peninsula, and, in 1383, their leader declared himself 'vicar' of the principality; his successor exchanged the title for that of 'prince' in 1396 (Fig. 16). It was from his widow's nephew that the Byzantine emperor was able to take the whole of the Peloponnese by 1432 (see p. 56), apart from a few points held by Venice; for to Modon and Coron the Venetians had added Argos (1388), Nauplia (1388) and Lepanto (1407). But the Byzantine reconquest was not to last long. By 1461 the advancing tide of Turkish success had engulfed the whole of the Peloponnese up to the limits of the Venetian colonies (see p. 76).

In the middle of the fourteenth century, the Byzantine rulers of the Peloponnese had strengthened their army by recruiting large numbers of Albanians. These mercenaries were followed by colonists, and a large number of Albanians then settled upon the waste lands of the province, where their descendants remain to this day.

THE DUCHY OF THE ARCHIPELAGO, 1207–1566

At the partition of 1204, the Greek islands had been allotted to Venice, but the government of the republic decided to leave their occupation to private citizens. Accordingly, Marco Sanudo, a nephew of the doge, set out with some companions to win a principality among the islands of the Cyclades (1207). They succeeded in founding a state that was in some ways the most stable of all those brought into being by the Fourth Crusade. Sanudo kept Naxos and some other islands for himself, and partitioned the surrounding islands amongst his fellow-freebooters. Thus at Andros and elsewhere arose those feudal castles whose ruins still dominate the landscape.

Sanudo had no wish to become merely a local governor under the republic, and so he acknowledged the overlordship of the Latin emperor who formed the islands into a duchy known sometimes as the duchy of Naxos, of 'the Dodekànesos' and of 'the Archipelago'. The nominal suzerainty was later transferred to Achaia (1236) and then to Naples (1267), though Venice more than once claimed overlordship. The duchy survived the revival of Byzantine power (see p. 56), and the Sanudo dynasty continued until 1383, when it was replaced by that of the usurper Francesco Crispo, a member of a Lombard family who had come to have possessions in Melos. The Crispi remained in power for the next two centuries.

Under the rule of the Crispi, Venetian influence became increasingly important in the affairs of the island barons, and Venice more than once took over the government of Andros, Naxos and Paros. But not even Venetian interference was able to save the islands from the Turkish raids which grew increasingly frequent. At last, in 1566, the Turkish conquest took place; for thirteen years a Jewish favourite of the Sultan, Joseph Nasi, ruled as an absentee duke, until the final incorporation of the duchy into Turkey in 1579. Nowhere else in Greece did Latin rule leave so many traces as among these islands of the Cyclades—in memorials, in language and in religion, and the Roman Church has remained important here up to this day.

THE COUNTY PALATINE OF CEPHALONIA, 1194–1483

Even before the Fourth Crusade, Matteo Orsini, a member of an Italian family, had made himself master of the islands of Cephalonia, Zante and Ithaca (1194). During the Venetian occupation of Corfu (1206–14), he acknowledged the supremacy of Venice, but afterwards transferred his allegiance to the prince of Achaia. His descendants became involved in the politics of Epirus, and ruled over that province from 1318 until it was reunited to the Byzantine empire in 1336 (see p. 66). Meanwhile, in 1324, the islands had been annexed outright by the Angevins to Achaia, and the county was not granted out again until 1357. It was then given to the Tocco family from Beneventum who united Santa Maura (Levkás) to the other islands. By 1418 the Tocci had also revived the continental dominion of the Orsini, and had made themselves masters of the country south of Janina (Fig. 19). The court of Cephalonia during these years was described by Froissart as a second fairyland. But family dissensions soon enabled the Turks to interfere; Janina was lost in 1430, and by 1449 Arta, Aetolia and Acarnania had also become Turkish. The islands likewise fell to the Turks in 1479, although with the exception of Santa Maura they were soon recovered by Venice and held for over three hundred years (*c.* 1482–1797); Santa Maura did not become Venetian until 1684.

THE DESPOTATE OF EPIRUS, 1204–1336

While the Byzantine empire was being appropriated by the crusaders, the difficult country of Epirus was seized by a representative of the imperial family, Michael Angelus Comnenus, who maintained his newly acquired territory against all comers. The court of Arta became, like that of Nicaea, a refuge for Greeks against the Latin invaders of the Aegean world. The second 'despot' of Epirus conquered the neighbouring kingdom of Salonica in 1223, and founded a new Greek empire of Salonica. This success both alarmed the Franks and also offended the rival Greek empire of Nicaea. In 1246, the Nicaean emperor was able to conquer the province of Salonica, but the Wallachian principality of Neopatras, to the south, was left independent until 1318 (see p. 58).

In the west, Epirus itself still remained free until the last of the direct line from Michael Angelus was killed, in 1318, by a member of the Orsini family of Cephalonia who then maintained the independence of the despotate until it was reunited to the Byzantine empire in 1336. Soon, however, the area was annexed by the expanding state of Serbia under Stephen Dushan (1349), and a large part of northern Greece fell under the control of the Serbs. On the break-up of the Serbian empire after Stephen's death in 1355, there was great confusion; Epirus was disputed by Serbs, Albanians and others (Fig. 16) until the southern portion was acquired by the Tocco family from Cephalonia in 1418 (see p. 65). By 1449, however, the area had passed under Turkish control, and with it the obscure people of Albania who, in the fourteenth century, had been expanding southwards towards Acarnania and Aetolia and even into Thessaly where the Vlachs had hitherto formed the bulk of the population.

VENETIAN POSSESSIONS, 1204–1797

Before 1204 Venice already occupied a commanding position in the eastern Mediterranean trade that played so great a part in the economic life of medieval Europe. That she could undertake the transport of the Fourth Crusade is in itself a measure of her power. Her gains at the partition of 1204 reflected these maritime interests, and marked a turning point in her history. While the Frankish adventurers occupied the mainland of Greece, Venetian influence was predominant in the islands and coasts of the Aegean. Modon and Coron, 'the right eye' of the republic, were important stations on the eastern route; Crete, purchased in 1204, was held, despite many insurrections, till 1669; Euboea, gained in 1209, was Venetian until 1470, and early in the fifteenth century large numbers of Albanians were induced to settle on the uncultivated lands of the island. But a map of territorial possessions does not do justice to Venetian enterprise in the Aegean, for frequently Venice acquired influence and trading rights without actual dominion and administrative responsibility. The Venetians who created the duchy of the Archipelago owed

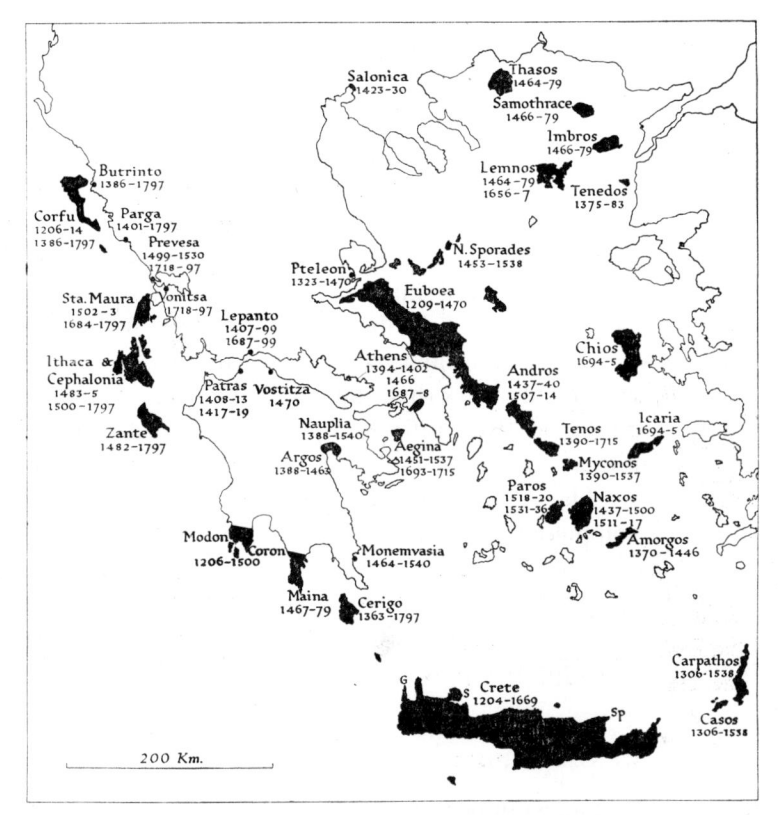

Fig. 17. Venetian possessions in the Greek lands
Based mainly on *The Cambridge Medieval History*, vol. IV, pp. 476–7 (Cambridge, 1923).

It is difficult to construct a really satisfactory map of Venetian possessions because sovereignty was sometimes not clearly defined, and Venice frequently acquired influence and control without administrative responsibility. Venetian citizens, too, held land from other powers, e.g. in the case of the duchy of the Archipelago (see p. 64). The dates on the map, moreover, do not take account of some changes in status, e.g. Venice paid tribute to the Turks for Zante from 1485 to 1699. Nor is any attempt made to indicate the occupation of the Peloponnese between 1685–7 and 1715 (Monemvasia was not taken until 1690). In Crete, after 1669, Venice still retained Grabusa (*G*) until 1691, and the island in Suda Bay (*S*) and Spinalonga (*Sp*) until 1715.

allegiance to the Latin empire; elsewhere, too, Venetian citizens held lands from other powers; thus a member of the Zorzi family of Venice in 1355 became marquess of Boudonitza, a dependency of the principality of Achaia.

In the centuries that followed the Fourth Crusade, Venice increased her colonies in the Aegean and the Peloponnese by purchase and by conquest. 'Never', we are told, 'was there a state so dependent on the sea.' Structurally, the Venetian empire was coming to consist of a series of strategic points, calling stations, islands, and merchant quarters in cities, all of which were strung along the greatest of medieval trade routes. Although these possessions fluctuated, the net result was an increase in dominion until, in the fifteenth century, Venetians and Turks were meeting at every point. The defence of the Aegean against the Turk had fallen to Venice. The first Turkish war lasted from 1464 to 1479, and thereafter there was intermittent warfare, with many oscillations in Venetian sovereignty (Fig. 17). Though the Venetian commander Morosini conquered the Peloponnese in 1685-7, the province was finally lost to the Turk in 1715. In that year, too, the last island that Venice held in the Aegean—Tenos—was also lost; the Ionian islands together with Cerigo and Cerigotto, however, she kept until 1797 (see p. 89).

GENOESE POSSESSIONS, *c.* 1261-1566

Genoa played a less important part than Venice in the history of the Aegean. She had no Byzantine tradition to pull her eastward, but soon, like Venice, she was benefiting by the carrying trade of the Crusades; the earliest treaty between Genoa and the Byzantine empire is dated 1155. Genoa took no part in the Fourth Crusade, but with the overthrow of the Latin empire in 1261 came the opportunity of the Genoese. In return for assisting the Greek empire of Nicaea, they exacted commercial privileges; the price was free trade throughout the empire, a monopoly of shipping in the Black Sea, and permission to found colonies in the Aegean. In the city of Constantinople, now restored to Byzantine hands, they were assigned the suburb of Galata as their special quarter, and they also obtained the rich city of Smyrna in Asia Minor. From the events of 1261, then, dates the rise of Genoa as an Aegean power (Fig. 18).

Genoese families now appeared in the islands. The Zaccaria were soon exploiting the alum mines of Phocea (1275) and the rich mastic plantations of Chios (1304); the latter island passed ultimately into the control of a Genoese chartered company whose partners, abandoning their own names, became known as 'the Giustiniani'.[1] The rich island of Lesbos passed in 1355 into the hands of the Gattilusio family which became connected by marriage with the Byzantine imperial house, and which extended its control to the nearby islands of Thasos, Lemnos, Samothrace and Imbros, as well as to Phocea in Asia Minor and to Aenos on the mainland of Thrace.

The vicissitudes of these and the other Genoese islands were many; and the rivalry between Venice and Genoa, breaking at times into open war, was the main key to the local politics of the Aegean world. But as the fourteenth century drew to a close, a new factor overshadowed this rivalry—the coming of the Turks. Though each city negotiated commercial treaties with the new enemy, they sometimes sank their differences in an attempt to meet this menace to western interference in the Aegean. One after another, the Genoese islands passed into Turkish hands. With the loss of Chios in 1566, Genoese sovereignty disappeared from the Aegean.

THE KNIGHTS OF RHODES, 1309–1522

At the break-up of the Byzantine empire in 1204, Rhodes was seized by a Greek noble, Leon Gabalas, but it was soon under

[1] This is the only example of this method of control by Latins in the Aegean. The company was known as the *maona*. Other examples of Genoese companies were the *maona* of Cyprus founded in 1374, and that of Corsica founded in 1378.

the control of Italian adventurers, who, during the thirteenth century, were compelled at times to acknowledge the overlordship of the emperor of Nicaea. Raided frequently by the Turks, it was occupied in 1309 by the Knights of St John, who, since the fall of the Holy Land in 1291, had lived in Cyprus. The dominion of the Knights soon stretched over the neighbouring islands which were governed on feudal principles.

Fig. 18. Genoese possessions in the Greek lands
Based on *The Cambridge Medieval History*, vol. IV, p. 477 (Cambridge, 1923).

The strategic situation of the islands in the eastern Mediterranean was important, for they formed a great fortress against the Turks. Many monuments still tell of their prosperity in the fourteenth century, despite Turkish raids. At length, in 1522, the Turks succeeded in occupying Rhodes, and the Knights were allowed to withdraw to Malta.

FRANKISH CIVILIZATION IN GREECE

The Frankish occupation formed a curious episode in the history of Greece. The newcomers from the west—Italians and Frenchmen, Catalans and Navarrese, Germans and Flemings—established a feudal constitution in all the states they founded. Thus, below the twelve barons of Achaia, for whom most information is available, there were greater and lesser vassals, then freemen, then serfs. Elsewhere there were variations, but the same general features of feudal society were to be found. To this land of opportunity came the younger sons of French noble houses seeking adventure and fortune. Of the court of Geoffrey de Villehardouin's successor in Achaia, the Venetian historian Marino Sanudo wrote: 'Knights came to the Morea from France, from Burgundy, and above all from Champagne, to follow him. Some came to amuse themselves, others to pay their debts, others again because of crimes which they had committed.'[1] Pope Honorius III in the thirteenth century could well speak of Greece as 'New France'. The social life of this feudal society, with its brilliant courts and gay tournaments, was a bright one; and a picture of the fine array of western chivalry has been preserved for us in the anonymous *Chronicle of the Morea*, versions of which exist in French, Italian and Aragonese as well as in Greek. The Greeks, apart from those in Crete, seem to have accepted the occupation with tameness, which contrasts with the frequent rebellions they raised under the Turks. Occasionally, especially in Achaia, old native families were to be found holding fiefs under the western barons.

At first, the Franks took over the existing Greek ecclesiastical organization, but installed Roman Catholic churchmen everywhere. There were fruitless attempts to reunite the churches of Rome and Constantinople, but the Roman faith made very little headway among the Greeks. Later on, towards the end

[1] W. Miller, *Essays in the Latin Orient*, p. 90 (Cambridge, 1921).

of the fourteenth century, the Greek Church recovered a good deal of ground, and some Orthodox bishops were allowed to return to their sees. The Greek people found in them an ally against their foreign rulers. It was in the Ionian islands and in the Cyclades that Roman Catholic influence was most permanent, and it survives up to the present day.

The Frankish occupation has left many traces upon the countryside, in great castles and isolated towers, but it made little mark upon the Greek people and their institutions. Conquerors and the conquered never really amalgamated except to produce some despised half-castes (*Gasmoûloi*) who usually sided with the Greeks. The new-comers did not come in sufficient numbers to obtain a firm grip on the country, and they remained to the end a series of garrisons in a foreign land. Their conquest became an episode, not a formative factor in the life of Greece. 'New France' was to pass away for ever before the advance of the Turk, leaving behind not much more than archaeological remains to recall the brilliant interlude of western chivalry.

3. BYZANTINE CIVILIZATION

LITERATURE

The prolific literary output of the Byzantines reflects every aspect of their life, culture and thought. Their literary tastes and scholarly pursuits were determined by an all-too-conscious effort to preserve and perpetuate the lore of classical Greece whose legitimate heirs they considered themselves to be, while their deep devotion to the Christian faith, their passion for theological discussion and the practical wisdom which distinguished them inspired a great variety of writings of considerable interest and originality. In secular poetry they cultivated the forms of classical Greek poetry, especially the epigram, and occasionally poets like Paul the Silentiary in the sixth century and George Pisides in the seventh succeeded in attaining wit and grace in their verse. There were a number of Byzantine historians beginning with Procopius and Agathias, both of whom wrote about the reign of Justinian, and ending with Laonicos Chalcocondyles, Sphrantzes, Ducas and Critobulos of Imbros, the four historians of the fall of Constantinople, in 1453. They all write about their own times and all strive to emulate the diction and manner of Herodotus, Thucydides or Polybius. This self-conscious atticism, at a time when the language was increasingly diverging from the prosody, grammar and vocabulary of Attic Greek, renders almost all educated secular writing produced during the Byzantine era frigid and rhetorical. For colour and freshness one has to turn to works of a popular character written for the most part by uneducated monks for a humbler public. Such are the numerous world chronicles, the Lives of Saints, or the Begging Poems of Ptochoprodromos. Also interesting is the emergence in the tenth century of an epic saga around Digenis Akritas, a legendary hero whose exploits in the eastern frontier of the empire are celebrated in a written epic and in many folk ballads. Contact with the Franks of the West resulted, from the twelfth century onwards, in a number of verse romances in the vernacular, influenced by western tales of chivalry as well as by the late Hellenistic romances.

Religious literature flourished widely and comprises theological, ascetical and liturgical works. It was a field in which the Byzantines excelled, producing mystical writings of great beauty, and religious poetry which reaches its highest level in the sixth century in the poetic genius of Romanos, whose hymns (*kontakia*) rank among the greatest achievements of ecclesiastical poetry.

Scholarly and educational activity centred chiefly on the literature of ancient Greece and continued on the whole the tradition of Alexandrian scholarship: textual and philological commentaries, lexica, anthologies, encyclopaedias and the production of copies of classical texts represent the invaluable contribution of the Byzantines to the preservation and transmission of the Greek classics.

ART

From its beginnings to the fifteenth century Byzantine art is marked in every phase of its development by an extraordinary vigour and an unusual wide range of output. It was the first great Christian art which sought to interpret the dogmas of faith in the realm of the visual and to establish conventions in an iconography which became an indispensable part of Orthodox worship. The interior decoration of churches (mosaics, frescoes, icons) was of supreme devotional significance and formed an integral part of the building design. It was intended not only to celebrate the glory of God but to help the congregation to communicate with the Divine by edifying and instructing them.

Various influences were at work in the development of Byzantine art, but from the start two main stylistic trends can be distinguished: the 'free and relaxed' style of the Hellenic tradition which the Byzantine artists had inherited from the Graeco-Roman world and which remained a living force, asserting itself in each of the 'Golden Ages' of Byzantine art— the Justinianic, the Macedonian, the Comnenian and the Palaeologan; and the marked tendency towards expressionism, abstraction or realism, all of which Byzantium may have absorbed from Oriental influences. Quite often all these styles are to be found in one composition, with remarkable results in the subtlety of representation. It seems certain that Byzantine art became highly centralized at quite an early stage. Constantinople took the lead in matters artistic and set the tone throughout the empire. Fine examples of this art have survived wherever the empire spread and even beyond its frontiers: the mosaic decoration of the Great Mosque of Damascus is the work of Byzantine artists. The mosaics of SS Cosmas and Damian in Rome, of San Vitale and St Apollinare in Classe in Ravenna, of St George and St Demetrius in Salonica, of Sancta Sophia, the Church of the Holy Apostles and Kahriye Djameh (Church of Chora) in Constantinople, of Daphni near Athens, or Hosios

Loukas near Delphi—to mention only a few—rank among the great masterpieces of pictorial art.

Equally superb is the Byzantine achievement in wall paintings and iconography. Greece is rich in churches decorated with frescoes of the best periods of Byzantine art, and the Byzantine Museum and the Benaki in Athens contain a representative collection of some very fine icon-paintings. The peninsula of Mr Athos should also be mentioned as one of the chief repositories of Byzantine culture and art. The minor arts too flourished during the Byzantine period. Many examples of decorative sculpture, ivory carvings, enamels, silver plate, ornamental tapestries, liturgical objects and illustrated manuscripts have survived.

ARCHITECTURE

In the fourth century various cities, Salonica, Ephesus and, above all, Constantinople, housed the Roman court and took over the tradition of Rome. The most sumptuous and permanent buildings were now churches, whether large congregational halls (*basilicas*) or centrally-planned domed buildings to mark holy sites (*martyria*), to serve as mausolea, or to enclose tanks for the public baptism of crowds of catechumens. The fourth- and fifth-century basilicas (e.g. St Demetrius and Haghia Paraskevi at Salonica) were spacious, purely Roman buildings, with apsidal east ends and timber roofs of low pitch. The baptisteries resemble the cold plunge-baths in Roman *Thermae*. The martyria and mausolea developed more original plans—a circle in a decagon, a cross, or a cross in an octagon. The best examples of each of these styles are the Tombs of Theodoric and Galla Placidia at Ravenna and the Santa Fosca at Torcello. The interior was veneered with marble for the full height of its lower arcades, and above that with mosaic. This decoration, taken from imperial Rome, remained the Byzantine ideal.

The threat of fire compelled architects to substitute vaults for timber roofs. The Romans had already used simple tunnel-vaults or cross-groined vaults (four tunnels intersecting at right angles over each bay). In Roman concrete these could span up to 100 ft, but the Byzantines lacked Roman *pozzuolana* and Roman slaves. Tunnels and cross-groined vaults, still used for smaller spans, were unstable over larger, when made of bricks or empty wine-jars. The circular dome was the obvious solution and architects soon learned to place this over a square compartment, supporting it on spherical triangles (pendentives) or corbelled arches (squinches) in the corners of the square. The main hall of Justinian's masterpiece, Sancta Sophia at Constantinople (A.D. 532-8), by far the largest Byzantine building, has three internal divisions, like the vaulted Basilica of Maxentius (*c*. A.D. 310) in Rome. But whereas the latter had three equal cross-vaulted bays, Sancta Sophia has a central dome and two lower semi-domes, giving a far more 'poetic' effect.

Justinian's architects also developed two other sorts of church, both like Sancta Sophia with a western vestibule (narthex): the polygonal nave, with apses (*exedrae*) opening from alternate sides (SS Sergius and Bacchus) or all sides (San Vitale, Ravenna); and the cruciform church, with a dome over the crossing and each arm (Holy Apostles at Constantinople, St John's at Ephesus and St Mark's at Venice). The second plan inspired all the later churches. The cross was enclosed in a rectangle, allowing space in the corners for the two virtually necessary rooms, the *prothesis* and *diakonikon*, each side of the eastern arm, or chancel. All three were now masked by a heavy screen, the *iconostasis*. In some churches the crossing remained small, but the whole building grew loftier (Holy Apostles, Salonica; Kahriyeh Djameh, Constantinople). In others dome and crossing grew larger, and absorbed parts of the other bays. This gives great spaciousness even to small interiors, as at Hosios Loukas and Daphni. The exterior was also more regarded now, and, as in Kahriyeh Djameh, some mouldings, borrowed from the West, enlivened the Byzantine flatness.

Compared with the churches, all Byzantine military and civil buildings, except the walls of Constantinople and perhaps Nicaea, are negligible.

4. TURKISH GREECE

THE OTTOMAN ADVANCE

It was at the request of a Byzantine emperor that the Ottoman Turks first came into Europe to fight against the Serbs. But having defeated the Serbs, they refused to return to their Asiatic homeland, and in 1354 established themselves on the European shores of the Dardanelles. A long and successful campaign in Thrace followed: Adrianople was captured in 1360, and the Turkish capital was then moved to this city from Brusa in Asia Minor. From this base in Thrace the Turkish conquest of south-eastern Europe began. The desperate effort of the Serbs, the Bulgars, the Vlachs and the Albanians to stay the progress of the Turks was shattered at Kossovo in 1389. The chronology of the Turkish advance is sometimes confusing, as the Christian states were frequently defeated and became tributary some years before they were completely annexed (Fig. 19).

The Latin states fell one after another during the next century. Macedonia (except for Salonica) was occupied by 1380; Salonica itself may have resisted until 1430. In 1393 Thessaly was annexed. The duchy of Athens was occupied in 1456–60; and by 1461 the Turks were also in complete control of the Peloponnese, apart from some coastal points held by the Venetians (see p. 63). In the north, Janina fell in 1430; the continental domain of the Tocco family had completely disappeared by 1449; and in 1479 the Turks extended their rule to the nearby Ionian islands, but they did not keep these for very long; Zante went to Venice in 1482, and Cephalonia and Ithaca in 1500; Santa Maura, however, except for a brief period (1502–3), did not become Venetian until 1684.

By the time that Constantinople itself had fallen in 1453, the Turks were in control of almost all the Greek mainland. Soon, the Aegean islands were mastered also. Lemnos, Imbros, Samothrace and Thasos were acquired in 1456–7, Lesbos in 1462, Euboea in 1470. But over a century was to elapse before

Turkish control was complete. Not until the duchy of Naxos and the island of Chios had fallen in 1566 were the Turks in as complete control of the Aegean Sea as of the Greek mainland; Crete itself did not fall until 1669, and the island of Tenos

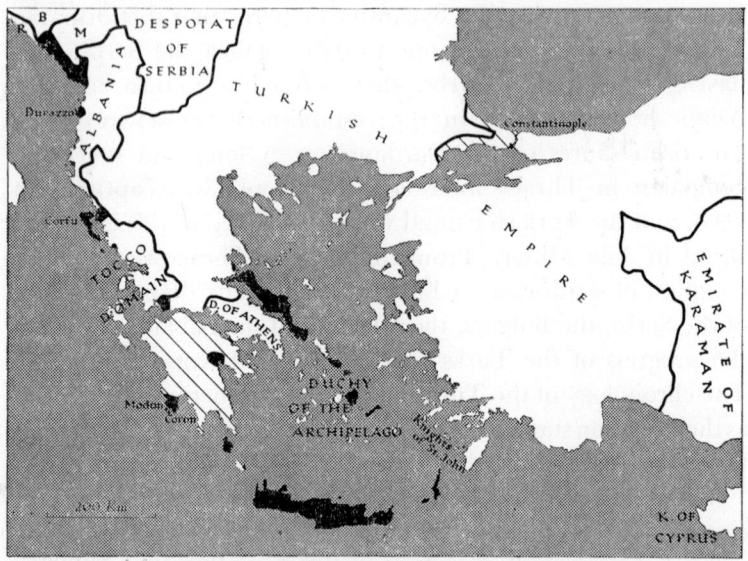

Fig. 19. Greece in 1440
Based on: (1) E. A. Freeman, *Atlas to the Historical Geography of Europe*, map 43 (London, 1903); W. R. Shepherd, *Historical Atlas*, p. 93 (London, 1930).
Venetian possessions are shown in black; B=Bosnia; M=Montenegro; R=Ragusa.

lingered on under Venetian sovereignty until as late as 1715. In the Aegean islands, a number of Albanians were settled, especially in the latter half of the sixteenth century, as part of a scheme of colonization.

TURKISH CONTROL OF GREECE

The Greek lands, divided among so many sovereignties since 1204, found unity once more in a foreign rule centred at Constantinople. The main features of the political organization of the Turkish lands were simple. The whole area was under the administration of the *beglerbeg* (lord of lords) of Rumili

(European Turkey) stationed at Sofia. In 1470, the Greek lands comprised six 'sanjaks' organized on a military basis: (1) Morea (Peloponnese), (2) Epirus, (3) Thessaly, (4) Salonica, (5) Euboea, Boeotia and Attica, (6) Aetolia and Acarnania. Other sanjaks were added as the islands and Crete were acquired. Each sanjak was divided into 'cazas' or subdistricts, of which, for example, there were twenty-three in the Morea. A great deal of the local administration, however, was left in the hands of the Greek 'archontes', or notables, of every town and even of every hamlet; these undertook, for example, the farming of taxes and the work of policing.

Greeks were used not only for local administration but also for more general administrative purposes. It was a feature of Turkish policy to use Christians themselves to hold together and govern the vast Turkish empire, and this policy reflected itself in the Church, in the army and in the civil service.

The Church

The Turks did not attempt any wholesale conversion of the Greeks to Islam, but sought to manage the Christian population through its own Church. Indeed, some Orthodox Christians had been in favour of the change by which a Turkish sultan replaced a Byzantine emperor inclined to reunion with Rome. As Voltaire said, the Greek clergy 'preferred the turban of a Turkish priest to the red hat of a Roman cardinal'. This hatred of the western Church enabled the sultan to interfere, and even to appear as a patron of the Orthodox faith. The Greek Patriarch was treated with great respect, and freedom of Christian worship was guaranteed. Here was an insurance against the possibility of a western and Catholic crusade to deliver the eastern lands. It is true that the Patriarch came more and more under the control of the Turkish authorities, but then the Christians themselves were soon intriguing and bidding for the office. It is true also that many Christian churches, even St Sophia itself, were converted into mosques wherever Moslems were numerous, and minarets disappeared from Macedonia and Thessaly only in the twentieth century with the Greco-Turkish exchange of populations. But still the fact remains that the Turkish régime was, with but few exceptions, a tolerant one.

The great financial distinction between true believers and Christians was the payment of the 'haratch', or capitation tax, by every male unbeliever over ten years of age (except by priests, by the blind, by the maimed and by old men). A Christian had also to pay twice the duty paid by a Moslem (5% as against 2½%) on imports and exports. Hardship, however, arose not from the legal taxes, but from various exactions by the provincial governors, so much so that in 1691 the central government prohibited the exaction of additional taxes on the plea of local necessity. Despite this, the Christians continued to suffer from the corruption of Turkish administration, but then so did their fellow-Moslems. Many Christians escaped either into Venetian territory or overseas. Some entered the Venetian employ as mercenaries, and the Greek 'stradioti' were known all over Europe. Numerous Epirote families settled across the waters in Calabria.

The Janissaries

There is a good deal of obscurity about the origin and working of the *corps d'élite* of the Turkish army, the janissaries (*yeni-tscheri*=new troops). About the year 1330 the corps was formed, recruited entirely from Christian children, taken at an early age (at about six or seven) and brought up as Moslems in a sort of military brotherhood, in which marriage was prohibited. From then on, every Christian father was compelled, at intervals of five years, or oftener, to make a declaration of the number of his sons, and one boy out of every five, or one out of every family, was taken by the officers of the sultan. The recruitment was enforced in all parts of the Ottoman empire in Europe, but mainly in Bosnia, Bulgaria and Albania. It is surprising that of the many insurrections against Turkish rule, only one (the Albanian agitation of 1565) seems to have been roused by this terrible tribute.

By the sixteenth century the janissaries numbered about 12,000–20,000, and had grown into a powerful and favoured corps; what was at first a curse came to be regarded by many parents as a blessing. There is even record of Moslems who lent their children to Christians so they might become members of so powerful a body. Creatures of the sultan, the janissaries in turn imposed their yoke upon him; they mutinied more than once, and in 1566 extorted the privilege of legal marriage, and membership of the body became to some extent hereditary. They lasted as a corps until 1826, but long before this they had ceased to be recruited from tribute-children; the last regular levy on children was in the year 1676. The result both of the levy, and of the migration of Greeks into Venetian territory and overseas, was a considerable diminution in the numbers of Greeks in the Greek lands. Indeed, by the end of the seventeenth century the time had come when 'a taxable infidel seemed a more valuable asset than a less remunerative believer in the true faith of Islam'.[1]

The Civil Service

The genius of the Turks was for conquest rather than administration, and so they used their conquered subjects to run the machinery of their empire. Some Greeks rose to high office; many even rose to the rank of Grand Vizier. Indeed, in the middle of the sixteenth century, the Venetians were reporting that the great offices in the Sultan's service were usually filled by Greeks and that many Turks were complaining of the favour shown to the Greeks. For some time the condition of this advancement was conversion to Islam, but about the middle of the seventeenth century the religious test was abolished for a number of the important offices of state, and in the following century the Grand Dragoman of the Porte (a secretary of state) was usually a Greek; so was the Grand

[1] W. Miller, *Essays on the Latin Orient*, p. 366 (Cambridge, 1921).

Dragoman of the Fleet; and the Morea, too, was placed under a native governor.

GREEK AND VENETIAN RESISTANCE

Although individual Greeks prospered in the Turkish empire, the Greek cause suffered; and when national and private interests clashed, the former only too often were sacrificed. This is not to say that all Greeks patiently endured the foreign yoke. Immediately after the conquest, assistance from the west had seemed possible, and there were many later proposals for a western crusade against the Ottoman power, but all these suggestions brought no substantial relief. A Spanish expedition in 1532, under the Genoese Andrea Doria, captured Coron and a great part of the Morea, but the Spaniards were expelled in the following year, and the Greeks were treated with great severity. Throughout the whole period of the Turkish occupation, Christian bandits known as 'klephts' maintained a semi-independent existence in the more mountainous regions north of the Isthmus. They preyed upon the more peaceful people of the plains, and to combat them the Turks organized a Christian gendarmerie known as 'armatoli'. The exploits of both are recorded in the ballad poetry of Greece.

The Christian defence now fell upon Venice. The first Venetian-Turkish war of 1463-79, which cost Venice both Argos and Euboea, was followed by repeated outbursts of hostilities for over two and a half centuries. Modon, Coron and Lepanto were lost in 1500, and, with the Turkish capture of Nauplia and Monemvasia in 1540, the last foothold of Venice in the Peloponnese disappeared; on the other hand, the Venetians had acquired a hold upon the Ionian islands of Zante (1482), Cephalonia and Ithaca (1500). In the Aegean, the Northern Sporades, Mykonos and Aegina were lost in the war of 1537-40. All that then remained to Venice were Crete, Tenos and the Ionian possessions.

Up to the middle of the sixteenth century, most of the islands of the Aegean, however, were still in western hands. The fall of the duchy of the Archipelago in 1566, and the capture of Chios from the Genoese in the same year, meant that the Turks were now in as complete control of the islands as of the mainland. The Turkish attack on Cyprus in 1570 produced a fresh outburst of warfare, and a large Christian fleet was collected with the help of the Papacy and of Spain. The Christian victory in the naval engagement off Lepanto (1571), famous though it has become, brought little relief to Greece. Roused by the prospect of help, the Greeks of the Peloponnese had risen to arms; but Christian counsels were divided; the last Greek resistance in Maina was quelled, and in 1573 the Venetians made a peace with the Turks that lasted until 1645.

During the seventy years of peace there were occasional Greek risings. In 1585 there was revolt in Acarnania and Aetolia, and again in 1611 there was another revolt around Janina. Early in the seventeenth century the restless people of Maina were also in rebellion and they were not reduced, in name at any rate, until 1614. During these years, and indeed during the whole period 1460-1684, piracy was a more important source of disturbance than revolt. The corsairs of North Africa, of Catalonia, Dalmatia, Genoa, Malta, Sicily and Tuscany, repeatedly plundered the coasts of Greece; some were Christians, some were Moslems, but, in any case, that made no difference to their victims. 'The unparalleled rapacity of these pirates devastated the maritime districts to such a degree that, even at the present day, many depopulated plains on the coasts of the Archipelago still indicate the fear which was long felt of dwelling near the sea.'[1] This was said even as late as the latter half of the nineteenth century.

During the Cretan war (1645-69) between Venice and the Turks, two rebellions were prompted by the Venetians in Greece. The Albanians of the Peloponnese rose in 1647, and in 1659 the people of Maina (who, incidentally, sold Christians to Turks as well as Turks to Christians) were able to sack Kalamata. By taking advantage of local feuds, the Turks were

[1] George Finlay, *A History of Greece*, vol. v, p. 57 (Oxford, 1877).

able to reduce the Mainotes, many of whom fled the country to Italy and to Corsica, where their descendants still live around Cargese. These diversions in the Morea could not prevent Crete from falling into Turkish hands in 1669, except for the three fortresses of Grabusa, Suda and Spinalonga (Fig. 17).

The renewal of war between Venice and Turkey in 1684 brought greater success to the Christian cause. In 1683, the Turks had been repulsed from Vienna; their best soldiers were engaged in Hungary, and the moment seemed ripe for western interference in Greece. The Venetian forces were under Francesco Morosini, and he entered into negotiation with the peoples of the two historic centres of resistance to the Turk— Epirus and Maina. In 1684 he captured the Ionian island of Santa Maura, and by August 1687 he was the possessor of all the Peloponnese, except Monemvasia (not reduced until 1690). He marched north of the Isthmus and captured Athens, but failed in an attack on Euboea. After long negotiations the Treaty of Carlowitz in 1699 gave Venice the whole of the Peloponnese.

The new province was in a sorry condition. Much of the land had gone out of cultivation; the neglect under Turkish administration had been aggravated by the destruction of war and by pestilence. According to one estimate, the population had fallen from over 200,000 inhabitants before the war to under 100,000. Venetian policy restored prosperity to the area; agriculture was improved; colonists were settled on empty lands, and many thousands of families arrived from the northern shores of the Gulf of Corinth. It has been estimated that the population of the province rose from 116,000 in 1692 to 177,000 in 1701, and to over 250,000 in 1708; and these figures are probably underestimates.[1] But although Venice improved the land, she failed to keep the sympathies of its people. The commercial policy of the republic hampered the trade of the area; Venetian soldiers were quartered on its inhabitants; there were religious difficulties between Roman Catholics and Orthodox. Soon, the Christian inhabitants of

[1] W. Miller, *Essays on the Latin Orient*, p. 418 (Cambridge, 1921).

the peninsula forgot the evils of the old regime. In 1710 one French traveller found the Greeks of Modon wishing for their return under Turkish domination, and envying the lot of those Greeks who still lived under it.[1]

Such were the conditions, when, in 1714, the Turks, having defeated Russia, were free to attempt the recapture of the peninsula. The campaign of 1715 was marked by striking Turkish victories and by mutinies in the Christian garrisons. Even Maina acknowledged the Turk; Tenos, the last Venetian island in the Aegean, also surrendered; and, in Crete, the last Venetian fortresses were likewise lost. By the treaty of Passarowitz in 1718, Venice relinquished her claim to the Peloponnese. Her most eastern possessions were now the islands of Cerigo and Cerigotto. Although she still held the Ionian Islands and four nearby places on the mainland, she ceased, from this time onward, to be an important factor in the fortunes of Greece.

But although Venice was no longer a decisive influence in the Greek world, the Venetian interlude was not without result. The material prosperity of the Greek lands continued to improve, and Turkish policy henceforward made a conscious attempt to placate the Greek subjects of the empire. The people of the Peloponnese were exempted from the land-tax for two years. Immigrants were exempted for three years, for the Turks were anxious to attract newcomers to settle on the wasted lands, and from this period dates another immigration of Albanians. At the heart of the empire, in Constantinople, an administrative aristocracy was developing among the Greek officials. Known as Phanariotes, from the 'Phanar' quarter of the city, these Greeks played an increasingly important part in administrative affairs during the eighteenth century. The four great Phanariote officers were those of dragoman of the Porte, dragoman of the Fleet, prince of Moldavia and prince of Wallachia. Around these great ones were crowds of minor Greek officials.

Moreover, if Venetian power was declining, so was Turkish

[1] A. de La Motraye, *Travels*, vol. I, p. 333 (London, 1723).

power, despite the victory of 1718. The Turkish failure to take Vienna in 1683 marked the transition from an expanding to a declining Turkey. In the north-west, Austria, and in the north-east, Russia, were soon to press back the Turkish frontiers. With the eighteenth century, too, came the beginnings of an effort to make the Greek lands independent.

RUSSIAN INTERFERENCE

Of the two rising enemies of the Turk, Russia was to exercise the most decisive influence upon Greek affairs. Russian interest in south-east Europe was a natural corollary to the expansion of the Russian state under Peter the Great (1689–1725) and his successors, and the Russo-Turkish wars were an inevitable consequence of a Russian Black Sea policy. Russian imperial agents appeared in various parts of European Turkey to prepare their fellow-Orthodox Christians for the day of liberation. The possibility of active resistance, however, did not come until after the middle of the century. In the sixties Russian agents were busily stirring up trouble in the historic centre of disaffection at Maina, and an English visitor to Greece in 1767 heard people frequently talk of their approaching deliverance through Russian aid. The Sultan appears to have shown but a careless contempt for these intrigues.

In 1768 the Russo-Turkish war broke out over the question of Poland, and two brothers named Orloff at once proceeded to Greece to organize an insurrection. The hopes of Catherine the Great were so high that Voltaire even thought it possible that Constantinople might soon become the capital of the Russian empire. But the small Russian force that landed in the Peloponnese in 1769 failed to rouse Greek national feeling. Many Greeks had no wish to exchange one foreign ruler for another, and were not prepared to swear allegiance to Catherine. The result was a complete defeat of the Russo-Greek forces by the Turks at Tripolitsa. But if the Russians had failed in the Peloponnese, they had been successful north of the Danube; and, too, the Russian fleet that appeared in the Aegean succeeded in occupying many of the Cyclades, which were greatly depopulated owing to corsairs and emigration. The war was ended in 1774 by the Treaty of Kutschuk Kainardji, by which Russia secured a firm grip upon the north shore of the Black Sea, and obtained also an international sanction for the rights of the Orthodox Christians of the Turkish empire. This vague stipulation was to provide a pretext for Russian interference in the domestic affairs of the Turkish empire.

During the early years of the peace, both Greeks and Turks suffered greatly from bands of Albanians who had been employed in the Turkish army but who now ravaged far and wide, both in the Peloponnese and to the north of the Isthmus. The condition of much of the countryside was desperate. The population of the Peloponnese (excluding Maina) had again been reduced to 100,000, and it was estimated that about 80,000 people had either died or emigrated; many had gone to the Crimea; over 12,000 had gone to Istria. The Albanian marauders were not put down until the dispatch of a Turkish expedition to the Peloponnese in 1779; some Albanians were induced to settle peacefully, others were exterminated. After this there was considerable improvement in the countryside; even the restless Mainotes were induced to pay regular tribute. Despite the plague of 1781–5, the population of the Peloponnese had greatly increased by the end of the century.

Russian interest did not abate after 1774. Catherine at one time suggested a restoration of the Byzantine empire, under her grandson, with Constantinople as its capital. Russian propaganda continued to be active in the Greek lands; a military academy for Greeks was established in Russia, and its pupils were selected from the principal Greek families by the Russian consuls. In 1783, a commercial treaty with the Sultan gave Greeks the right to trade under the Russian flag. From now onwards, Greek shipping spread actively over the Mediterranean, and increasing commercial prosperity contributed to the new sense of Hellenic unity that was developing during the years.

In 1787 Russo-Turkish antagonism once more flared into war over the question of the Crimea, and Russian agents scattered manifestos throughout Greece, inviting co-operation against the Turk. This succeeded in rousing the Albanian Christians around Suli, but it was evident that they were not sufficiently strong to provide a major diversion in the war. Nor were the exploits of pirates in the Aegean, infamous though they were, sufficient to turn the scales of warfare against the Turk. In 1792, Catherine, without consulting her Greek supporters, concluded the Treaty of Jassy with the Sultan; this treaty extended the Russian frontier to the Dniester in the north, and provided for a general amnesty for all Greeks involved in the war. By this time, however, a new factor in the form of the French Revolution had appeared to complicate the policies of all European states.

THE RISE OF GREEK NATIONAL FEELING

The struggle for Greek independence was to come about not merely as an instrument of Russian policy but as a result of rising national self-consciousness among the Greeks themselves. The French Revolution, breaking out in 1789, was a powerful stimulus to every people in Europe, and the enthusiasm of its rallying cries—Liberty and Freedom—found a responsive answer in Greece. One of the warmest supporters of the new ideas was Constantine Rhigas (1760–98), born at Velestino. It was he who wrote the famous Greek version of the Marseillaise, paraphrased by Byron as 'Sons of the Greeks, arise'. It was he, too, who founded a *Hetairía*, a society to promote Greek patriotic sentiment and to provide the Greeks with arms. Believing that the influence of the French Revolution would shortly lead to action in the Balkans, he went to Vienna to organize the movement among exiled Greeks and their sympathizers. From here, he published many Greek translations of foreign works, not in classical Greek but in the common tongue. He also formed a collection of national songs which, though not published until sixteen years after his death, was passed from hand to hand in manuscript, arousing patriotic enthusiasm everywhere in Greece. His work was cut short, for he was handed over by the Austrian government to the Turks, and was shot in 1798.

The death of Rhigas did nothing to abate the intellectual ferment that was active among the Greeks, and one indication of this was the work of Adamantios Korais (1748-1833). He was the son of a merchant of Smyrna, though from 1782 onwards he lived in France (in Paris itself after 1788). Inspired by the French Revolution he devoted himself to furthering the cause of Greek independence. Laying great stress on the classical inheritance of the Greeks, he sought to systematize the written language of his country in accordance with classical tradition. The result, something between the classical tongue and the common speech, was not merely of academic interest; for, in Greece as in other countries, the codifying of the written language, so that it became intelligible to all peoples and classes, was a powerful factor in calling into being a new nation, and the name of Korais must ever remain an important one in the story of the Greek revolt. Nor was Korais the only man to work along these lines. In the Ionian islands, a school of writers was busily at work collecting folk songs to feed Greek patriotism with memories of its past glory and heroism. It is true they wrote in the popular tongue and did not follow the systematization of Korais, but both schools of thought were symptoms of an educational revival and of the new feeling of nationality in Greece.

Despite the great influence of the French Revolution upon Greece, the Revolutionary and Napoleonic wars hardly touched Greece itself. In 1797, the Venetian Republic was extinguished and the Ionian islands were occupied by the French as a stepping-stone to the East. The general commanding the French troops was instructed: 'Be careful in issuing proclamations to the Greeks to make plenty of reference to Athens and Sparta.' Napoleon himself addressed the Mainotes as 'worthy descendants of the Spartans who alone among the ancient Greeks knew the secret of preserving political liberty'. The common fear of French interference in Greece even drew together for a short time those irreconcilable foes, the Tsar and the Sultan; France was forced to evacuate the Ionian islands in the following year, and in 1800 they became a federal republic under the joint protection of Russia and Turkey. But the unnatural allies were soon at war, and in 1807 the islands were ceded to France. They were taken by the British in 1809–10, and emerged in 1815 as a protectorate under British control, and so they remained until 1864.

The Congress of Vienna in 1815 did not attempt to solve the problem of south-eastern Europe, and Greece remained part of the Sultan's domain. There were, however, signs everywhere of the new spirit of Greek nationality. A new *Hetairía* had been created at Odessa in 1814, and its influence now extended throughout European Turkey. Thus the Albanians in Greece felt as Greek as the Greeks, and were to play a great part in the liberation to come. A feeling of expectancy was evident among the Phanariotes of Constantinople as well as among the bishops of the Orthodox Church. Travellers who returned from Greece brought away the impression that a crisis was at hand.

In the meantime, Turkish administration continued steadily to decline. Inefficiency and corruption were to be encountered everywhere. The local officials of the empire were straining after independence, and a series of rude shocks prepared the way for the Greek insurrection. Serbia had been in revolt since 1804, and an Albanian adventurer, Mehemet Ali, had become virtually independent in Egypt. Another Turkish official, Ali Pasha of Janina, had also become independent in Epirus, and, with Turkish action against the rebel, a favourable moment had arrived for the war of liberation. The first outbreak against the Turk in Moldavia and Wallachia (1821) was soon quelled. But before this northern revolt was over, the Greeks of the Peloponnese had risen and the struggle for Greek independence had begun.

CHAPTER III

MODERN GREECE, 1821-1939

1. THE WAR OF INDEPENDENCE, 1821-32

THE PREPARATION FOR WAR

THE literary and classical revival of the late eighteenth century was merged with the ferment of ideas produced by the 'Enlightenment' and the French Revolution. But the rise of Russia at the expense of Turkey led the Greek clergy and people to renew an older and simpler dream of freedom, in which the expulsion of the Turks and possession of land were more prominent than the purification of language or ideas. The Greeks had never been fully disarmed: the *klephts* of the Peloponnese, half brigands and half patriots, had become more daring than ever. Napoleon sent emissaries from Italy to the Peloponnese in 1797, and hundreds of peasant warriors enlisted in the Ionian regiment of the French Republic, which had momentarily annexed these islands. Many Greeks looked also to Ali Pasha of Janina, who was conducting, with French backing, a spirited struggle for his own independence in Epirus. Finally, the Greek (and Albanian) sailors, particularly those of the islands of Hydra and Spezzia (Spétsai) off the eastern coast of Argolis, were rising in wealth and confidence, and felt little fear of the Turkish navy, which was manned by unreliable Greek crews and commanded by Turkish officers often ignorant of the sea.

The men who created or revived the more or less secret society, *Filikí Hetairía*, at Odessa in 1814 were rather revolutionary than traditionalist in temper. It was active among the hellenizing elements in Wallachia and Moldavia and among Greeks engaged in shipping and trade with Constantinople and the Black Sea; but its influence in Greece was limited until 1819–20, and its activities were then soon merged in the general movement which was hardly secret any longer. Encouraged by some of the Russian Consuls in Turkey, but not countenanced by the Russian Government, the society's agents glorified Russia as the expected leader of a crusade. The meeting between Napoleon and the Tsar at Tilsit (1807) had been followed by a new Russian war against Turkey; and the Peace Treaty of Bucharest (1812) between Tsar and Sultan left a number of still unsettled disputes which might lead to a diplomatic rupture at any time. It was true that the statesmen at Vienna in 1814–15 agreed on a conservative system in Europe, and could ill afford an upheaval in the Balkans. But the Quadruple Alliance did not include any guarantee of the Turkish empire; while the Holy Alliance, and the character of Alexander I who initiated it, implicitly excluded any such idea. The Greek patriots expected help from the Tsar or at least from his Corfiot minister, Capo d'Istria; they were hardly aware of the Tsar's growing distrust of revolutionary movements anywhere. In spite of appearances, therefore, the Levant was in no such state of tranquillity as the Sultan, Metternich, and most of the European merchants desired.

THE STRUGGLE, 1821–27

The War of Independence could not have been won by the Greeks without the armed intervention of foreign Powers; but, equally, the movement could hardly have been permanently suppressed if these Powers had held aloof. The Powers were led to intervene, partly in order to remove the deadlock which threatened constant disturbance and piracy in the Aegean, but also by the pressure of public opinion at home; and the very success of the Greeks in creating this deadlock was due rather to the spirit which animated them than to their physical resources in so unequal a struggle.

The signal for revolt was given in March 1821 by a raid upon Jassy and Bucharest from Russian territory; but this ill-considered enterprise was disavowed by the Tsar, and was finally suppressed in June without eliciting any sympathy from the Romanian peasantry. Meanwhile, in April, a spontaneous but ill-coordinated rising in the Peloponnese, led by the clergy, the 'primates' (landowners and magistrates) and many armed chieftains, began with a wholesale extermination of the Turks. Turkish reprisals, including the execution of the Patriarch at Constantinople, led to the departure of the Russian ambassador and a formal rupture of relations. For the next four years the other Powers attempted, with diminishing success, to prevent the revolt in Greece from becoming the occasion of a general attack by Russia upon Turkey, which might be followed by an upheaval all over Europe. England, no less than Austria, was anxious to keep the Tsar quiet. Both were relieved when Capo d'Istria, the advocate of a forward policy, had to retire in 1822; but in Switzerland, for the next five years, he was active in promoting sympathy and relief for the Greeks. And, whereas Metternich hoped to see the revolt soon quietly suppressed, Canning began to see an opportunity either of intervening alone to England's advantage or, if that were impossible, of joining hands with the Tsar in order to keep some control over the issue. In either case, the Greeks were likely to profit.

In spite of personal, sectional and regional quarrels, much savage cruelty and a great lack of discipline, the Greeks showed themselves to be brave soldiers and skilful sailors. The Peloponnese was nearly cleared of the Turks, who failed to open the way for its reconquest either by way of Attica and the Isthmus or across the Gulf of Corinth. The Turks underrated their enemies and failed at first to secure the coasts and islands against the Greek ships under Andreas Miaoulis. During this respite the Greeks were unable to organize their government on a firm basis. An assembly, not recognized by rival bodies, produced in January 1822 a little-heeded 'Constitution of Epidaurus', and elected the Phanariote Alexander Mavrokordato as President. The military chieftains resented the attempt to form a regular government. But the 'European' Greeks had on their side both the wealthy islanders and the European Committees which were collecting funds (in England chiefly under Byron's influence); between them, they held the purse-strings, and by the end of 1824 their authority seemed to be well established.

Meanwhile, the Sultan purchased the help of his nominal vassal, Mehemet Ali, Pasha of Egypt, by allowing him to subdue and occupy Crete and by promising further rewards for the conquest of the Peloponnese. Miaoulis was no longer able to deny the sea passages to their combined fleets. Early in 1825, Mehemet's son Ibrahim landed an Arab army of more than 10,000 men at Modon in the south, and soon overran a great part of the Peloponnese, without, however, being strong enough to reduce it systematically. North of the Isthmus, Missolonghi (Mesolóngion) held out in the west until April 1826, two years after Byron's death there, and the Moslem forces could not recover Attica until the French philhellene Fabvier was forced to surrender the Acropolis in June 1827. By this time the prospect of foreign intervention was at last taking shape.

FOREIGN INTERVENTION, 1827–29

At the eleventh hour the Greek provisional government had just agreed on a compromise between the factions: the 'Russian' party of Kolokotronis and the chieftains secured in April the election of Capo d'Istria (henceforward known as Capodistrias) as President for seven years; the choice of Sir Richard Church and of Lord Cochrane to command the Greek forces on land and at sea was a concession to the 'English' party of the islanders and some of the primates; the 'French' party of Kolettis, whose support came mainly from north of the Isthmus, was satisfied by the publication in May 1827 of the extremely democratic 'Constitution of Troizen'. Nauplia was still in Greek hands, and Ibrahim, when he took the field again in

April, still found so many centres of armed resistance that he adopted a new policy of systematic devastation among the vineyards of Messenia and Elis.

Before his death in December 1825, Tsar Alexander I had already ceased to discuss the Greek question with his continental allies, and leaned towards the more active policy which his successor Nicholas I was to pursue more resolutely. Canning disliked the double prospect of an Egyptian occupation in Greece and of Greek piracy in the Aegean, but he was hardly in a position to move alone in response to a Greek appeal for British protection (June 1825). The upshot was the Protocol signed by the duke of Wellington at St Petersburg on 4 April 1826. The two governments agreed to impose on both parties, by means of joint or separate mediation, a settlement giving to the Greeks, within unspecified boundaries, an autonomous but tributary status, with compensation for the Turkish proprietors. On 29 April the Assembly made a formal request for mediation on this basis, but staked out its claim for the future by arguing for the inclusion of every region, subdued or not, that had taken up arms during the revolt.

Even before the Protocol was signed, the Tsar sent an ultimatum to the Sultan requiring negotiation on outstanding Russo-Turkish disputes, and the resulting Convention of Akkerman (October 1826) was a diplomatic success for Russia. The Bourbon government of France, to whom a section of the Greeks had also appealed, desired to share, not in a revolution, but in a crusade. This prolonged but enlarged the negotiations. The tripartite Treaty of London (6 July 1827), signed during Canning's brief premiership, added little to the proposals of the Protocol, but an additional article provided for sending a combined fleet to Greek waters in order to enforce an armistice on both parties—'without however taking any part in the hostilities'. Both parties accepted the armistice, but neither Ibrahim on land, nor the English philhellene Hastings at sea, ceased operations. Stratford Canning at Constantinople went a little beyond his instructions by referring in a private letter to cannon-shot as the final arbiter; this was repeated by Admiral Codrington to his captains. By such ambiguities the governments were able to avoid direct responsibility for the decisive conflict in the Bay of Navarino on 20 October, when the Turkish and Egyptian fleets were destroyed by the naval squadrons of England, Russia and France. Metternich might call this encounter a 'frightful catastrophe', and Wellington, who came into office in January 1828, might describe it as an 'untoward event'; but the ambassadors had already left Constantinople, and England was not released from her obligations under the treaty even if Russia should separately pursue the quarrel to the point of war.

The Egyptians soon evacuated the Peloponnese, after a mere show of resistance to a French force, which arrived in the name of the three Powers and which stayed there from 1828 to 1833. But the Sultan would not yield. He had denounced the Convention of Akkerman and almost invited the Russian declaration of war (April 1828); nothing but a disastrous second campaign forced him to accede to the Treaty of London as part of the peace treaty signed at Adrianople (14 September 1829) in the presence of a Russian army.

THE NEW KINGDOM, 1829-32

The future status and the frontiers of Greece were still undetermined. Wellington thought that a small independent state under a European sovereign would be less open to Russian influence than a larger territory still tributary to Turkey. As President, Capodistrias was somewhat unjustly suspected by England and France of being a tool of the Tsar. His services to Greece have been underrated, but in attempting personal rule he had not sufficient means of enforcing it; faction and anarchy culminated in his assassination (October 1831). Meanwhile Prince Leopold of Saxe-Coburg, soon to be the first king of Belgium, whose name had been canvassed as early as 1825, accepted and then declined the throne of Greece (February–May 1830); it was accepted in May 1832 by King Louis I of Bavaria, an enthusiastic philhellene, for his younger son Otho, then aged 17 (see table on p. 102). Delegates from Thessaly, Epirus, Chios and Crete attended the fourth National Assembly (August 1829), but these regions were in full Turkish occupation. Wellington wanted at first to liberate only the Peloponnese and the lesser islands, excluding even Euboea; but the three ambassadors in conference at Poros (December 1828) had recommended a more generous settlement, and public opinion could not conceive a Greece without Athens at least. The northern frontier, as offered to Leopold in 1830, ran south-westwards from the Gulf of Zeitoun to the mouth of the Aspropotamos; but Palmerston was able to secure for Otho in 1832 the line proposed at Poros in 1828, from the Gulf of Volos in the east to the Gulf of Arta (Amvrakía) in the west, including Acarnania but leaving the northern shore of both gulfs (and the southern point of the latter) in Turkish hands (Fig. 20). A Turkish garrison remained in the Acropolis until March 1833, and Athens was a mere village when it became the capital of Greece.

Among the islands, the ambassadors had proposed to include both Samos and Crete, with the support of Palmerston in opposition. But Palmerston in office could not or would not reverse the decision of 1830, which was based on the view that Samos (like Chios and Mytilene) was too near the coast of Asia Minor, and Crete too rich and distant a prize, with its strong Turkish minority, to be entrusted to the infant state. Samos obtained, and Chios recovered, a tolerably autonomous status, though Samos was badly misgoverned and Chios never recovered its old prosperity after the Turkish massacre of the islanders in 1822. Crete was restored to the Sultan in 1840 after fifteen years under Egyptian rule; two generations of periodical risings passed before the Turkish garrison was removed in 1898, and the Cretan Greeks' desire for full union with Greece was not satisfied until 1912.

Fig. 20. The growth of Greece

Based on (1) R. Muir and G. Philip, *Historical Atlas*, p. 86, 6th ed. (London, 1924); (2) I. Bowman, *The New World*, pp. 403 and 515, 4th ed. (New York, 1928).

The frontier of 1881 was modified in 1897 when a number of small points were retroceded to Turkey. The Treaty of Sèvres (August 1920) gave Greece the greater part of Eastern Thrace and also Smyrna, the latter subject to a plebiscite in five years' time. These provisions came to nothing after the disaster of September 1922 (see p. 120), and were cancelled by the treaty of Lausanne (July 1923).

2. THE REIGN OF OTHO I, *1833–62*

Since Leopold's withdrawal had been grounded partly on rumours of opposition, the Powers did not consult the Greeks in advance about their next choice. Russia stipulated against any Constitution as a condition of advancing her share of the promised loan of 60,000,000 francs from the three Powers. The Bavarian Regents for the young King Otho, who landed at Nauplia on 6 February 1833, determined to administer the country from the centre, giving office only to the most 'European' Greeks such as Trikoupis, Kolettis and Mavrokordato. Bavarian ministers soon gave place to Greeks; but, on coming of age in 1835, Otho himself presided over his Cabinet. Much was gained in the first ten years of Bavarian rule, but the leaders and veterans of the revolution were ill content, and some of them kept the tradition of local insurrections alive for many years. Officials nominated and removable by the Crown filled the place that had been occupied under the Turks by the primates and clergy in a crude form of local self-government. The establishment of an autocephalous state Church was unpopular, lacking the consent of the Patriarch until 1852, and coming from a king for whom as a Roman Catholic no Orthodox rite of coronation was possible. Centralization, police supervision, taxation and statistics became the order of the day.

Although the bloodless revolution of September 1843, which forced the king to promise a Constitution, was managed by the military men, Orthodox and Russian in their sympathies, the first prime ministers under the Constitution of 1844 were Mavrokordato, who was associated with the 'English' party, and then his rival Kolettis, who was favoured by the French. Both of them shared the official belief in centralization; but, whereas the former wanted the Greeks to put their modest house in order before looking to expand, the latter shared the more popular view that expansion was the first condition for improvement. Wearing the national dress and surrounded by patriots of the 'national party', Kolettis gained the sympathy of the king, and still more of the energetic queen. After his death in 1847, memories of the War of Independence were kept alive in the names of succeeding ministers. It was intended that the nominated Senate (Yerousía) of twenty-seven members should be a conservative check upon the Chamber of Deputies (Vouli) elected by universal manhood suffrage, but in practice the Senate soon became a platform for criticism by the Opposition.

Nationalist sentiment was stirred by Palmerston's over-hasty blockade of the Piraeus in 1850 for the sake of dubious monetary claims (a proceeding endorsed by a small majority in the Commons but censured in the House of Lords), and more permanently by the rising agitation in the Ionian islands for union with Greece. Since the islands had come under British protection in 1815, successive governors had done much to improve their material prosperity, already proportionately much greater than that of Greece itself. But the constitutional reforms of 1849, greatly relaxing the constraints imposed in 1817, did no more than past coercion to allay unrest. The Greek character of the islands emerged from beneath the upper layer of Italianate society on which the English government, like its Venetian predecessors, had hitherto relied for support.

The progress of nationalist and democratic feelings was not in itself a danger to the dynasty. The king and queen were now thorough 'Greeks', and were never so popular as when their impulse to support insurrections in Epirus and Thessaly during the Crimean war was rudely checked by an Anglo-French military occupation of the Piraeus (1854–7). But after 1859 the Greek desire to imitate Garibaldi could hardly be shared by the German king, although he would not agree to renounce future attempts against Turkey as the condition for accepting Lord John Russell's offer of the Ionian islands. At the same time, a new generation of politicians was growing up, nursed at the University of Athens in the principles of the French Revolution; the rising spirit of opposition was heralded by the election of Epaminondas Delegeorges to the Chamber in 1859. In October 1862 a rising in Acarnania, following a revolt in February of the garrisons at Nauplia and elsewhere, brought the king and queen hurriedly back in their yacht from a voyage round the coastal ports, only to find the garrison of Athens in revolt and a provisional government already set up. They sailed away on 24 October and retired to Bamberg, where the ex-king died four years later.

Otho was somewhat pedantic and Amalia often impulsive;

but later generations have given a more generous recognition both to their sincerity and to the progress of Greece under their rule. In thirty years, population and shipping had alike been doubled, and foreign trade (no doubt at its lowest ebb in 1833) had been more than quadrupled, only to be more than doubled again in the next decade. Athens had grown from a village into a small city, and Piraeus from almost nothing into a busy port. Without repudiating a special relation to the protecting powers, the king had done his best to make Greece a state more nearly independent in fact; and, without adding to its territory during his reign, he had rather encouraged than repressed the assertion of its future claims.

3. THE REIGN OF GEORGE I, 1863–1913

The revolution itself was bloodless, but faction spread into minor civil war, while the three Powers tried to find a new ruler. In order to exclude a nephew of the Tsar, who was favoured by the Russians and the French, the British government insisted on respecting the Protocol of 3 February 1830, which disqualified members of the Powers' reigning families. In spite of this, the National Assembly ratified an overwhelming plebiscite in favour of Prince Alfred, Queen Victoria's second son; but three months later they accepted the second son of the heir to the Danish throne, whose supporters in the plebiscite (like those in favour of a Greek by birth) had numbered only six. This settlement was embodied in a Treaty between Denmark and the three Powers (13 July 1863); in October, after 30 years, the Greeks again welcomed a stranger aged 17 as their king (see table on p. 102).

A speculative hope, which had moved many to ask for Prince Alfred, had become a public assurance with the proposal for the Danish Prince—England's free consent to the union of the Ionian islands with Greece (Fig. 20). The cession of the islands, completed by a treaty between Greece and the

MODERN GREECE: DYNASTIC TABLE

(1) *Bavarian House*

Maximilian I, Elector (1799), then first king (1805) of Bavaria, d. 1825

Louis I, King of Bavaria, abd. 1848

Maximilian II, King of Bavaria

Otho = Amalia of Oldenburg
b. 1816. OTHO, King of Greece, 1833, abd. 1862, d. 1866

(2) *House of Schleswig-Holstein-Sonderburg-Glücksburg*

Christian IX, King of Denmark, b. 1818, d. 1906

Frederick VIII, King of Denmark

Alexandra = Edward VII, King of England

b. 1846, William = Olga of Russia
became GEORGE I, King of the Hellenes, 1863;
assassinated, 1913

3 other sons
1 daughter

CONSTANTINE I = Sophia of Prussia
b. 1868, King of the Hellenes, 1913
Compelled to withdraw, 1917, in favour of Alexander
Returned, 1920, on Alexander's death
Abd. 1922, in favour of George, who had withdrawn with him in 1917; d. 1923

George, High Commissioner in Crete, 1898–1906

b. 1893, ALEXANDER
King of the Hellenes, 1917, d. 1920

b. 1890, GEORGE II = Elizabeth of Romania
King of the Hellenes, 1922
Withdrew, Dec. 1923, without abdicating
(REPUBLIC, 1924–1935)
Restored, 1935; d. 1947

b. 1901, PAUL = Frederika of Brunswick
King of the Hellenes, 1947, d. 1964

Sophia b. 1940, CONSTANTINE II = Anne-Marie   Irene
King of the Hellenes, 1964   of Denmark

three Powers on 29 March 1864, was partly a sacrifice, but also a means of escape from a diplomatic deadlock and a relief from trying to govern in face of a Greek unionist Assembly. The islanders gained at first moral rather than material satisfaction; the upper classes were ill content, and the clergy objected to the inevitable transfer of authority from the Patriarch at Constantinople to the Synod in Athens. Yet the cession was an unprecedented gesture by a Great Power, and an immense gain to Greece in wealth, population and prestige, and also in the admixture of an aristocratic culture which had never been subjected to the Turks and was rooted in centuries of Venetian rule.

The title of George I as 'King of the Hellenes' (not 'King of Hellas') indicated that he must be a constitutional or even a democratic ruler. It is a tribute to his tact that he was able for nearly fifty years to keep his footing in the system set up by the Constitution of 1864, with only occasional resort to the dismissal of an undefeated ministry or to his right of forming an extra-parliamentary Cabinet. The first crisis of the reign was occasioned by the condition of Crete. Behind the tale of fiscal, judicial and educational grievances was the desire for union or at least for autonomy, which inspired the desperate struggles of the insurrection of 1866. The proposal of Napoleon III and the Tsar for an open Cretan plebiscite was supported by all the Powers except England; but neither Derby nor Gladstone would contemplate anything more than autonomy. The Sultan formulated an Organic Statute which became the nominal law for the next ten years. Feeling in Athens had been running high in favour of combining support for the Cretans with a new bid for Thessaly and Epirus; but in February 1869 a new premier had to agree, under pressure from the Powers in conference, to a declaration renouncing aggression against Turkey. Another set-back for Greek ambitions was the creation of the Bulgarian Exarchate in 1870 by the Turks at the prompting of the Russians: for different reasons, both saw the advantage of isolating Orthodox Slavs in European Turkey from the Greek influence of the Patriarch. About the same time, internal quarrels were aggravated by nice questions of constitutional legality.

Factious passions, easily aroused, were as easily forgotten in a common wave of patriotic feeling during the Russo-Turkish War of 1877–8. But the Greeks had little sympathy for the Slavs in revolt, and still less for the increasingly Pan-Slav

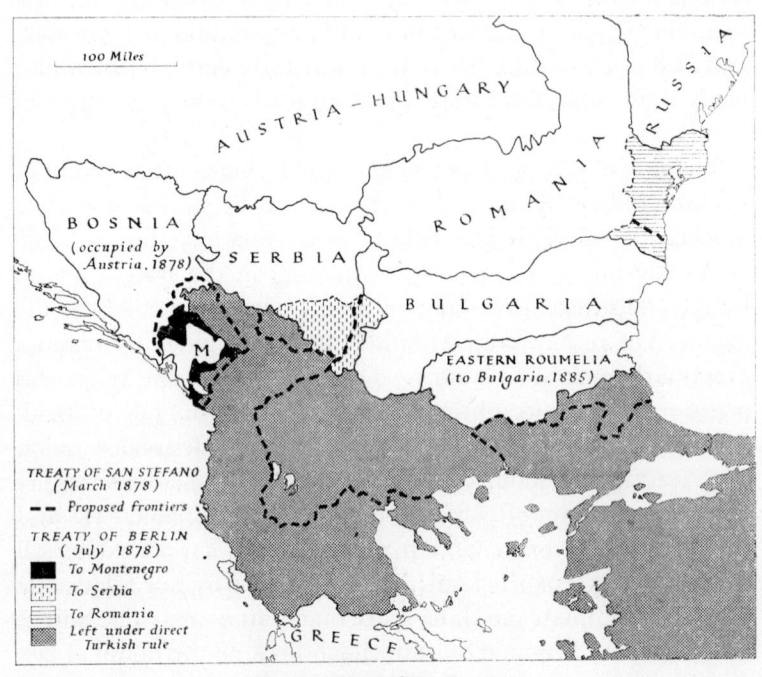

Fig. 21. The Balkans in 1878

Based on (1) *The Cambridge Modern History Atlas*, map 119, 2nd ed. (Cambridge, 1924); (2) C. Grant Robertson and J. G. Bartholomew, *An Historical Atlas of Modern Europe*, plates 23–25, 2nd ed. (Oxford, 1924).

policy of Russia. Their public resolution 'to occupy the Greek provinces of Turkey' (2 February 1878) came too late, and was followed so quickly by an armistice between Russia and Turkey that the Greek army never marched. Volunteers supported a short-lived movement in Epirus; the more serious risings in Thessaly and Crete were brought to an end by the mediation of British consuls and by the Turkish undertaking at San Stefano to adhere more strictly to the Organic Statute in Crete and to extend its principles to the provinces of Turkey in Europe. At the Congress of Berlin, which undid the Slav character of the Russian Treaty of San Stefano (Fig. 21), England unsuccessfully supported the Greeks' claim to direct representation, but secured for them an undertaking by the Powers to press upon the Sultan an improvement in their northern frontier so as to run from the mouth of the Salamvrias (Piniós) to that of the Kalamas (Thíamis) opposite Corfu.

The Turks were resigned to the loss of Thessaly, the richer but more indisputably Hellenic region; but they clung to Janina, Preveza and Arta in the west—a region which they and the Moslem minority described as part of 'Albania', while to the Greeks it formed a part (and only the southern part) of 'Epirus'. Finally a Conference, from which Greece was excluded, led to a Convention (24 May 1881) which left Janina and Preveza to Turkey but gave to Greece the town and district of Arta as well as almost the whole of Thessaly (Fig. 22). The Cretan Christians were for the moment not ill-satisfied with the concessions made in the Pact of Halepa (October 1878). When Cyprus was unexpectedly ceded in 1878 to Britain (subject to a tribute to the Sultan), the Greek majority there were as yet more grateful for liberation from Turkey than critical of the fiscal burdens and constitutional restrictions of virtual Crown Colony rule.

Fruitless mobilizations, in 1881 and again in 1886, only added to the public debt. The bellicose Deligiannis, premier for the first time in 1885, was ousted by his senior and more realistic rival Trikoupis, whose periods of office, now as earlier, were spent in trying to make good by economic reforms the expenses of the 'National Party's' policy of expansion. Trikoupis lived to appease the beginnings of a new outbreak in Crete (1889), but died in 1896, at the moment when the inability of Turkish governors to restrain the Moslem minority produced the final insurrection. This time, in spite of the Powers, Deligiannis was supported by the king as well as by all parties in arming for war, both in Crete and on the continent. Turkey replied to the incursion of irregular bands into Macedonia by a declaration of war (April 1897): a month later, the Powers had to intervene to save the nation from defeat and the dynasty from overthrow in a conflict undertaken against their advice. Certain strategic points along the northern frontier were retroceded to Turkey (Fig. 22), and the Powers

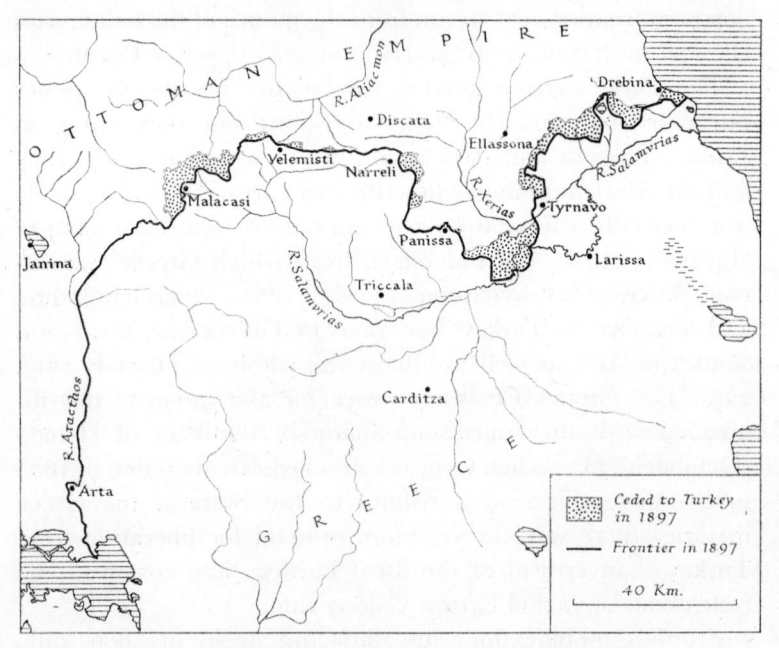

Fig. 22. Rectification of the Turco-Greek frontier, 1897
Based on 'Map to illustrate the rectification of the Turco-Greek frontier in 1897'. Lithographed at the Intelligence Division, W.O., Feb. 1898 (I.D.W.O. no. 1317): the map is on a scale of 1:400,000.

instituted a Commission of Control over sufficient Greek revenues to serve the interest of the indemnity to Turkey and of older national debts also. One half of the Cretan problem was settled (November 1898) by a four-Power occupation of the chief towns and by appointing as High Commissioner the Greek king's second son, Prince George, who did much to pacify the island and to make its autonomy a reality. After a disagreement with his Cretan councillor, Eleutherios Venizelos, and a proclamation of union with Greece by the Cretan opposition, Prince George resigned in 1906: the island was being rapidly and peacefully hellenized under his successor, and the remaining international troops had just been withdrawn, when the Near-Eastern crisis of 1908 produced another but still premature proclamation of union.

In Macedonia, the Sultan had discovered an ideal method of fostering Balkan rivalries by showing favour in turn to the different 'nationalities' which he there misgoverned. After the creation of the Exarchate in 1870, Bulgarian churches and schools had been at first encouraged. But the creation of a virtually independent Bulgaria in 1878, and the inclusion of Eastern Roumelia in 1885, followed by the growing violence of Bulgarian agitation after 1895, led the Sultan to show some favour to the Serbs of Macedonia, and also the Vlachs, whom the Romanians had lately begun to claim as their kinsmen. It suited the Turks in 1905 for the first time to give the Vlachs distinct privileges, in such a way as to instigate a diplomatic rupture between Romania and Greece. Of the rival claims in Macedonia, the Sultan most feared those of the Greeks and made fewest concessions to them. In spite of the Powers' programme of reforms (1903), the reign of terror of the Bulgarian Macedonian Committees became so bad that in 1904 the Greeks organized rival armed bands under klephts and even army officers. In 1905, the Sultan was forced by a naval demonstration to accept the measures of international control, which had been arranged by the Powers and were later prolonged in March 1908 for six years. But the experiment had done little to pacify the province before it became the starting point of a novel and momentous revolution.

Since the suspension in 1878 of the Turkish Constitution, hastily conceded two years earlier, Abdul Hamid had enjoyed an Indian summer of bureaucratic power. Administrative despotism and foreign control were alike resented by a party of 'Young Turkish' reformers; their secret 'Committee of Union and Progress', founded at Geneva in 1891, was transferred to Paris and then in 1906 to Salonica, where it spread rapidly among the army officers, with the sympathy of the Jews and Freemasons. When Enver Bey proclaimed the Constitution in Macedonia and threatened to march on Constantinople, the Sultan gave way the next day, 24 July 1908, and the Powers optimistically agreed to withdraw their controls. But the proclamation of Prince Ferdinand as independent 'Tsar of the Bulgarians', and the simultaneous annexation of Bosnia and Herzegovina by Austria (5-7 October 1908), combined with dissensions in the Young Turkish Parliament to produce a counter-revolution at the capital (13 April 1909). Thereupon the Committee's Macedonian army marched on Constantinople, deposed Abdul Hamid (27 April 1909), and came to terms with Bulgaria and Austria at the expense of the Serbs, whose friends in Russia failed them.

The Greek government stood aloof from this crisis in the history of the Turks and the Balkan Slavs, and also dared not accept the renewed proclamation of union made by a Cretan provisional government. Although the remaining European troops left the island, the Young Turks insisted on forcing Greece under threat of war to disavow the agitation in Crete, Macedonia and Epirus, and to place the future of Crete once more in the hands of the Powers (August 1909). This humiliation led to the seizure of power at Athens by the newly formed Military League of officers, who were dissatisfied with the handling of the Cretan question; they invited to Athens the Cretan leader Venizelos, who was technically a Greek subject. Victorious in the elections which followed his appointment (18 October 1910) as prime minister, Venizelos succeeded in persuading the Military League to dissolve itself in return for such a revision of the Constitution of 1864 as should make military intervention in politics unnecessary; this was carried out (January-June 1911) by the 'Second Revisionary National

Assembly'. The elections for the next ordinary Chamber (25 March 1912) gave him 150 out of 181 members, including all but one of those from north of the Isthmus: always his popularity was to be greatest in the newest and frontier regions, and least secure in the conservative Ionian Islands.

Venizelos's advent to power began a stormy period of triumphs and disasters, of which King George I lived only to see the beginning: on 18 March 1913 he was assassinated by a Greek in the newly occupied city of Salonica, after the virtual union of Crete to Greece and a few months before the fiftieth anniversary of his accession. Between the unhappy Turkish war of 1897 and the appointment of Venizelos as prime minister in 1910, the king's prudent restraint prevented criticism of the dynasty from becoming serious; before and after those dates he had been generally popular. During his reign, the Ionian islands, Thessaly and Arta, and finally Crete, had been incorporated (Fig. 20); population had been trebled and its density doubled; foreign trade and the tonnage of merchant shipping had alike been more than trebled. Brigandage had been much reduced, nearly 4000 km. of roads and over 1000 km. of railway constructed, and the way was now opening at last for connexion by rail with Europe. Unfortunately, the corruption of politics and the violent intervention of the army had not been eliminated by the surgical operation of 1911.

4. THE CRISIS OF 1912–23

THE BALKAN WARS, 1912–14

The First Balkan War

The Balkan peoples soon perceived that the Young Turks were more nationalist than liberal. Then in September 1911 the Italians took occasion to make war on Turkey for the possession of Tripoli and Cyrenaica, which they had long coveted; they brought pressure to bear by occupying Rhodes, Cos, Leipsos and ten islands of the Dodecanese (April–May

1912). A congress of island delegates declared, however, for union with Greece, and the Treaty of Lausanne (18 October 1912), which ended the war with Turkey, provided (in vain) that the Italians should leave these islands as soon as the Turkish evacuation of the two African provinces (now known as Libya) should be complete. Thus the Turkish revival, and the ambitions of Italy, gave the Greeks new reasons for thinking that no time must be lost in making sure of their share in the 'Turkish inheritance'.

Venizelos had already renewed relations with Romania and made overtures to Bulgaria. Bulgaria first negotiated with Serbia a Treaty of Alliance (13 March 1912), followed by a Military Convention (12 May), envisaging offensive action against Turkey and providing for the division of the spoils; her Treaty with Greece (29 May) remained defensive in form, but was soon followed by a Military Convention. By September 1912, Montenegro had also come to understandings with the three larger Balkan States. Early in October she declared war on Turkey, the other three States sent an ultimatum which could have but one answer, and the Greek Chamber completed the annexation of Crete by admitting its deputies and appointing a governor. On 17 October Turkey declared war on Montenegro, Bulgaria and Serbia, but made a bid for Greek neutrality. Venizelos, however, with his eyes on Macedonia, fulfilled his obligations to Bulgaria by declaring war on Turkey (18 October). The Greeks took a full share in the sweeping victory of the Balkan Allies. The army of the Crown Prince Constantine cleared southern and western Macedonia and entered Salonica on 8 November, only to be joined there by a rival and suspicious Bulgarian force. The armistice signed on 3 December 1912 did not include the Greeks, but the Turks acquiesced, under pressure from the Powers, in the full demands made by the Allies at the London Conference. Thereupon Enver Bey overthrew the government, repudiated the terms and renewed the war on 3 February 1913; but Janina surrendered to the Greek Crown Prince on 6 March (twelve days before he became King Constantine), Adrianople fell to the Bulgarians, and Scutari to the Montenegrins. By the Treaty of London (30 May 1913) Turkey ceded collectively to the Balkan Allies all her territory in Europe (apart from Albania), except Constantinople and its approaches within a line drawn from Enez (Aínos) on the Aegean to Midia on the Black Sea. Crete was finally ceded to Greece, but the fate of the Turkish Aegean islands and of Albania was to be settled by the Powers.

The Second Balkan War

The previous decision of the Powers (20 December 1912), under pressure from Austria and Italy, to accept the principle of an independent Albania, thus depriving Montenegro of Scutari, Serbia of access to the Adriatic, and Greece of 'Northern Epirus', led directly to the second Balkan War. The partition of Macedonia became more crucial than ever. In face of Bulgarian provocations, Serbia and Greece made an alliance on 2 June, and replied to a Bulgar attack at the end of the month by a general advance. In a short but bloody campaign, the Serbs invaded Bulgaria, the Greeks seized the whole of Macedonia and most of the Thracian coast, and the Romanians took the opportunity to occupy the southern Dobrudja without firing a shot. By a treaty with Bulgaria signed at Constantinople on 29 September 1913, Turkey recovered Enez, Adrianople and Kirk-Kilisse, which it had already reoccupied, and also pushed the frontier a little northwards from Midia on the Black Sea. The Treaty of Bucharest (10 August 1913) between Bulgaria and her Balkan enemies gave most of Macedonia to the Greeks; the eastern frontier now reached the Aegean at the mouth of the Mesta (Néstos), excluding Xanthe but including the coveted tobacco port of Kavalla (Fig. 23).

The peace treaty between Greece and Turkey (14 November 1913) left to the decision of the Powers the two most important questions of the islands and Albania. Among the Turkish Aegean islands, nine had been occupied by the Greeks during the war; in addition, the Assembly of Samos, which had often been in conflict with its princes, proclaimed union with Greece, and was officially annexed by a Greek force on 15 March 1913. In February 1914 the Powers recognized Greek sovereignty over all these islands except Tenedos and Imbros; but for the Italians, the Greeks would no doubt have occupied the Dodecanese also during the Balkan War. The Powers made it a

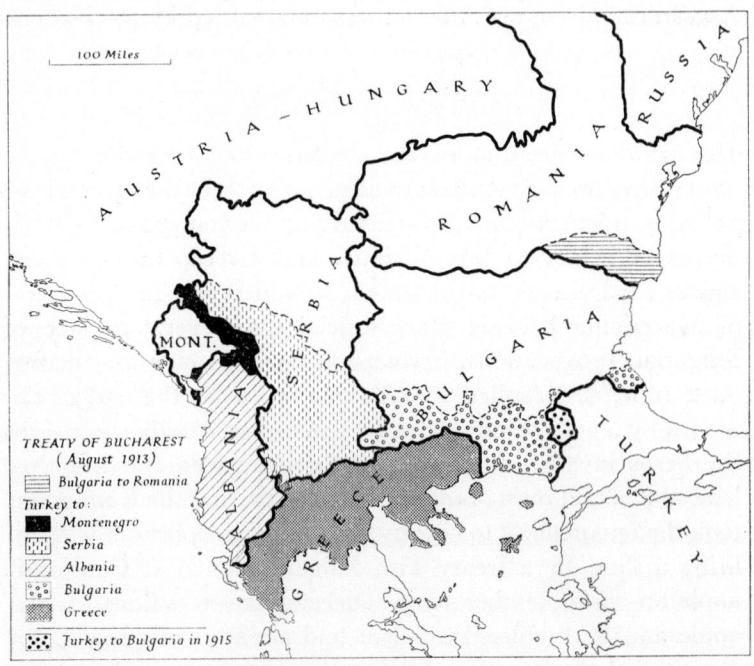

Fig. 23. The Balkans, 1912–13

Based on C. Grant Robertson and J. G. Bartholomew, *An Historical Atlas of Modern Europe*, plate 25, 2nd ed. (Oxford, 1924).

condition of their award that the Greeks should withdraw from those districts of northern Epirus (Santi Quaranta, Chimarra, Argyrokastro and Koritsa) which they had occupied during the war but now had to surrender to the new state of Albania. But before the Greek troops had gone, the Greeks in these districts obtained a limited autonomy under international supervision by an arrangement made at Corfu on 17 May.

Prince William of Wied, the chosen ruler of Albania, who arrived at Durazzo in March, had no authority outside that port and little enough within it.

THE WAR OF 1914–18

Thus the outbreak of the European War in August 1914 was for the Greeks, as for their Balkan neighbours, only the intensification of a crisis which had begun two years earlier. The first signs of the fateful rift between King Constantine and Venizelos appeared at once. Both men were popular, Venizelos as architect of the Balkan alliance and Cretan union, Constantine for his leading part in the Balkan campaign. But their sympathies in the war, as well as their expectations of its outcome, were sharply opposed. The king admired the German army, and declined with regret an invitation from his brother-in-law the Kaiser to join the Central Powers. The Cretan statesman was more impressed by the naval power of the Entente countries (also the original guarantors of Greece), by their economic ties with Greece, and by the strength of their case in the eyes of the world. Having assured Serbia that, although he could not move against Austria, he would help her to repel any Bulgarian attack, he made it clear (23 August) that Greece would be ready to join the Entente Powers against a Turkish attack in return for a guarantee against the Bulgarian danger. A fortnight later, having got their leave to reoccupy northern Epirus, he advised the king to concert plans with the Allies for an occupation of Gallipoli; but Greece remained neutral when England declared war on Turkey (5 November). In two further memoranda to the king (January 1915), he supported England's invitation to reconstitute the Balkan alliance by surrendering Kavalla to the Bulgarians in return for Allied promises of 'important compensations' on the coast of Asia Minor. In February, he persuaded a Crown Council of former prime ministers to recommend the dispatch of one division to Gallipoli.

Dismissed by the king (6 March), Venizelos kept a majority of nearly 60 at the elections held on 13 June, returned to office on 23 August, and at once renewed his pledges to Serbia against a Bulgarian attack. When Bulgaria mobilized in September, he persuaded the reluctant king to mobilize too, and to invite France and England to supply the army that Serbia lacked; before Constantine could change his mind, French troops began to disembark at Salonica. On 4 October the king again dismissed him, and again dissolved the Chamber after it had defeated the new ministry. This government, controlled by the Palace and the General Staff, was pledged to 'benevolent neutrality' towards the Allies and to the view that the Treaty with Serbia applied only to a purely Balkan conflict. Serbia was overrun before Allied help could reach her, and Venizelos's liberal party abstained from the elections (19 December). A Bulgarian force was allowed to occupy Fort Roupel, one of the keys to eastern Macedonia (May 1916).

Greek confidence in the Allies' intentions had not been improved by the Treaty of London (26 April 1915), which was known to have assigned the Dodecanese to Italy in full sovereignty, and to have arranged a partition of Albania more favourable to Italy than to Greece. Confidence in the Allies' power was also weakened by their inability to help Serbia or to force the Dardanelles. With the fall of Venizelos, the Allies, distrusting the king's no longer benevolent neutrality, introduced martial law at Salonica, replaced the Greek troops in Epirus by Italians, and demanded the demobilization of the Greek army, a 'non-political' government and fresh elections. Venizelos sailed for Crete, appealed to the Greeks to 'save what may still be saved', landed at Salonica (5 October 1916) and there organized a provisional government which soon declared war on Germany and Bulgaria.

Greece now had two governments: that of Venizelos, supported throughout the newly won regions, but not yet formally recognized by the Allies beyond the limits of its actual authority; that of Constantine, supported by his League of Reservists in the provinces of old Greece, and behaving so as to make itself intolerable to the Allies. The king gained by Athenian resentment at the drastic measures of the Allies, who expelled the enemy legations from Athens, obtained full control of the Piraeus and of the recently completed railway to Salonica, and punished Greek resistance to a landing party (1 December) by blockading the coasts and insisting on the removal of all Greek troops and equipment to the Peloponnese. America's entry into the war (April 1917), and the failure of the king's appeals to Berlin for an attack on Venizelist Macedonia, forced him to show less open hostility to the Allies; but they in turn had lost patience, and presented an ultimatum requiring his immediate abdication, and intimating also that the Crown Prince George, suspected of pro-German sympathies, would not be acceptable. The next day (12 June 1917) King Constantine appointed his second son, Alexander, in his place, avoiding a formal abdication, and left Greece with his family for Switzerland. The French deported some of his supporters to Corsica, and occupied Athens.

At the end of June 1917 Venizelos, as prime minister of a reunited government, declared war on the Central Powers and recalled the Chamber of June 1915, all but ten of whose members joined in a vote of confidence. A large number of anti-Venizelist civil servants and officers were removed, and, although most of the former had been reinstated by 1920, many of the latter remained as an irreconcilable and dangerous element in politics. The Allied army had been pinned at Salonica for a year after landing there in October 1915. With the help of Serbian forces brought there from Corfu, they had been able in November 1916 to recover at Monastir a small corner of Serbian territory; in July 1917 a pact signed at Corfu announced the projected union of the Yugoslavs in a single state. By the spring of 1918, 250,000 Greeks had been remobilized. But it was not until September 1918 that the combined French, English, Greek and Serbian armies began the offensive which led to the capitulation of Bulgaria, the abdication of King Ferdinand (4 October), the recovery of Belgrade, and the signature of an armistice by Turkey on 30 October 1918 (Fig. 24).

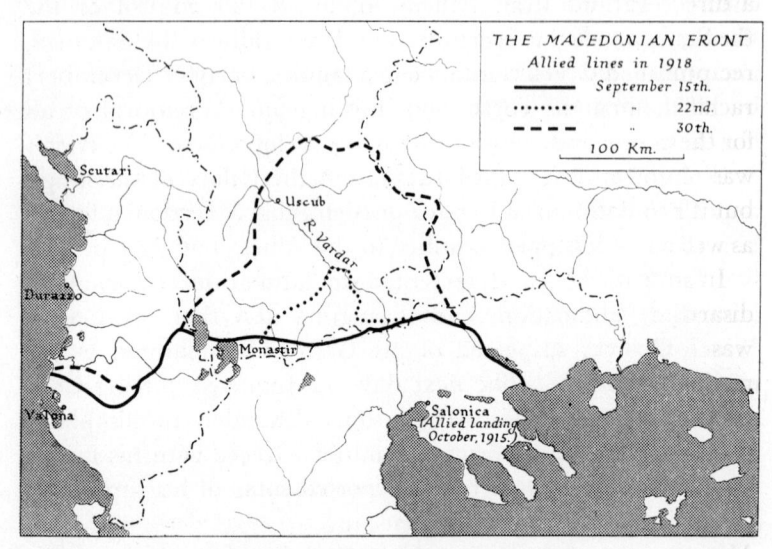

Fig. 24. The Macedonian Front, 1918
Based on H. W. V. Temperley, *A History of the Peace Conference*, vol. IV, p. 14 (London, 1921).
The allied line was held by Italians, French, Greek, Serbian and British troops; facing them were Germans west of the valley of the Vardar and Bulgarians to the east.

THE PEACE SETTLEMENT, 1919–23

The personality of Venizelos impressed itself strongly at the Peace Conference. Once more Bulgaria paid dearly for the miscalculations of her rulers: by the Treaty of Neuilly (27 November 1919) she was partly disarmed and had to restore the southern Dobrudja to Romania, while Greece not only recovered eastern Macedonia but also cut Bulgaria off from the Aegean by obtaining western Thrace with the small port and railway of Dedeagach (renamed Alexandroúpolis). The Treaty stipulations for giving Bulgaria economic outlets to the sea were to be a cause of endless argument: while the Bulgarians looked for the recovery of Dedeagach, and the Greeks offered alternative facilities by rail westwards to Salonica, both parties were too suspicious to agree upon the natural solution—a direct and not very difficult outlet by rail from Sofia down the Struma valley to Salonica. The Treaty also provided for 'the reciprocal and voluntary emigration of persons belonging to racial minorities'. This provision was not so important as that for the compulsory Greco-Turkish exchange of populations that was to come in 1923, because far fewer people were involved; but it helped to make the northern frontier of Greece an ethnic as well as a political one (Fig. 25).

In spite of the armistice terms, the Turks could not easily be disarmed in Asia Minor, and the final settlement with them was long delayed by dissensions among the Powers, by the rashness of the Greeks, and by the revolution which was re-creating Turkey herself. The Greeks wanted to keep the future of Constantinople open by making it an international city, and were represented in the Allied garrison there. Asking for a large part of the coast of Asia Minor, they were allowed in May 1919 to occupy Smyrna and in December to reoccupy northern Epirus. Early in 1920, in view of the unexpected strength of the hostile Kemalist movement, the Allied Supreme Council decided to keep the Sultan at Constantinople but to allow the Greek army to pacify Thrace and also Asia Minor northwards from Smyrna to the Dardanelles.

The Treaty of Sèvres (signed on 10 August 1920 but never ratified) was highly favourable to Greek ambitions: Greece was to obtain Adrianople and all eastern Thrace to Chatalja within 20 miles of the capital, together with Gallipoli and the northern shore of the Sea of Marmora (subject to an International Commission for the Straits). Smyrna and its hinterland were placed under Greek administration, with provision for a local parliament which might opt after five years for incorporation in Greece (Fig. 20): Venizelos's aim was to provide a check on Turkish nationalism and a refuge for the Greeks of Asia Minor (scattered, but numbering a million or

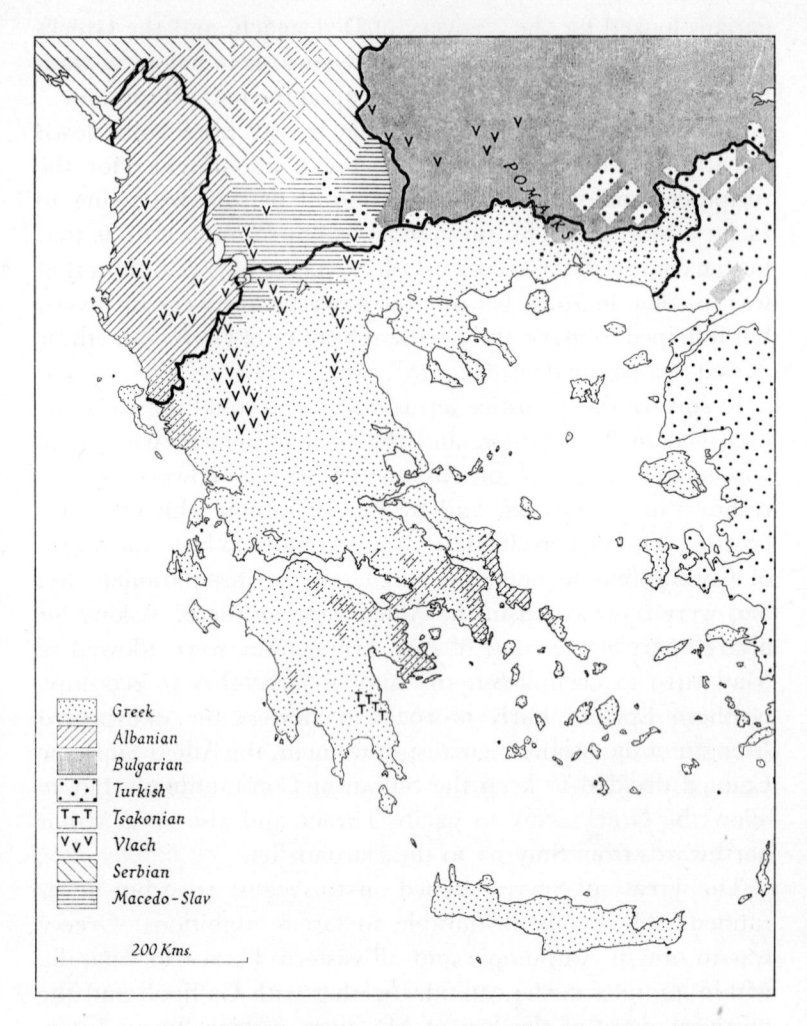

Fig. 25. The languages of Greece and adjoining areas

Based mainly on (1) *South-East Europe: Ethnographical Map*, Geographical Section, General Staff, No. 3703a (1918); (2) map in *Greek Refugee Settlement* (League of Nations, Geneva, 1926); (3) *Grande Atlante del Touring Club Italiano*, plate 16 (3rd ed. Roma, 1933); (4) *A Gazetteer of Greece*, Fig. (Permanent Committee on Geographical Names, London, 1942).

The distribution of Vlachs is based on the G.S.G.S. map and differs from that of Fig. 12.

more) in case of oppression. Turkey ceded all the Aegean islands which had already been occupied, but the fate of some remained uncertain until 1923 (see p. 121).

The population of Venizelist Greece had swollen in eight years from under three to six and a half millions. But the triumph was short-lived. The country was exhausted by war and prolonged mobilization, and exasperated by the corruption of adventurers attached to Venizelos's party and profiting by his absorption in making war or peace. Six weeks after the Chamber had unanimously endorsed the treaties, the accidental death of King Alexander (25 October 1920) fatally revived the one issue that Venizelos most wished to avoid. His preference was for a constitutional monarchy, and he offered the Crown to Constantine's third son, Prince Paul; but Paul refused it, as properly belonging to his father or his elder brother George. Venizelos's opponents then all combined to defeat him by more than two to one at the elections (14 November), and, after his departure and the removal of his officials, arranged a plebiscite (5 December) in which the Venizelists abstained and all but a handful of over a million Greeks voted for the return of King Constantine. A fortnight later the king reached Athens after more than three years of exile. Probably the revival of Turkey and the jealousy of Italy would have deprived even a Venizelist Greece of the full harvest of the Treaty of Sèvres; in addition, the Allies now refused to recognize Constantine and withdrew their financial support. France made haste to secure herself in Syria by a reconciliation with Ankara (20 October 1921). In England, Mr Lloyd George's pro-Greek policy was feared, not only in official quarters as likely to offend Moslem sentiment in India, but also by the public as likely to delay complete demobilization.

Meanwhile the three Powers (England, France and Italy) which met in London (February–March 1921) to discuss a revision of the Treaty of Sèvres in Turkey's favour, were confirmed in their views by the failure of a preliminary Greek attack (March–April). In a second offensive, the Greek army came within 60 miles of Ankara (July), but had to retreat again after a costly defeat at the River Sakaria (26 August). Constantine, who had rejected Allied offers to mediate in the spring, now placed the fate of Greece unconditionally in the hands of Lord Curzon and the Powers (December 1921), and carried on at home a policy of revenge against the Venizelists. His minister Gounaris ignored one defeat in the Chamber (March 1922); and, although he resigned in May when he could no longer conceal the Powers' proposals (note of 26 March) for the evacuation of Asia Minor, he formed a new coalition. At the end of August the Turks took the offensive and entered Smyrna a fortnight later (9 September 1922). Most of the city was burned to the ground amid the confusion of escaping Greek civilians and soldiers. Before resigning, the Greek government ordered demobilization of the demoralized army.

The consequence of this disaster haunted Greek politics for fifteen years or more. When Colonel Plastiras headed a revolution among units of the army assembled in Chios, King Constantine abdicated (September 1922) in favour of his eldest son George II (who had been excluded as pro-German by the Powers two years earlier), and died next year at Palermo. Six of his leading advisers, including his prime minister and commander-in-chief, were among those tried by a revolutionary court martial of eleven officers (only two of whom, however, were Venizelists), and were shot on 29 November 1922. This unusual violence was due to panic, and to revulsion in Athens against a government which had long concealed by grandiose promises the real weakness of Greece's changed situation. The execution of civilian politicians shocked those of other countries, but Lord Curzon, presiding over the Conference which had just met at Lausanne, did not break off relations with the revolutionary government.

The settlement with Kemalist Turkey was at last completed by the Treaty of Lausanne (24 July 1923). For the most part, the treaty merely confirmed the changes in the Treaty of Sèvres already brought about by intervening events or decisions of the Powers. It also substantially confirmed the arrangements for a compulsory Greco-Turkish exchange of population that had been agreed by the Convention of Lausanne in January of the same year. The elimination of the Greeks from Asia Minor was a fact which the Powers, themselves in part responsible for the adventure, could only temper by the arrangements made for an exchange of populations (Figs. 25 and 26). A revision of the frontier in Thrace had already been settled at Paris in March 1922, and Turkey now recovered the line of the Maritsa which she held in 1914. In November 1921 the Conference of Ambassadors had restored northern Epirus to Albania, with the frontier of 1914. Tenedos and Imbros, reserved for Turkey in 1914 but occupied by the Powers during the war and handed over to Greece after the Treaty of Sèvres, were now to be demilitarized along with the Greek islands of Lemnos and Samothrace.

An agreement, wrung from Italy by Venizelos at the height of his power (29 July 1919) and confirmed in 1920 by the Treaty of Sèvres, had assigned to Greece the islands of the Dodecanese, with the important exception of Rhodes which was to exercise an option by plebiscite within five years (1919) or fifteen years (1920) after the supposed case of the cession of Cyprus to Greece by England. This agreement was repudiated by Italy in 1922, the Treaty of Sèvres being still unratified; and at Lausanne all these islands were ceded by Turkey unconditionally to Italy. The Italians argued that their first conditional promise of evacuation, made to Turkey in 1912, was overridden by the Allies' offer of the islands to Italy in the Treaty of London (April 1915) and by the state of war with Turkey which followed; and that their second promise of evacuation, made in 1919-20 in favour of Greece, was overridden by the non-ratification and general revision of the Treaty of Sèvres, and by the non-fulfilment of the condition which applied only to Rhodes. But the real reason lay in their *de facto* occupation since 1912 and in their intention, carried

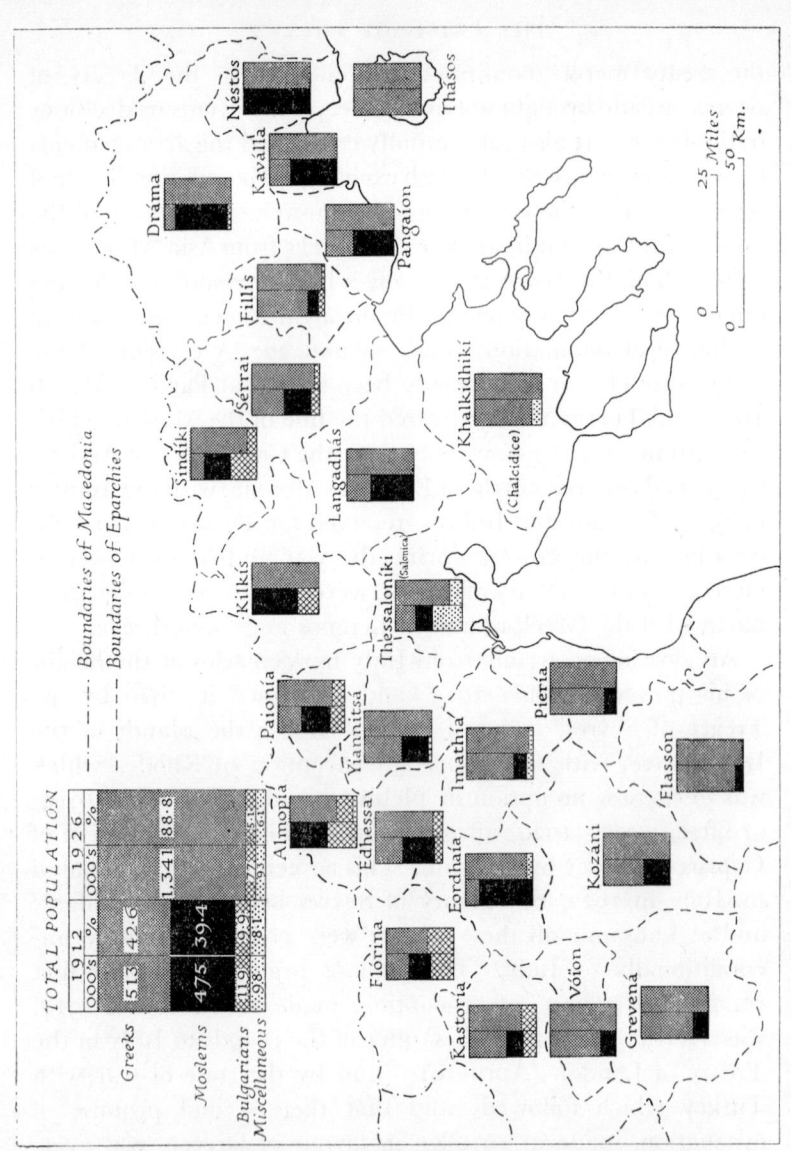

Fig. 26. Major ethnic groups in Macedonia, 1912 and 1926

Based on a map in *Greek Refugee Settlement* (League of Nations, Geneva, 1926). The main feature of the map is the disappearance of the Moslem element. There is also a reduction in the number of Bulgarians in many eparchies; 'Macedo-Slavs' are included under the heading 'Bulgarians'. The large rectangle shows the changes in the ethnic composition of Macedonia as a whole.

122

out gradually, of developing naval and air bases there. The islands remained directly under the Italian Foreign Office, and the inhabitants had no chance of expressing any desire for union with Greece.

Cyprus, with about 350,000 inhabitants (one-fifth Turks), had been occupied by England in return for her services to Turkey in 1878, annexed in 1914 when she declared war on Turkey, and momentarily offered to Greece in October 1915 on the unfulfilled condition that Greece would immediately enter the war. But England promised France in 1916 not to alienate Cyprus (so near to Syria) without French consent; its cession by Turkey to England at Sèvres was confirmed at Lausanne and it became a Crown Colony in name, as it had long been in effect, by Letters Patent of 10 March 1925. At the same time the number of elected members of the Legislative Council was increased, but not so as to give an elected Greek majority. The annual tribute of about £93,000, due to Turkey by the Convention of 1878, had been assigned from the first to the service of the Ottoman debt; proving a heavy burden on the island, it was soon partly offset by variable grants from the Treasury (fixed in 1910 at £50,000), and then wholly remitted (1928) in return for a small annual contribution of £10,000 for imperial defence. The island was not used as a strategical base, and was somewhat neglected. In 1925 and 1929 the elected members petitioned for redress of grievances and for union with Greece; the decisive rejection of the latter demand by both Conservative and Labour governments did not put an end to financial and educational grievances. A budget dispute in 1931 led to riots at the capital and demonstrations involving about one-third of the villages. As a result of this episode, the Legislative Council was suspended. The agitation for union, which hardly existed before 1919, met with some sympathy in Greece, but no encouragement from Venizelos; it was hampered by the islanders' knowledge of the much heavier financial burdens laid on post-war Greece.

The Treaty of Lausanne put an end to an almost continuous

foreign crisis of more than ten years' duration. The Greeks, discouraged but acquiescent, began to see that their 'Great Idea' could hardly be realized in full and that defence of their gains by reconciliation with their neighbours was more urgent than further expansion. In spite of recent set-backs, those gains were great indeed. But reconciliation abroad was bound to be slow in coming, at least while the domestic crisis was still unsolved.

5. DOMESTIC AFFAIRS, 1923-40

THE REPUBLIC OF 1923-35

After the abdication of Constantine in September 1922, the country had to face the issue between Republicans and Royalists—an issue easily confused with that between Venizelists and anti-Venizelists. The Populists, who favoured a democratic monarchy, abstained from the elections (December 1923), in which the Venizelists won 200 and the Republicans 120 seats; but the latter had such energetic backing from officers of the army and navy that the young King George II left Greece without formally abdicating. Invited by the National Assembly, Venizelos made a brief reappearance as prime minister (January 1924), but returned to Paris when his proposal for a plebiscite, to be followed by a general election, was opposed by the Republicans. Supported by the Republican Officers' League, the new premier Papanastasiou first used a vote of the Assembly to proclaim the Republic on 25 March 1924 and then held a plebiscite (13 April) in which more than two-thirds of the voters confirmed his action.

In June 1925 the leader of this Officers' League, General Pangalos, overthrew the next ministry, dissolved the Assembly which had completed the draft of a Constitution, issued by proclamation a modified Republican Constitution (30 September 1925), and promised to submit it for ratification after fresh elections. But in January 1926 he announced his intention to concentrate all executive and administrative powers in his own hands, postponed any election indefinitely, and suspended the whole of the new Constitution except the first Article which declared Greece to be a Republic. Security of tenure for the civil service was suspended, and newspapers were forbidden to publish any protests. Without extolling dictatorship in principle, Pangalos professed to be overriding Athenian party politics in the interests of the country as a whole, and promised to revive the Constitution with increased powers for the President shortly to be elected. By skilful manœuvres he secured his own election as President in April 1926. Four months later he was overthrown by General Kondilis, a former associate whom he had exiled. After dissolving the Republican Guard of Pangalos by force, Kondilis thereupon offered to dissolve his own party (National Republicans) and to give up the premiership after the general election fixed for November 1926. This example of public spirit made possible a Coalition government of leading Royalists and Republicans to match a Chamber in which the latter had only a small majority. Under Republican pressure, and working on the previous Assembly's draft of 1925, the new Chamber at last adopted the final text of the Republican Constitution on 2 June 1927. But the resignation of the Royalist Tsaldaris, and then of the Republican leader Papanastasiou, soon weakened a hitherto surprisingly successful coalition.

Venizelos still corresponded with friends and supporters in Greece, and his figure loomed large. After a long visit to Crete he came to Athens in March 1928, reassumed the leadership of his old party, and on 3 July took office once more, forming a government which was supported by two-thirds of the new Chamber. Once more his record during four and a half years of power (1928–1932) was to be one of striking success in foreign policy and of growing difficulties at home. At home, his construction of a Senate under the Constitution of 1927 had no popular appeal, he was unable to promise lower taxation, and his wise reconciliation with Turkey in 1930 (see p. 130) was denounced by Royalists as betraying the interests of Greece. In principle a constitutional monarchist, he thereby lost the full confidence of the Republicans; in practice friendly to the republican experiment and long opposed to the restoration of any member of Constantine's family, he was thereby exposed to the unjust imputation of being nothing more nor less than a Venizelist. The currency crisis of 1931 began a ding-dong struggle in which Venizelos was first momentarily defeated by the Republicans in the Chamber and then lost ground in two successive elections (September 1932, February 1933) to the 'Populist' party of the moderate Royalist Tsaldaris. When Venizelos resigned for the third and last time in nine months, Tsaldaris once more formed a government (10 March 1933), restoring the decided Royalist Metaxas as Minister of the Interior and the anti-parliamentary, now almost Royalist, Kondilis as Minister of War, but dropping Papanastasiou, the symbol of republicanism in the last two Cabinets.

Tsaldaris remained in office for two and a half years, and presided over the transition to monarchy. His party held a majority in the Chamber, but the Venizelists in opposition controlled the Senate, which was thus able to block measures passed by the Chamber. The opposition argued that in such a case a joint meeting of Senate and Chamber was obligatory; the government, that it was merely permitted. Extreme Royalists like Metaxas were in favour of suspending the Constitution, on the ground that the Senate's obstructive tactics made government impossible. On the other side, the Republicans alleged, not without reason, that ministers supported by the Populist party were undermining the Republican Constitution by favouring the movement for restoration of the monarchy. General Plastiras, who had begun the revolution in Chios in 1922, twice attempted a Republican military coup (March 1933 and March 1935). On the second and more serious occasion, the insurgent officers were overpowered in Athens, and Plastiras's own movement in Macedonia was forestalled at Salonica. When the cruiser *Averoff* put to sea with some smaller ships and joined the movement, Venizelos, who was in Crete, was momentarily persuaded to lead it, but he soon withdrew to Rhodes and thence to Paris, while the warships surrendered themselves to the government. This episode probably convinced him that the Royalists had the upper hand; he was to give a provisional blessing to the restored monarchy before his death on 18 March 1936. The attempted *coup* was followed by some death sentences, and by a purge in the civil service and the army. The Chamber was then dissolved, the Senate abolished, and the security of tenure of judges and civil servants suspended. The Liberals and Republicans abstained from the elections held on 9 June 1935, so that the monarchists almost monopolized the new Chamber; but the extreme Royalists were still a minority among them.

A fifth National Assembly for constitutional revision empowered the government to hold a free plebiscite; but General Kondilis, backed by the most decided enemies of the Republic, first forced Tsaldaris to declare himself openly for a monarchy, then replaced him as prime minister (10 October), got the new Chamber to declare in favour of the monarchical form of government and the Constitution of 1911, and himself became regent in the name of King George II. After all this, the plebiscite (3 November 1935), in which 97% of the votes were said to have been cast in favour of the king's return, was merely a matter of form. The Republicans alleged that the secrecy of the ballot was not observed, and that many Royalists cast more than one vote. Against this, it was argued that the Greeks were tired of the Venizelist feud with Constantine's family, and had postponed a change until now only through fear of civil war and loss of political liberties. But, with their rapidly increasing economic dependence on Nazi Germany (which hurt the towns but benefited the peasantry), the tide was setting not only against the Republic but against constitutional monarchy too.

KING GEORGE II AND GENERAL METAXAS, 1935-41

King George II, who had lived mostly in England since he left Greece in 1923, attempted reconciliation by discarding the parties which had secured his return in November 1935. He insisted on a general amnesty, got rid of Kondilis, who died shortly afterwards, and dissolved the Chamber with a view to constitutional revision by a new National Assembly. But the free elections held in January 1936 produced a deadlock like those of 1933, exposing incidentally the unreliability of the recent plebiscite: fifteen Communists held the balance between 143 Monarchists and 142 Liberals, Republicans and Agrarians. On the death of the king's non-party premier Demertzig in April, General John Metaxas, who did not share the king's belief in the value of parliament, obtained the consent of the Chamber to an adjournment for five months, governing meanwhile by decree. His path was smoothed by the death of several political veterans—not only Kondilis (31 January) and Demertzig (13 April), but also Venizelos (18 March) and Tsaldaris (15 May). Konduriotis, the first President of the Republic (1924–1929), had died in August 1935; his successor, Zaimis, who had also formerly been ten times prime minister, died in September 1936 at the age of 81. Nevertheless, Metaxas met with obstruction from the political parties and from the recently appointed legislative commission of forty deputies. The Communists' appearance of strength was accidental, but he used their threat of a general strike to convince the king that constitutional monarchy was impossible in Greece and to get his consent to decrees dissolving the Chamber and declaring martial law (4 August 1936). No date for new elections was fixed, and constitutional guarantees of liberty of the subject were suspended.

The virtual dictatorship inaugurated by General Metaxas, in imitation of Mussolini and Hitler, was still unshaken when he died in January 1941, successfully defending his country against the Italian attack, and before the onrush of the German invaders. His dictatorship was more intelligent than that of General Pangalos ten years earlier. In a broadcast address (10 August 1936) he began by appealing to the youth of Greece against outworn politicians, parties and parliaments. He announced and partly carried out a programme of social reforms, coupled with rearmament. Without pursuing his initial suggestions for a 'corporative State', he introduced minimum wages, insurances and maternity benefits, organized youth movements and started a ten-year programme of public works. Since the depression which started in 1929, the Greeks had already doubled wheat production and increased industrial output by more than 50%, in an effort to reduce imports and so offset the falling market for their two main export crops— tobacco and currants. Clearing agreements with Germany enabled them to sell these crops at high prices in Reichsmarks; but these marks remained in Germany as a credit fund with which Greece might buy (also at high prices) such armaments and industrial products as Germany could spare—not always what Greece most wanted. Finding a large unused credit in Reichsmarks, Metaxas had no choice but to buy from Germany; but he declared his readiness to trade with England if she would undertake to buy a definite quantity of tobacco or currants.

Opposition to the new regime continued for a time. The Athenians disliked a censorship which affected not only the press but University studies and even the speeches of Pericles, or those of Antigone in the theatre; moreover, a form of government which silenced opposition was certainly distasteful in principle to the country as a whole. But after some critics had been banished to the islands in 1938, there was no more trouble. The Greeks knew that it was not easy for them to combine political liberties with unity, in face of dangers from authoritarian neighbours. When war came, the Republican officers were allowed to rejoin the army and the Greeks were united as they had never been during the war of 1914–18.

6. FOREIGN AFFAIRS, 1923-40

RELATIONS WITH TURKEY

The problem of migration and resettlement, which overshadowed all else for some years after 1922, was partly domestic and partly international. Few countries have had to undergo such an upheaval as this migration, which suddenly increased the population of Greece on balance by about 20% without adding to its territory and within a few months of military defeat and political revolution.

The gradual absorption of the refugees made possible the reconciliation with Turkey which was the main achievement of Venizelos during 1928-1932. The negotiations, begun in 1929, were hindered by fears of naval rivalry, which Venizelos allayed by advising the Chamber to build light craft only. A final Convention about the exchange of populations (10 June 1930) prepared public opinion for his visit to Ankara and signature there of a Treaty of neutrality, conciliation and arbitration, a Protocol on parity of naval armaments, and a commercial Convention (all signed 30 October 1930 and ratified 5 October 1931). The Greek people followed his lead and ceased to look on the Turks as their natural enemies. Old ambitions were tacitly abandoned. 'The ghost of the Roman Empire, which had so long haunted the Near East, was finally exorcised.' Relations continued to improve: in 1932 Greece warmly supported the admission of Turkey to the League of Nations, and a ten-year agreement for consultation and guarantee of frontiers was signed on 14 September 1933. Nor did Greece make any objection to the Montreux Convention of 20 July 1936, by which Turkey recovered full strategical control of the Straits, and Greece incidentally regained the right to fortify the islands of Lemnos and Samothrace.

RELATIONS WITH THE BALKAN POWERS

The Pact of 1930 between Greece and Turkey was preceded by other Balkan agreements. Both parties acknowledged the help of Italy, which had already made its own pacts with Turkey (30 May 1928) and with Greece (23 September 1928). Greece already had a pact with Romania (21 March 1928); in announcing the pact with Italy, Venizelos declared that the question of the Dodecanese no longer existed, and soon afterwards (November 1928) he made an agreement with Albania. By the treaties of November 1926 and November 1927 Albania had become almost a protectorate of Italy; Mussolini was anxious to strengthen his position there by promoting Balkan pacts under Italian patronage rather than under that of France, Yugoslavia and the Little Entente. The Yugoslav government, fearing isolation in the Balkans, ratified at last its conventions of 1924 and 1925 with Italy, and accepted Venizelos's offer (October 1928) to negotiate on outstanding differences. Yugoslavia had taken offence in 1924 at the terms of a Greek agreement with Bulgaria about minorities, and had denounced the alliance of 1913; negotiations for its renewal had failed in 1925. A settlement (1926) of Yugoslav claims relating to port and railway facilities at Salonica was rejected by the Greek Chamber in 1927; but the initiative of Venizelos led at last to the signature of six protocols relating to these claims, and of a pact between the two countries (27 March 1929). Yugoslavia was linked with Romania in the Little Entente, and had a pact with Turkey dating from 1925. A Bulgarian treaty with Turkey (6 March 1929), and an agreement with Yugoslavia on frontier questions only (26 September 1929 and 14 February 1930), added to the links in this chain of pacts, which was greatly strengthened by the reconciliation between Greece and Turkey; Bulgaria, the one 'unsatisfied' Balkan state, was still on bad terms with Greece and had no general pact with Yugoslavia; the differences between them were hard to bridge, and public opinion was suspicious in all three countries. With this exception, the moment seemed favourable for discussion of a Balkan entente or even of a Balkan federal pact. Common economic problems pointed in the same direction.

In October 1930 the first of a series of unofficial 'Balkan Conferences' was held at Athens. Greek, Turkish, Yugoslav, Romanian, Albanian and Bulgarian delegations were present, together with observers sent by the governments. The initiative came from Papanastasiou, the Republican leader, and Venizelos gave it his blessing. The Conference agreed on a regular constitution, chose a Balkan flag and hymn, advocated an annual meeting of foreign ministers, and set up a committee to draft a Balkan pact against war, and for mutual help. Other committees suggested postal union and co-operation in the fields of social legislation and economics. But Bulgaria protested, with sympathetic Italian comment, because the agenda excluded concrete applications of minority questions and confined discussion to the general principles. A second unofficial Balkan Conference was held in October 1931, when 200 delegates were welcomed by the Turkish government at Istanbul and afterwards by Kemal himself at Ankara. This Conference initiated a Balkan Chamber of Commerce but made little progress in the direction of a draft Balkan pact: the Bulgarians reopened the minorities question, and even threatened to raise the still more thorny question of revision of frontiers. The third Conference met at Bucharest in October 1932, and the fourth at Salonica in November 1933, both continuing the non-political discussions, but avoiding consideration of a political pact. A fifth Conference, arranged for Belgrade in 1934, was cancelled owing to Yugoslav fears that it might endanger the progress of their separate negotiations with Bulgaria, which had just produced a commercial treaty in May 1934. Official discussions between Greece and Bulgaria had been confined mainly to the subject of financial claims; a temporary settlement made in 1927 was upset by the Hoover moratorium on war debts (1931), and a final settlement, discussed in 1933, was delayed by Bulgaria's refusal to abandon her claims for revision of the peace treaties.

The modest success of these unofficial Conferences, and still more the need to resist revisionist claims which had the support of Italy and Germany, led Greece, Turkey, Yugoslavia and Romania, in spite of Bulgarian abstention, to sign a Pact (9 February 1934), including a mutual guarantee of frontiers and promise of consultation. A protocol explained that the obligations of the Pact would arise if any Balkan state should join another Power in aggression against one of the signatories. But the force of this protocol was lessened by declarations which excluded any obligation for Turkey to fight Russia or for Greece to fight any greater Power; the Turks feared that revisionist Bulgaria might join Russia in attacking Romania, the Greeks that she might join Italy in attacking Yugoslavia. With these reservations the Pact was ratified by the Greek Senate, and registered at Geneva in October 1934. Meeting again at Ankara in the autumn, the same states adopted statutes for a Balkan Entente, modelled on those of the Little Entente—a combination equally opposed to revision of the peace treaties.

The Balkan Pact of 1934 reflected a certain distrust of Italy, which was deepened by the Franco-Italian agreement of January 1935; Greek opinion in particular was very hostile to Italy throughout the Abyssinian dispute. When 'sanctions' had been withdrawn in July 1936, Italy assured these states that she intended no retaliation; but the visit of Dr Schacht to Athens in June, and German press discussion of collaboration between Germany and Italy in the Balkans, made the value of such assurances doubtful. Nevertheless, General Metaxas, in power since April 1936, was generally considered to be an admirer of Italy and Germany; in the Balkan Conference at Belgrade (May 1936) he showed that he was anxious to minimize the commitments of Greece under the pact, at least until his programme of rearmament should have made some progress. He was well aware that Greece must take account of the British navy, as well as of the German or Italian army, and showed less readiness than Bulgaria to submit completely to German economic predominance. But in Balkan politics he preferred isolation, at the risk of having to fight Bulgaria without support, to far-reaching security pacts involving the danger of conflict with the Axis Powers. Holding that the interests of Greece were Mediterranean, not continental, he clung to the friendship of Turkey and tried to avoid giving offence to the protagonists in the impending conflict. Romania also leaned towards isolation after the fall in August 1936 of M. Titulescu, a leading exponent of 'collective security'. The mood in the Balkan capitals began to be that of *sauve qui peut.*

It was natural that Yugoslavia, conscious that the solidity of both the Little Entente and the Balkan Entente was weakening, should seek to reinsure herself elsewhere. Her pact with Bulgaria (24 January 1937), although vague and brief, was intended to have the same symbolic importance as the pact between Greece and Turkey seven years earlier. Her political and commercial treaties with Italy (25 March 1937) were more warmly welcomed in the Italian than in the Yugoslav press. For the sake of breaking up the Little Entente, it cost Italy nothing to make reassuring statements about her intentions in Albania, and it was worth while for Germany to relax for a time in Italy's favour her own economic hold on Yugoslavia. In spite of being partly responsible for it, both Greece and Romania felt misgivings about the new Yugoslav policy, but they made the best of it by joining next year with Yugoslavia and Turkey in coming to terms with Bulgaria. This Pact of Salonica (31 July 1938) appeared to restore and extend the common front of the Balkan States; but the four 'satisfied' states, whose Pact of 1934 had originally been directed against Bulgaria, now had to admit her on terms which showed how the successes of the revisionist 'Axis Powers' had weakened their own position. Bulgaria still did not undertake to guarantee existing frontiers, and legalized her own rearmament by getting release from the military clauses of the Treaty of Neuilly (1919) in return for nothing more than a promise not to seek revision by force. Revision by force soon became the order of the day.

7. MODERN GREEK LITERATURE

After the fall of Constantinople the Byzantine tradition of learning passed to Rome, Florence and Venice, while popular literature came mostly from Crete which had been under Venetian occupation since the Fourth Crusade. Out of the beginnings of a Greco-Venetian culture there sprang up in Crete during the seventeenth century a small but healthy crop of literary works, all written after Italian models, all full of life and colour, with no memory of ancient Greece, but all unmistakably Greek in character and feeling. These works, the religious play *Abraham's Sacrifice*, the *Erophile*, which has been called 'an Elizabethan tragedy of love and blood', the postoral comedy *Gyparis*, and the best known of all (and most widely read in Greece to this day), the *Erotokritos*, a romantic epic, and a few more, are all written in demotic, or popular Greek, with a Cretan flavour which indicates their origin and adds to their charm.

The Turkish conquest of Crete in 1669 brought this phase to an end, but its stirrings were heard in the Ionian Islands where a school of poetry emerged headed by Dionysios Solomos (1798–1857), who was born in Zante and spent most of his life in Corfu. He remains in quality, as well as in time, the first poet of the Greek Kingdom, who pointed the way for all subsequent Greek poetry. Like Wordsworth he believed that the purest poetry was written in the simplest language, and for that he drew both from the rich tradition of Greek folk poetry and from the cultivated poetry of Crete. He elevated the demotic language to a refined artistic medium capable of expressing with simplicity and power his feelings for nature, freedom, truth, love and death. The first few stanzas of his *Hymn to Liberty* were adopted as the national anthem of Greece. Also from the Ionian Islands came two notable contemporaries of Solomos: Andreas Kalvos, who wrote lyric odes of great beauty in an idiosyncratic purist language; and Aristoteles Valaoritis, a romantic poet of uneven merit, who modelled his patriotic verse on the heroic popular ballads.

The literary scene in Athens was dominated for a long period by a school of poets, all of whom wrote in the *katharévousa* or purist Greek (see p. 88). All came under the influence of the weaker aspects of French romanticism. The reaction came in the 1880's when the controversy over the language question flared up in a violent form as a result of the publication of a polemical work, *My Journey*, by John Psycharis, who advocated the abolition of the *katharévousa* and the adoption of the demotic as the language of the state, scholarship and literature. His theories were fiercely opposed by scholars, but were welcomed by men of letters. This conflict brought about a re-assessment of Greek values which was quickened by a renewed interest in Greek folklore and folk poetry. Out of this restlessness a new poetic movement was born. The young poets and writers who sought to link modern Greek literature with its traditions and at the same time to bring it in line with contemporary European trends rallied round Kostes Palamas (1859-1943). An unusual creative vitality followed, especially in the field of poetry. Parnassianism, symbolism and surrealism were all represented. Palamas, whose output, both in verse and in prose, was prodigious, was the central personality for over fifty years and exercised an immense influence on the development of Greek poetry. Angelos Sikelianos (1884-1951), drawing his inspiration from the classical and Christian tradition, added a new tone to Greek poetry. George Seferis (b. 1900), the third major poet of this century, was awarded the Nobel prize for literature in 1963. His first poems, which appeared in 1931, revealed a new sensibility and a remarkable assimilation of the Greek tradition. This was expressed in terms of a modern symbolism, and in his terse and allusive verse the broken statues of antiquity, Odysseus and his companions, or the wreck of a ship in the bay of Poros, acquire a haunting reality. A unique figure is Constantine Cavafy (1868-1933), a poet who lived and worked in Alexandria and was remote from the literary movements of the Greek mainland. His poetry has a refined aestheticism and melancholy at the transience of youth and sensual pleasures, and is often inspired by moments in ancient and later Greek history in which he brings out with poignancy the irony, humour, or pathos of a situation.

Modern Greek prose is represented by numerous short-story writers and novelists like Emmanuel Roidis (1835–1904), Gregorios Xenopoulos (1862–1951), Stratis Myrivilis, Elias Venezis, George Theotokas, Nikos Kazantzakis (1885–1957) whose novels have been translated into many European languages, and Pantelis Prevelakis. On the whole, modern Greek prose-writing is perhaps somewhat below the high level reached by poetry, though in some of the delightful short novels of Vassilis Vassilikos (b. 1933), which have appeared recently, there is good evidence that prose writers are becoming more sophisticated and more accomplished in their craft.

CHAPTER IV

MODERN GREECE, 1939-64

1. RELATIONS WITH THE FASCIST POWERS

THE anxieties about Italian intentions which impelled the Greek government to strengthen its relations with other Balkan powers were soon justified. In April 1939, after Hitler had completed the destruction of Czechoslovakia, Mussolini invaded Albania on Easter Monday and overran it virtually without a struggle. The Greek government saw that more drastic precautions were necessary, and communicated to the British government its fears for Corfu. On 13 April the British and French governments announced a unilateral guarantee of Greece's territorial integrity, which also extended to Romania. The Italians denied that they had any aggressive intentions against Greek territory, and gave evidence of good will by withdrawing troops from the Greco-Albanian frontier in September, and also by reaffirming their pact of friendship with Greece, signed in 1928, later in the same month. A friendly exchange of notes on 30 September closed the affair so far as immediate diplomatic contact was concerned, but clearly the Greeks could not look at the future with complacence.

The government continued its efforts to consolidate the Balkan Entente. They tried to persuade Bulgaria to join, by offering the Bulgarians a free zone in Salonica, like that of the Yugoslavs, but without success. More important were their continued negotiations with Britain and France, and indirectly also those of Britain and France with Turkey. One outcome of the former was an Anglo-Greek financial agreement, though its effectiveness was limited by the fact that Germany had a strong position in the Greek economy, as the main customer for the main export product, tobacco; and also by the resentment felt in London at the failure of the Greeks to settle the payments due on past loans. The chief matter for satisfaction to the Greeks was the announcement, in May and June, of Anglo-Turkish and Franco-Turkish agreements on mutual aid against aggression in the Mediterranean area. The agreements were reformulated in October 1939 (after the outbreak of the second world war) in a tripartite treaty to the same effect. There were, however, qualifying clauses in the treaty which in the event provided Turkey with loopholes, so that the Turks did not actually declare war on the Axis powers until the second world war was nearly finished.

The Greeks rightly judged that their security would depend primarily on their own efforts. Although Metaxas reaffirmed Greek neutrality in September 1939, on the outbreak of the second world war, public opinion was strongly on the side of Britain and France. In 1940, especially after the fall of France and the declaration of war by Mussolini on Hitler's side, the Greeks began preparing for war with a calm courage and a deliberate lack of ostentation or provocation which impressed and moved every foreign observer. The call-up of certain extra categories of men began in May, and on 4 June Metaxas made a speech warning his people of the danger. The Italian government began to bombard him with notes of complaint and protest, particularly against the Greeks' condonation of British violations of their neutrality. It is a fact that such breaches took place, and were condoned: it would have taken an impossibly severe Greek government to prevent them, in the current state of public opinion. Nevertheless, Metaxas reaffirmed Greek neutrality on 5 August, and Mussolini reaffirmed his friendly intentions, while 'unidentified' aircraft attacked Greek ships at sea and other incidents took place which were generally ascribed to Italian provocation. Finally, on 15 August, the Greek light cruiser *Helle*, which was in the harbour of the island of Tenos to attend the Feast of the Assumption, was torpedoed and sunk by a submarine of whose nationality there was never the slightest doubt. At the same time Mussolini began to accuse the Greeks of official responsibility for the murder of one Daut Hodja, an Albanian bandit killed in a border brawl.

Metaxas ordered mobilization to take place unobtrusively in September 1940, but continued to maintain the forms of neutrality by undertaking commercial negotiations with Germany and appealing privately to Hitler to restrain his ally. But after the meeting of Hitler and Mussolini at the Brenner Pass in October, it was clear that no respite was likely. On 26 October Mussolini accused the Greek army of violating the Albanian frontier, no doubt for the sake of his own public opinion. On 27 October a reception was held at the Italian Legation in Athens: Metaxas was present, and no indication was given that war was imminent. Early the following morning the Italian Minister called on Metaxas to deliver an ultimatum, while Italian troops in Albania were already crossing the frontier. Metaxas replied with one word—'No!'—which has become the most famous retort in Greek history since Leonidas at Thermopylae told the Persians to 'Come and get it!' Greek public opinion received the declaration of war with enthusiasm and almost with relief. Greece thus voluntarily became Britain's only combatant ally at the darkest moment of the war. If it was Britain's 'finest hour', it was also Greece's.

Such British help as was available, which was very limited, was immediately sent to Greece, supported by a military mission and a loan of £5 million. Naval support was valuable, but the biggest impression was made by the small number of R.A.F. aircraft which appeared over the Albanian front. It was, however, almost entirely due to the Greek army, of which Metaxas was himself Commander-in-Chief with General Alexander Papagos as Chief of Staff, that the Italian invasion was repulsed. Within a few days, Greek troops crossed the frontier into Albania, and occupied the principal towns in the south: Koritsa in November and Argyrokastron in December. Southern Albania was looked upon in Greece as essentially Greek territory, and known as 'Northern Epirus'. Having a large Greek-speaking Orthodox population, it was expected to be incorporated into Greece at the peace settlement. But after these initial successes, the tide of war turned against the Greeks. They never captured Valona, the principal port of southern Albania; and at the end of January 1941 Metaxas died, leaving the fate of his country in weaker and less decisive hands.

It was becoming apparent that Hitler would have to come to the rescue of Mussolini in the Balkans. A more important motive, known for certain only in retrospect, was that Hitler had already decided to attack Russia, and needed security on his southern flank. German troops therefore began moving into Hungary, Romania and Bulgaria early in 1941, with the consent of their respective governments, which recognized that the only way of avoiding submission to Hitler was by submission to Stalin. Only Yugoslavia held out for a time. Meanwhile, the British government, in anticipation of Hitler's intentions, tried to persuade the Greek government to allow a British expeditionary force to land in Greece, in fulfilment of the guarantee of April 1939. So long as Metaxas lived, he insisted that British troops should land in Greece only after the Germans had crossed the Danube or entered Bulgaria, and then only if the British force were sufficient to ensure that a front could be held. His specific requirements were more exacting than the British government could meet at the time, having also to face an Italian threat to Egypt from the Libyan desert. After Metaxas' death, his successor, Alexander Koryzis, a mild and unbelligerent banker, reaffirmed his predecessor's requirements and asked again if they could be met. As a consequence of British successes against the Italians in the North African desert, it now seemed that they could. After a visit to Athens by a number of high-ranking British visitors (including Anthony Eden, the Foreign Secretary, General Dill, the C.I.G.S., and General Wavell, the Commander-in-Chief of the Middle East) the Greek government decided to accept the proffered British force as adequate. It began to arrive in Piraeus harbour during March, watched by all the officials of the German Legation in Athens, which was formally neutral.

There was now no doubt that Hitler intended to attack Greece. Although censorship tried to prevent Greek opinion from anticipating the worst, a notable 'open letter' to Hitler was published by a leading editor, Vlakhos, in his paper, the *Kathimeriní*, which correctly expressed the determination of virtually every Greek to fight to the last. The attack was delayed while Hitler tried to bring Yugoslavia to submission. He persuaded the Yugoslav Regent and Prime Minister in March to adhere to the German-Italian alliance, but a popular revolution in Belgrade a few days later overthrew the government, ended the Regency, and brought the boy-king Peter to the throne. Staff talks began a few days later between the Yugoslavs and the western allies, but it was too late. On 6 April the Germans attacked both Yugoslavia and Greece, Hitler's lust for revenge being particularly concentrated on the city of Belgrade. Yugoslavia was overrun in a few days, and Greece was invaded simultaneously from Bulgaria, Albania and Yugoslavia.

The possibility of successfully forming a defensive front in Greece had already been prejudiced by a disastrous misunderstanding between the Greek and British military authorities, the cause of which has never been cleared up. The British believed that it had been agreed that General Papagos should withdraw his forward divisions from northern and north-eastern Greece to the line of the River Aliakmon, south-west of Salonica, where the British expeditionary force would join them to form a front. Papagos believed it had been agreed that he should not do this until the British had first ascertained the Yugoslav government's intentions, since if Yugoslavia joined in resisting the Germans it might be possible to hold Salonica and even to eliminate the Italians in Albania altogether. He had waited in vain for a report on this matter from the British Military Mission, until it was too late to carry out an orderly withdrawal. The result was that good Greek divisions were overrun in the north-east, and the Aliakmon Line was too thinly held. The Balkan front began to crumble in a few days.

On 18 April the Prime Minister, Koryzis, committed suicide, and another former banker, Emmanuel Tsouderos, was appointed by King George in his place, after the king had briefly acted as prime minister himself. Two days later a corps commander, General Tsolakoglou, signed an armistice in the north without authority. Papagos repudiated his action, but proposed to the British commander, General Wilson, that the British force should be withdrawn from Greece. He promised every possible help in extricating them—a promise that was amply fulfilled, and with a lack of recrimination almost unexampled between allies. The withdrawal and evacuation went on through the last ten days of April and into the first week of May. The king escaped with his new government to Crete, of which Tsouderos was a native, and a large part of the British expeditionary force, including a high proportion of Australians and New Zealanders, was also transported to Crete by the Royal Navy, though losses were naturally heavy. On 30 April the Germans appointed General Tsolakoglou Prime Minister. On 20 May they launched an attack on Crete with parachutists and airborne troops, and overran the island after a ferocious battle ten days later. The king and his government, as well as a high proportion of the allied troops, were evacuated to Egypt.

2. *THE ENEMY OCCUPATION*

By 1 June 1941 the Germans had the whole of Greece under their domination, but they never effectively occupied more than a limited geographical extent of the country. The Bulgarians were allowed to annex the north-eastern corner (Eastern Macedonia and Western Thrace); the Italians were invited into Athens, where their reception was not respectful; and the Germans themselves took charge of the principal routes of communication, which were important to them in view of their impending incursion into North Africa, where the Italians had also suffered a humiliating setback. The greater part of Greece, being covered in mountain ranges with very

Fig. 27. The Occupation of Greece, 1941
Based on official sources.

inadequate communications, was left largely to itself; and that meant, in many cases, that it was left to starvation. But it also meant that it was left to the guerilla bands which soon formed themselves out of the remnants of the Greek army and the less law-abiding sections of the mountain population (Fig. 27).

During the enemy occupation, from 1941 to 1944 (and even into 1945 in the case of Crete and some other islands), the history of Greece divided into two streams, which flowed in their respective courses almost independently of each other.

In Greece itself, there was a succession of collaborating governments, a restless and suffering population, and a resistance movement which developed great strength and far-reaching political ambitions. Outside Greece, the legitimate government under the king continued to be recognized by the allies, dividing its time between London and Egypt, and exercising control over Greek subjects and armed forces in the Middle East. There was some communication between the two divisions of Greek life, but it was irregular and imperfect. Individual travellers contrived to escape from Greece *via* Turkey from time to time during the occupation, and among them were important political and military figures. There were also numerous clandestine wireless links between Greece and the outside world; but most of them were under British control, in the sense that all outgoing traffic passed through British headquarters, and in many cases the Greeks in charge of the transmissions were chosen, trained and controlled by the British authorities.

Partly because the communications were so imperfect, and partly because the Greek government in exile regarded their substance as tendentious, the gulf between occupied Greece and the free Greek world grew dangerously wide, and grave misunderstandings took place. The most serious was the failure of the government in exile to appreciate the strength of anti-monarchist feeling which developed in occupied Greece. For a variety of reasons, the resistance was led largely by Communist and Venizelist elements, who agreed in opposing the return of the king after the war. The leading Communists had been in prison when the Germans arrived in Greece; and by an incredible act of folly (no doubt because the Soviet Union was still Germany's ally) the Germans released many of them, whereupon they went into hiding and began to organize resistance, especially after the German attack on Russia in June 1941. The leading Venizelists, though few of them were in prison, had played no active part in Greece during Metaxas's dictatorship, since there was no parliament or recognized opposition, and those who were serving officers had all been dismissed. They therefore provided a pool of active, able men, who were pro-allied but anti-monarchist, from which a resistance movement could readily be formed. Officers and politicians who had supported the Metaxas regime, on the other hand, were discredited and disheartened by defeat. Many escaped abroad, most of the rest stayed at home to await events, and only a few turned their minds to resistance.

Two, if not three, separate Greek worlds thus came into existence. In occupied Greece, apart from the puppet governments, which were held in universal contempt, the predominant idea—though not necessarily the idea of the majority—was that after the war the old social and economic order would be swept away, and some of the most forceful personalities intended to sweep away the monarchy with it. Among the Greeks in exile, the old order still held sway, and the return of the king after the war was taken for granted. Apart from the handful of collaborators, both the Greeks in Greece and those abroad were firmly loyal to the Allies. Naturally in each of the two worlds strong elements of the other were also embedded, but they did not serve to bridge the gulf. The British government supported the king and his government as the legitimate rulers of Greece, but they also needed the help of the resistance in Greece. The consequent embarrassment of policy was aggravated when the Americans joined the alliance, since although President Roosevelt joined Churchill in personally supporting the king, many American officials and politicians tended to judge the anti-monarchist leaders of the resistance as more deserving of political support. During the early years of the occupation, however, these differences were concealed by the exigencies of the war effort and the struggle for survival.

Resistance began sporadically. In Athens, small groups were formed, from patriotic, pro-allied and idealistic motives, to carry out sabotage and intelligence for the allies, and to help escaped prisoners-of-war and the starving population. Since students played a prominent role, in 1942 the university was closed. Soon, larger organizations were developed, particularly by the Communist Party of Greece (*Kommunistikón Kómma Elládos*—KKE), whose first major success was to frustrate the recruitment of labour for export to Germany. In the mountainous provinces, again small groups were first formed, either from remnants of the army or from the brigands who had been active at all stages of Greek history. Larger organizations gradually absorbed and expanded them in 1942: firstly, the National Popular Liberation Army (*Ethnikós Laikós Apeleftherotikós Stratós*—ELAS), under the political direction of the National Liberation Front (*Ethnikón Apeleftherotikón Métopon*—EAM), which was nominally an all-party coalition but in reality a creation of the Communists; secondly, the National Republican Greek Army (*Ethnikós Dimokratikós Ellinikós Stratós*—EDES); and others of less note. The first major success of these forces was the destruction of the Gorgopotamos railway viaduct in November 1942, carried out in conjunction with a small British parachute force which thereafter became the British Military Mission to the Greek guerillas. In the same month the first puppet prime minister, Tsolakoglou, resigned and was replaced by a former university professor, Logothetopoulos, who had a German wife.

Outside Greece, the king's government under Tsouderos continued to act in the people's name. Greece was admitted to membership of the United Nations and signed their declaration. An agreement was made with the British government on the employment of Greek forces under British command, and with the U.S.A. for Lend-Lease supplies. The government also succeeded in making arrangements for Swedish ships to carry food to the starving population of Greece. Looking to the future, an agreement was signed with the Yugoslav government in exile to form the basis of a post-war Balkan Union, but events overtook the good intention. The most difficult problem for the future was to assure the status of the king, who was widely regarded as having broken his constitutional oath when he allowed General Metaxas to set up a dictatorship. In the summer of 1942, the first important politician to escape from Greece, Panayiotis Kanellopoulos, who was made Deputy Prime Minister under Tsouderos, confirmed the strength of feeling in Greece about this question. Later in the year, Tsouderos publicly stated on behalf of the king that after the war the Greek people would have the final say in determining their new conditions of life. But this did not satisfy the leaders of the resistance. The uneasy stirrings of the Greek political world became evident early in 1943, when a major re-shuffle of the government in exile took place in March and the king established his residence in Cairo; while in Athens Logothetopoulos was removed in April and replaced by John Rallis, who remained the puppet Prime Minister till the end of the occupation.

The resistance leaders in the mountains were also quarrelling, not solely or even mainly about the constitutional question of the monarchy. All the main military leaders were by background anti-monarchist: Colonel Stephanos Saraphis and Colonel Dimitrios Psaros, who led small independent armies, had both been cashiered in 1935 for supporting the last Venizelist rising; and Colonel Napoleon Zervas, the leader of EDES, had taken part in more than one republican *coup d'état* in the 1920's. But the prospect of Communism, embodied in EAM/ELAS, began to overshadow the constitutional question, and affected them in different ways. Zervas decided to make his peace with the monarchy as the lesser evil, and under British persuasion he exchanged amicable messages with the king. Saraphis and Psaros were both attacked by ELAS during 1943, and both were defeated and captured. Saraphis then changed sides, and became the titular Commander-in-Chief of ELAS. Psaros held out, and with the help of British intervention he was released and allowed to re-form his force; but it played no further effective role, and in 1944 it was again destroyed by ELAS, and Psaros was murdered. The leading figure in these atrocious operations was the Communist Athanasios Claras, known by the pseudonym of Aris Veloukhiotis. The policy was that of the Communist Party (KKE) working through EAM, but Aris was a rebellious personality who often acted irresponsibly on his own initiative.

By the middle of 1943, when North Africa was cleared of the enemy and the invasion of Southern Europe was imminent, a critical situation had arisen in Greece. It was assumed by most Greeks that the invasion would take place in Greece, and the course of allied preparations corroborated this impression, in some cases deliberately in order to deceive the Germans. The guerilla leaders were persuaded to stop quarrelling and unite their forces in order to disrupt all German communications through Greece in July 1943, as part of an allied deception operation. The price of the necessary supplies was that they should all sign an agreement, drafted by the British Military Mission, constituting themselves as 'National Bands of Greek Guerillas'. They all did so, and the operation was successful; but it deceived the Greeks, including the Communists, as well as the Germans. Although the expected invasion took place in Italy instead of Greece, the KKE nevertheless calculated that the Germans would be out of Greece before the end of 1943 and acted accordingly. A joint mission of guerilla leaders was sent to Cairo in a British aircraft in July 1943 from a landing-ground constructed in the mountains, and the Communist spokesmen presented demands to the king and Tsouderos which were unacceptable. On their return to Greece by the same means, the Communists launched an attack on all rival guerilla forces, intending to destroy the opposition in anticipation of the end of the occupation. They were strengthened by a windfall of Italian weapons, acquired in August when the Pinerolo Division surrendered to the British Military Mission just as Mussolini's régime was falling in Italy. The attack by ELAS on its rivals was successful, except against Zervas, who held EDES together on his native territory in north-west Greece (Epirus).

Under British pressure, the king made several attempts to satisfy the less extravagant demands of the more moderate resistance leaders. In July 1943 he promised a 'fully representative' government upon the liberation, to be followed by elections to a Constituent Assembly within six months; in November he declared that 'when the hour of liberation struck, he would examine anew the date of his return'. But early in 1944 the anti-monarchist infection spread to the Greek armed forces in Egypt. A mutiny broke out, which the British and loyal Greek forces suppressed. Tsouderos resigned after a disagreement with the king just before the mutiny, and was succeeded by Sophoklis Venizelos (a son of the great Cretan), who resigned in his turn after a few days. George Papandreou, a Venizelist who had recently escaped from Greece, was then asked to form a government. He decided to convene a conference in the Lebanon to create a government of national unity, with the participation of resistance leaders. The Communists had already formed a provisional administration called the Political Committee of National Liberation (*Politiki Epitropí Ethnikís Apeleftheróseos*—PEEA) in the mountains, but they sent representatives to the Lebanon Conference. Their representatives (including Saraphis and several Communists) agreed to join Papandreou's Government of National Unity, but PEEA repudiated their decision, again at Communist dictation. Negotiations continued through the summer of 1944, while all efforts by ELAS to destroy Zervas' forces failed and the withdrawal of the Germans became obviously imminent, though a year later than the Communists had expected. They finally decided in August to join Papandreou's government, no doubt hoping to subvert it from within. An almost bloodless take-over of Athens and most of Greece by the allies followed in October 1944, as the Germans withdrew northwards.

By November 1944 the atmosphere had worsened again. When the British commander, General Scobie, ordered the dissolution of the guerilla forces, EAM refused and the Communist ministers left Papandreou's government. Early in December violence broke out in Athens between the Greek and British authorities on the one side and EAM/ELAS on the other. Representatives of the U.S.A. in Athens were ordered to remain neutral. After weeks of fierce fighting, during which Zervas's forces were driven out of Epirus and almost all of Greece fell into Communist hands except parts of Athens, Salonica, Patras and the islands, ELAS were finally defeated by large British reinforcements from Italy. Churchill and Eden personally intervened in the bitter quarrel, arriving in Athens on Christmas Day. Papandreou resigned at the end of December, being succeeded by General Plastiras, the famous Republican of the 1920's and titular leader of EDES. Still more significant, the king, now in London, agreed not to return to Greece until he should be recalled by a plebiscite; and more reluctantly, he appointed the Archbishop of Athens, Damaskinos, as Regent. Negotiations for a truce with ELAS began on 10 January 1945 and succeeded three days later. ELAS agreed to surrender their arms, which turned out to be more numerous than had been expected. In February a conference between the Greek government, the British Ambassador, and EAM/ELAS was held at Varkiza, near Athens. It ended in agreement on liberal reforms, an amnesty for political crimes, and a plebiscite to be held on the monarchy under international supervision. The surrender of ELAS was repudiated by Aris Veloukhiotis, who took to the hills again, where he was killed by security forces in the summer. The problems of reconstruction had now to be faced in the most unpromising circumstances, though with liberal help from UNRRA and the allies.

3. POST-WAR TROUBLES

The liberation of Greece from enemy occupation became complete only with the surrender of Germany in May 1945, since German troops had remained in Crete and other islands (including the Dodecanese, which still belonged to Italy) after their withdrawal from the mainland in October 1944. The five years which followed were in some ways no less painful than the preceding five years of war and occupation. The problems of reconstruction fell into several categories, all of which were interlocked and interacted on each other. First, there was the problem of economic disorganization. The administration had entirely broken down, especially in the provinces; towns and villages had been largely destroyed and the population had been reduced by starvation, fighting and deliberate reprisals; road and rail communications were at a standstill; ports had been put out of action and shipping sunk; the currency was ruined by galloping inflation; foreign trade, on which Greece depended for essential food-supplies, was non-existent, and in particular Greece's most important customer (Germany) for her most important product (tobacco) was virtually destroyed. The Greeks' dependence on foreign aid, whether British, American or international, was to continue for many years.

The second category of problems was social, political and constitutional. The division between the Greeks who had escaped abroad, including the government and some of the armed forces, and those who had spent the war in Greece, remained to be reconciled. So did that between those in Greece who had resisted the occupation and those who had acquiesced or even collaborated in it; so did that between monarchists and republicans, and that between Communists and the rest. Parliamentary democracy had also to be restored, having been in abeyance since 1936; and the personal position of King George had to be regulated. Finally, in the third category, there were the problems of Greece's foreign relations. These had to be revised and re-established in many different directions: with Greece's traditional allies, in particular Britain and France; with her most important new ally, the United States; with her ex-enemies, particularly Germany and Italy;

with the Soviet Union and the Communist *bloc*, particularly Greece's three northern neighbours, Albania, Yugoslavia and Bulgaria; and with the principal neutral and newly independent countries of the Eastern Mediterranean.

Unlike other occupied countries, Greece was to enjoy no period of respite for reconstruction. All the problems made themselves felt at once, and were reflected at once in the development of the political situation. In April 1945 General Plastiras was forced to resign, having come under attack for compromising sentiments he was alleged to have expressed while living in France during the war, and he was succeeded as Prime Minister by Admiral Voulgaris at the head of a non-political or 'service' government. The leading figure in the new government was the eminent economist, Professor Varvaressos, who put forward a vigorous but exacting plan for economic recovery in June. Two months later, when his plan was shelved, he resigned.

The prestige of the 'service' government progressively declined: it had no solution to the problem of inflation, nor to that of the political prisoners, both collaborators and Communists, who congested the gaols throughout the country; nor could it make any practical headway with its commitment to hold free elections by the end of the year. In September the Regent, Archbishop Damaskinos, visited England and was warmly received; but he was unable to bring back what he chiefly hoped for—increased economic aid and support for Greece's territorial claims against Albania and Bulgaria. He had also hoped, and many British philhellenes had urged, that the British colony of Cyprus might be ceded to Greece, especially as the cession by Italy of the Dodecanese was already promised. But he received only the personal honour of a G.C.M.G.

In October Voulgaris resigned, nominally because of opposition to his announcement of elections in January. A prolonged political crisis followed, during which the Regent himself became Prime Minister for a few days. Themistoklis Sophoulis and Sophoklis Venizelos successively failed to form governments, and one formed by Panayiotis Kanellopoulos on 1 November lasted less than three weeks. It was succeeded by a slightly more stable government composed of relatively youthful politicians of the Centre, some of whom had distinguished themselves in the Resistance, again under the aged Sophoulis. The new government boldly tackled the problem of restoring parliamentary democracy by proclaiming an amnesty and the withdrawal of 60,000 prosecutions in December, and announcing elections for 31 March 1946. The British, French and United States governments accepted invitations, which were made under the terms of the Varkiza Agreement, to form a mission to supervise the elections (the Allied Mission for Observing the Greek Elections—AMFOGE), but the Soviet government refused the invitation on the ground that it would constitute interference in Greece's internal affairs. They also used the first meeting of the U.N. Security Council in January 1946 to demand the withdrawal of British troops from Greece, without success.

The elections were nevertheless held and resulted in a 60% poll, of which the Populist Party led by Constantine Tsaldaris won more than half. AMFOGE reported that the result had been fairly achieved, but the Communists claimed that all those who had abstained would have voted for them. Tsaldaris became Prime Minister on 18 April, and announced that a referendum on the future position of the monarchy would be held on 1 September. In June a sharp dispute took place in Parliament about the form of the referendum, since the question posed by the government was whether or not King George should return to his throne, not, as the opposition desired, whether Greece should be a monarchy or a republic. However, the government had its way; in August the Anglo-American mission (from which the French had withdrawn) expressed approval of the state of the register; and on 1 September the Greeks voted by a large majority (1,166,512 out of 1,861,146 registered voters) in favour of the King's return. He arrived in Greece on 28 September for his second restoration, to confront a rapidly deteriorating situation. Fighting had broken out in northern Greece in May, and in the Peloponnese in November. The economic situation was catastrophic, despite an increase of aid from Britain and a loan from the U.S.A. Inflation continued; rebuilding and the restoration of communications were at a standstill; and in the absence of rationing there were grave abuses in the distribution of food. The country was on the brink of civil war; nor were the grievances confined to the Communists.

In December 1946 Tsaldaris complained to the United Nations that the Yugoslav government was helping to promote rebellion in Greece. The U.N. agreed to send an investigating commission, which arrived in January. In the same month Tsaldaris resigned, and was succeeded by Dimitrios Maximos, an elder statesman of the right wing who formed a somewhat wider cabinet in which General (as he now was) Napoleon Zervas, the former leader of EDES, became Minister of Public Order. An event more portentous for the future in the same month was the arrival of a U.S. economic mission to investigate Greece's needs, which were of growing interest to the United States government because the task of supporting Greece was already beginning to look beyond the powers of Britain alone. On 12 March President Truman announced his famous plan, the 'Truman Doctrine', for economic aid to Greece and Turkey, beginning with the provision of $400,000. The first American Mission for Aid to Greece arrived in Athens in July.

Meanwhile King George had died suddenly in March. His successor was his younger brother, Paul, who found himself inheriting a country threatened by disaster. The report of the first U.N. Commission, which broadly supported Greek complaints, was the subject of violent dispute by the Communist *bloc* at the United Nations, and a vote in the Security Council to continue its work was vetoed by the Soviet representative on 29 July. The Secretary-General, Trygve Lie, nevertheless ruled that the United Nations Special Commission on the

Balkans (UNSCOB) was still in existence. Greece had thus become one of the first major themes of dispute in the cold war.

Twice during 1947, in June and December, the Greek Communist rebels in northern Greece tried to seize the town of Konitsa, near the Albanian border, in order to establish a capital and to demand international recognition. The Greek government was therefore faced with a full-scale civil war, in which the Communist states on the northern borders were undoubtedly helping the rebels. Attempts to react with equal vigour were handicapped at first by public opinion in Athens, where left-wing sympathies were still surprisingly strong. Maximos's government, for instance, was compelled to resign after complaints at the ruthless methods of General Zervas in preserving public order, though later it did not pass unobserved that a man whom Zervas had arrested, and whom the following government released, was responsible for assassinating a senior Minister in the streets of Athens. The new government was formed in August by a coalition between Tsaldaris and Sophoulis; and for the next two and a half years, until the Communist rebellion was suppressed, Greece continued to be ruled by governments of 'national unity' on an inter-party basis.

The new government offered an amnesty to the rebels, which was ignored. In November a joint General Staff was created by the Greek and United States governments. On 24 December the Greek Communist leader, Markos Vaphiadis, proclaimed an independent government in the northern mountains. UNSCOB, which was now back at work in Greece, urged that no government should recognize the régime of Markos; nor did any do so—not even, curiously enough, the Communist governments which were supporting him and which had recently established the Cominform in Belgrade. For a time, however, all seemed to go well with Markos's forces, although their efforts to capture Konitsa were repulsed. Whenever they were defeated in local actions, they could withdraw across the northern frontiers to reorganize and re-equip. Moreover, they took with them many thousands of Greek children, who could be trained later in countries of the Communist *bloc* to continue the struggle. In 1948 the Communists were able to extend their operations over an even larger extent of Greece than had been held by the guerillas during the German occupation, including the Peloponnese and Attica up to the suburbs of Athens.

There was little to cheer the Greek population during 1948. Among the few items of good news was the formal completion of the cession to Greece of the Dodecanese islands by Italy as part of the peace treaty; and in November a treaty of Amity, Commerce and Navigation was signed with Italy—the first with any ex-enemy. During the summer the Corinth Canal was reopened and the railway viaduct over the River Gorgopotamos (destroyed by guerillas and British officers in 1942) was repaired; but it was an indication of the tragic situation that such necessary reconstruction had to wait three years after the end of the war. The road from Athens to Salonica was also repaired at great speed with American aid, and reopened in mid-1948, but only to military traffic in convoys. Meanwhile, about 700,000 refugees—nearly 10% of the population—had fled from the fighting in the north, and almost all of them were homeless. At the end of October Martial Law was proclaimed throughout Greece. In November Sophoulis resigned, but re-formed an almost identical government a few days later. It was a measure of the desperate state of affairs that although no one could devise any effective alternative government, Sophoulis won a vote of confidence on his reappointment only by 168 votes to 167.

When exactly the tide turned is not easy to say. The Americans made a notable contribution by the vigour with which they re-equipped the Greek forces and repaired the communications, especially the roads into the interior, without which it was impossible to defeat the rebels or guarantee the safety of loyal villages. The support of most members of the United Nations was also staunch: against Soviet opposition, the General Assembly expressly condemned Albania, Yugoslavia and Bulgaria for aiding the rebellion, on the basis of an UNSCOB report in November 1948. Changes in the leadership both of the Greek government and forces, and of the Communists, also played a part.

In January 1949 General Papagos, who had been in command against the Italians in Albania in 1940–41 and later a prisoner of war in Germany, was appointed Commander-in-Chief; and in the same month a new coalition government was formed under Sophoulis again, in which Alexander Diomedes was Deputy Prime Minister and virtually the effective leader. In the following month Markos was deposed from the Communist leadership and never heard of again. He was succeeded as head of the War Council by Nikos Zakhariadis and as Prime Minister by Partsalidis. These changes were perhaps connected with the great upheaval in the Communist camp which led to the breach between Tito and Stalin, the expulsion of Yugoslavia from the Cominform in the summer of 1948, and the Yugoslav decision to close the frontier with Greece in July 1949. Certainly this last decision was a major factor in bringing the Communist rebellion to defeat.

It was already apparent that only aid from the north kept the rebellion going. Early in 1949 the Peloponnese was cleared of rebels; most of the leading Communists in Athens were under lock and key by April; and in the same month the process of clearing the north also began, with such good results that in July some 100,000 refugees were able to return to their homes. The end of the rebellion was then not long delayed. After Tito had closed the Greco-Yugoslav frontier, the decisive battles were fought in August. The rebels were helped by fire from Albania, but the lack of freedom to manœuvre into and out of Yugoslavia was fatal to them. On 6 September the government announced the virtual end of the war, which was acknowledged by the rebel radio in October with an announcement of the 'temporary cessation' of hostilities. Shortly before the climax of the struggle, Sophoulis had died in June, still holding office as Prime Minister, and it was left to his successor, Diomedes, to proclaim the victory and to face the problems of reconstruction.

The problems were formidable, and Diomedes did not last long to face them. Inflation was still unchecked: prices were rising, the balance of trade was seriously adverse, industrial unrest was growing; and even the civil servants struck in protest against the high cost of living. Diomedes resigned in January 1950 after a breach with his colleague, Venizelos. It was the end of the Liberal-Populist coalition, which was succeeded by a 'caretaker' government under Ion Theotokis, to prepare for elections in March. Grave though the situation was, however, at least internal security was no longer a source of anxiety. It was announced that all death sentences for treason passed by military courts were to be reviewed; and Martial Law was lifted before the elections. Two further signs of the historic watershed across which Greece was now passing were the beginning of the withdrawal of British service missions, and the opening of discussions with the Yugoslavs to re-establish diplomatic relations and restore communications. The general election of March 1950 also marked the end of an era: the alternate dominance of the Populists under Tsaldaris and the Liberals under Venizelos was broken by the emergence of a new party, the National Progressive Union of the Centre (EPEK), led by General Plastiras and Tsouderos.

As a result of the elections, none of the three main parties could form a government without the support or acquiescence of one of the other two. Tsaldaris refused to try; Venizelos tried, but resigned after two weeks, not without some pressure from the United States Ambassador—itself a new phenomenon in Greek politics. Plastiras formed a government with Liberal support in April, but lost the support of Venizelos when he released a large proportion of the detained rebels. Venizelos then formed a purely Liberal government in May, which lasted until September, when he lost a vote of confidence. He next formed a new government with the support of the Populists under Tsaldaris, but resigned in November after a dispute with Tsaldaris, and formed yet another coalition with a small minority party, the Democratic Socialists. The coalition was generally supported by EPEK, and lasted until June 1951, when the Democratic Socialists resigned. Venizelos continued in office, with the help of the Populists and EPEK in turn, but only for another month. This period of unstable coalition government ended in the late summer of 1951 with the break-up of EPEK, from which Tsouderos withdrew, and the dissolution of Parliament to enable new elections to be held on the basis of an electoral law aimed at promoting the emergence of fewer and larger parties.

The need for a more stable kind of parliamentary democracy was strongly felt in this uneasy period, and was accentuated by the extreme gravity of the international events which coincided with it. Two months after the elections of 1950, the Korean War broke out, and Greece hastened to offer a brigade and an Air Force contingent to serve under the United Nations. The outbreak of the war had far-reaching consequences for Greece as for other European countries. The fear of aggression in Europe led to the invitation to Greece and Turkey to become associated with the North Atlantic Treaty Organization for Mediterranean affairs, and later (in 1951) to full membership. It also led to a closer association of Greece with both Yugoslavia and Turkey for local defence in the Balkan area. American military aid was increased, but financial aid for economic reconstruction was cut in the autumn of 1950, partly as an indication of disapproval of the unsatisfactory political situation. That situation failed to improve, and consequently gave the western world an unfortunate impression of Greek irresponsibility. One of those who felt the justice of allied disapproval most keenly was Alexander Papagos, who had been promoted Field-Marshal and Commander-in-Chief of all the armed forces in 1950. Accordingly he resigned all his appointments in May 1951, and two months later announced the formation of what he called, in imitation of General de Gaulle's *Rassemblement Français*, the 'Greek Rally' to fight the forthcoming elections.

4. THE BEGINNING OF RECONSTRUCTION

It is from the elections of September 1951, although they again failed to produce a decisive result, that the beginning of Greece's reconstruction can be dated. Under a new system of what was called 'modified proportional representation', the Greek Rally won 36% of the votes and 114 seats out of 250. The election was also notable for the first re-emergence of the Communists as a parliamentary party, under the guise of the Union of the Democratic Left (EDA), which won 10 seats. Since no party had an overall majority, and since Papagos refused to enter any coalition—and indeed unsuccessfully demanded that new elections should be held at once on a simple majority system—a coalition of the familiar kind was formed by Plastiras with the Liberals. Papagos announced that he would support the government in its foreign policy, which was one of loyalty to NATO and support for the United Nations, but not on its domestic policy, which included a wide Pacification Bill to wind up the aftermath of the civil war.

It was clear that the government could not have a long life; nor, according to Papagos, could the system of government of which it was typical. Nevertheless a number of important events marked its single year of office. Greece became a full member of NATO in October 1951 and was elected to the Security Council in December. UNSCOB was withdrawn, having served its purpose. A new constitution was promulgated on 1 January 1952, in which a major innovation was that strikes were forbidden in the civil service. Cordial relations were developed with Italy, Turkey and Yugoslavia; and the Yugoslavs even returned some of the Greek children carried off in the civil war. Increasing attention was paid to Middle Eastern affairs, particularly in Egypt: Greece recognized, by implication, the Egyptian claim to the Sudan in June 1952, and also expressed an interest in the abortive Anglo-American plan for a Middle East Defence Organization in September.

Fig. 28. Modern Greece

In October, however, the scene was dramatically changed by a new general election, in which Field-Marshal Papagos at last had his own way. A new electoral law, strongly supported by the United States government, prescribed the majority system of election and an increased number of seats, from 250 to 300. The Greek Rally won an absolute majority with 239 seats, and all the remaining 61 seats went to a coalition of the remains of EPEK with the Liberals. The Communist-backed EDA lost all its seats; and a few weeks later it was publicly linked with the organization of a secret Communist cell uncovered in Athens. The longest period of stable government in modern Greek history was then inaugurated.

Papagos's Minister of Co-ordination, Spyros Markezinis, announced an economic plan on lines laid down by Professor Varvaressos in 1945, and visited the U.S.A. in April 1953 to seek American aid for agricultural improvements and the development of electric power and industry. A drastic reduction of the Civil Service was set in motion with some five thousand retirements. The *drachma* was devalued in April, and in August the first post-war budget to anticipate a surplus was introduced. The improvement of the economic situation was marked, although the American contribution was still considerable and indispensable. Papagos's firm hand was generally respected: an attempt to organize a general strike in protest at his measures in June 1953 was not widely successful. Greece's recovery was now well under way, though a disastrous earthquake in the Ionian Islands in August came as a reminder that her troubles were still not at an end. The difficulties of economic reconstruction were illustrated by the resignation of Markezinis in April 1954.

The most important developments during Papagos's tenure of office, which lasted until his death in October 1955, were in the field of foreign affairs. There took place both an improvement and an extension of Greece's international relations, marred however by one painful exception—the prolonged dispute over Cyprus. The trend of improvement affected particularly Greek relations with her northern neighbours. With Bulgaria efforts to normalize relations were partially successful in 1953-54: frontier disputes were settled, prisoners were exchanged, but full diplomatic relations were not yet restored, nor would the Bulgarian government agree to pay reparations arising from the second world war. In 1955 a somewhat similar partial *rapprochement* took place with Albania, whose government proposed the establishment of diplomatic relations but refused to agree to Greece's condition, that the status of Northern Epirus (the Greek term for Southern Albania) should be regarded as still open until settled by a peace conference. Other members of the Soviet *bloc*, no doubt influenced by the post-Stalinist thaw, made friendly overtures towards Greece. Young Greeks who had been carried off during the civil war were returned from Hungary, Romania and Czechoslovakia; and during 1954 trade agreements were signed by the Greek government with Czechoslovakia, Romania and the Soviet Union. An indication of the extension of Greece's international connections was the signature during the same year of trade agreements with Spain, Israel and the German Federal Republic.

Much more striking than any of these minor improvements, however, was the development under Papagos's direction of the Balkan Alliance with Turkey and Yugoslavia. Staff conversations took place in 1952, and led to the signature at Ankara on 28 February 1953 of a defence treaty between the three Balkan neighbours, which was heartily approved by Greece's western allies. The Greek government was anxious to carry the arrangements still further. In June 1954 Marshal Tito was invited to visit Athens, an event which set the seal on the restoration of the traditional amity between Greece and Yugoslavia. On 9 August of the same year a formal alliance between Greece, Turkey and Yugoslavia was signed at Bled.

It was modelled on the North Atlantic Treaty, and contained provisions not only for the creation of a combined General Staff but also for co-operation in non-military fields and for some common political institutions. The Permanent Council met for the first time in Ankara in February 1955, and the General Staff in Belgrade two months later. These arrangements were to prove, in the event, a dead letter, and the alliance cannot be said ever to have worked effectively in practice. In part the reason was that it never needed to do so, because the danger of Soviet aggression in the Balkans, against which the alliance was directed, disappeared with the policy of 'de-Stalinization' and the restoration of at least civil relations between Tito and Khrushchev. But a more decisive reason was the steady deterioration of relations between Greece and Turkey after 1954, as the dispute over Cyprus came to a head.

5. THE CYPRUS DISPUTE

The Greeks had long hoped for the cession of Cyprus to Greece by the British government. Indeed, the cry of '*Énosis*' (union with Greece) had been heard in Cyprus as soon as the British arrived there in 1878, and had been constantly echoed on the Greek mainland ever since. An unofficial plebiscite was held in Cyprus in January 1950, organized by the Church under the direction of the Archbishop, who held his office by popular election and was expected to regard himself as a national leader or 'Ethnarch'. Since none of the Turkish population of the island (amounting to about 80,000 out of a total of nearly half a million) took part in the plebiscite, the result was an overwhelming vote in favour of *énosis*.

When a Cypriot delegation visited Athens, on its way to the United Nations to communicate the result, the Greek government of the day expressed the hope that Britain would respond to the wishes of the Cypriot people, but added that it would handle the question in due time within the framework of its traditional friendship with the British. The same policy was reiterated on many subsequent occasions, culminating in a formal statement by Papagos on 18 March 1954. By this time, however, the movement in favour of *énosis* was under the vigorous direction of Archbishop Makarios, and violence was already being considered as the only recourse by Colonel George Grivas, a Cypriot-born officer of the Greek Army who had played a minor and disreputable role in the closing stages of the German occupation of Greece.

Under pressure from Makarios, and also stimulated by riots

in Athens and stung by a succession of rebuffs from the British government, Papagos finally notified the United Nations in August 1954 that Greece wished the future of Cyprus to be considered by the General Assembly. In December the United Nations resolved not to consider the question 'for the time being'. Renewed rioting in Athens and Salonica was severely suppressed by Papagos, who would have preferred to find a way of dropping the matter. But circumstances became too strong for him. An organized campaign of violence, led by Grivas, began in Cyprus during April 1955. In Greece, there was a deterioration of the economic situation, from which some distraction was desirable; there was bitter disappointment in the public mind both with Britain and with the U.S.A., whose representatives voted with the British at the U.N.; there were other troubles at home, including a recrudescence of Communist activity and a new earthquake disaster in the neighbourhood of Volos; and there was almost universal sympathy with the Greek Cypriot rebellion under Grivas. Greece's foreign policy began to deviate perceptibly, against Papagos's personal inclinations, in the direction of the neutralist, anti-colonialist, and even pro-Soviet trends of the day. In the hope of stemming the tide, the British government invited the Greek and Turkish governments in June to attend a conference in London on the Eastern Mediterranean, at which Cyprus could be included in the agenda. The Turks quickly accepted; Makarios protested against the Turks even being invited; the Greeks accepted only after several days' hesitation.

The conference met at the end of August, and resulted only in a re-statement of familiar positions: the Greeks insisting that they would accept no settlement of the Cypriot question which excluded the possibility of *énosis*; the Turks that they would accept none which did not exclude that possibility; the British that they would concede self-government to the island if the Greeks and the Turks could agree on terms, but without any ultimate commitment on sovereignty. The deadlock was made worse by an outbreak of anti-Greek violence in Istanbul and Smyrna on 6 September, which was later proved (after the overthrow of the Turkish government in 1960) to have been officially inspired and organized. The Turks offered apologies and amends, but the Greeks angrily withdrew from a number of inter-allied occasions, including the NATO exercises in the Eastern Mediterranean. The North Atlantic Council considered the painful situation, without result. To make matters worse, the United Nations refused in September to include Cyprus on the agenda of the forthcoming General Assembly. On 4 October Papagos died.

It had been expected that Papagos would be succeeded by his Foreign Minister, Stephanos Stephanopoulos. Instead, the King summoned the comparatively unknown Minister of Communications and Public Works, Constantine Karamanlis. His policy did not differ from that of Papagos, whose loyal supporter he had been, but he tried vigorously to recover control of a situation which had progressively slipped from the dying Field-Marshal's hands. In November he conducted secret conversations with the British government, of which the Turks were informed, and the tension decreased. At the beginning of December it was announced that the Greek appeal to the United Nations would not be renewed, and at the end of the month a Greek emissary was sent to Cyprus, where he met Makarios and the newly appointed governor, Field-Marshal Sir John Harding, the former Chief of the Imperial General Staff. The year ended in an atmosphere of relative optimism.

Karamanlis then dissolved Parliament in January 1956 and held a general election on 9 February under a new and complicated electoral law. He also formed a new party, the National Radical Union (ERE), to replace Papagos's Greek Rally. Since the electoral law favoured large rather than small parties, practically the whole of the opposition formed a single electoral combination, ranging from the Populists to the crypto-Communists. This combination won almost exactly 50% of the votes, but only 145 seats out of 300. The remaining 155 were won by Karamanlis, who thus had a narrow majority although ERE won only 45.7% of the votes. It was the first general election in which women voted, and in the new government a woman held office for the first time.

Unfortunately, so far as Cyprus was concerned, the turn of the year proved to have been a false dawn. For this there were two principal reasons. One was that the appointment of a Field-Marshal as governor convinced the Greeks that Britain intended to pursue a repressive policy in Cyprus. The other was that Grivas's organization, known as the National Organization of Cypriot Combatants (*Ethnikí Orgánosis Kypríon Agonistón*—EOKA), began to get out of hand. As was later proved from captured documents and admitted in retrospect, the outbreak of violence had enjoyed the blessing and approval of Archbishop Makarios, to whom Grivas (operating under the pseudonym of Dighenis Akritas, a legendary Greek hero) constantly referred as his leader; but that is not to say that the relations of the two men were easy. When it appeared, early in 1956, that Makarios was about to negotiate a settlement with the new governor, Grivas put out leaflets denouncing the negotiations and swearing to continue the struggle. Under such pressures, Makarios hardened his attitude towards the negotiations; and the British government insisted on terms, particularly with regard to an amnesty, which he could not accept. Early in March the negotiations broke down, and on 9 March Makarios was deported to the Seychelles Islands. The next day the Greek Ambassador was recalled from London, and on 13 March the Greek appeal to the United Nations was renewed.

Karamanlis still hoped for a compromise and a reconciliation. He rejected the foreign policy of neutralism and abandonment of the western alliance, which had been advocated by his opponents at the general election. In March the Greeks again took part in NATO manœuvres. In the speech from the throne at the opening of the new Parliament on 2 April, King Paul reaffirmed the Greeks' desire for *énosis* but deplored the deterioration in allied relations. When the Soviet Foreign Minister, Shepilov, visited Athens on his way back to Moscow from Egypt in June, Karamanlis rebuffed his offers of aid. But the situation continued to grow worse during the summer. The terrorism of EOKA, which had originally been directed chiefly against Greeks who failed to support *énosis*, was increasingly turned against Turkish Cypriots and British troops. An angry exchange took place between Karamanlis and Eden when the latter insisted that Cyprus was essential as a British base to safeguard oil supplies from the Middle East. Within a few weeks sharp point was given to this argument when President Nasser announced the nationalization of the Suez Canal Company at the end of July. Greece was the only country, apart from Egypt, which refused an invitation to attend the conference convened in London in August by the British and French governments to discuss the crisis over the Suez Canal. For the next three years the Greeks sought their friendships increasingly outside the circle of the western alliances.

An unexpected development during August 1956 was the announcement of a truce by EOKA. The governor of Cyprus, however, chose to interpret it as an indication of willingness to surrender, and responded to it in that sense, with the result that fighting was resumed after a short interval. The bloodshed grew still worse during the Anglo-French campaign against Egypt, part of which was mounted from Cyprus, but there was never any danger that the British forces would lose control of the island. The Greeks, however, were confirmed in their determination by mounting hopes of success at the United Nations.

When the British government sent Lord Radcliffe to Cyprus to prepare a new constitution, the Greek government rejected the resultant draft in December without consideration or discussion, although it would probably have proved, on examination and trial, to have offered them their last chance of achieving *énosis* eventually through constitutional means.

Public opinion generally believed—though it is doubtful whether the belief was shared by Karamanlis, who visited the U.S.A. in the autumn of 1956—that pressure at the United Nations would give them what they wanted in the end. Nevertheless the resolution on Cyprus passed by the General Assembly in February 1957 was only moderately encouraging to the Greeks. It urged a 'peaceful, democratic and just solution' and the resumption of negotiations to that end. Greece, Turkey and Britain all agreed; but whereas the Greeks construed the intention to be negotiations between Britain and 'the people of Cyprus', the Turks and the British construed it to be between the three governments concerned.

It thus seemed impossible to renew the negotiations which all parties claimed to desire. The good offices of NATO were offered, but rejected by Greece. A compromise was reached on the position of Archbishop Makarios after he had made an ambiguous statement deploring violence in March: he was released from the Seychelles but not allowed to return to Cyprus. Towards her old allies and new friends Greece's policy continued to be neither hot nor cold. Diplomatic relations were renewed with Romania in 1956, but a Romanian proposal in September 1957 for an enlargement of the Balkan Pact to include Romania, Bulgaria and Albania was rejected by Greece, although it was rather surprisingly accepted in principle by Yugoslavia. The Balkan Pact was in fact already regarded as a dead letter by the Greeks, though the Yugoslav Vice-President Kardelj was politely received in Athens in October.

Towards Turkey the feelings of the Greeks were inevitably still bitter, but as a friendly gesture the defences of Leros, a Greek island in the Dodecanese close to the Turkish coast, were dismantled. Towards the U.S.A. Greek sentiments were naturally divided. The American refusal to support their claim to *énosis* was resented, but Greece's economic and military dependence remained inescapable. An agreement on U.S. bases in Greece had existed since 1953, and the allegation that Karamanlis had agreed to allow the Americans to establish rockets on Greek soil was strongly pressed against him by the opposition in 1957. The Greek government also endorsed the 'Eisenhower Doctrine' on the Middle East, but refused to allow American aircraft to land on Greek aerodromes during the 'air-lift' to Jordan in September 1957. On the other hand, the Greeks were somewhat disenchanted in their new-found friendship with President Nasser when the policy of 'Egyptianization' of foreign businesses severely hit the large Greek community in Egypt.

The Greeks continued to court the 'unaligned' countries, including the former colonies of western powers, with the object of mustering a sufficient majority at the United Nations, which meant in effect two-thirds of the General Assembly. In September 1957 Greece succeeded in having a motion for the 'self-determination' of Cyprus inscribed on the U.N. agenda, and Makarios (who had installed himself in Athens) left for New York to press it home. Two events in October encouraged the hopes of the Greeks: Sir John Harding was replaced as governor of Cyprus by Sir Hugh Foot, a member of the Colonial Service with a liberal reputation; and the British Labour Party Conference voted in support of self-determination for Cyprus without partition—partition being the solution now advocated by the Turks and seriously considered by the British Conservative government. The United Nations, however, again proved a disappointment. Although the Greek motion was passed by both the Political Committee and the General Assembly, the majority in the latter was less than two-thirds and therefore ineffective. The United States again voted against Greece, and in retaliation U.S. installations in Athens were damaged by bombs. The trend towards neutralism and even towards co-operation with the Soviet *bloc* gathered strength.

During 1958 many new and some surprising associations were formed. Commercial discussions with the United Arab Republic and Yugoslavia were followed by trade agreements with the Soviet Union, Poland and Japan, and controls on trade with Communist China (imposed to please the Americans) were relaxed. Agreements were also concluded with Albania, on clearing mines from the Corfu strait, and with Bulgaria on frontier issues. Among the interchanges made during the year were visits by the King and Queen of Greece to the Lebanon; by the Foreign Minister to meet his Egyptian and Yugoslav colleagues at Brioni; and by the Spanish Foreign Minister and Sudanese Vice-President to Athens. Relations with the British government, on the other hand, were frigid. Nothing came of visits to Athens by the British Foreign Secretary, Selwyn Lloyd, and Sir Hugh Foot in February. The new Prime Minister, Harold Macmillan, had no more success when he came in August, to expound a new plan put forward by the British government for a 'partnership' of Britain, Greece and Turkey in the administration of Cyprus.

It seemed, however, that Karamanlis was anxious not to be carried away into desperate courses by the extreme feelings of public opinion, the press and opposition, and even some of his own colleagues. In March 1958 he resigned, after the defection from his government of two ministers with their supporters, and held a general election on 11 May. The principal issues exploited against him were the weakness of his policy over Cyprus and the allegation that he had agreed, or was about to agree, to the establishment of U.S. missile bases in Greece. It was therefore a highly significant victory when he increased his strength in Parliament, under a voting system known as 'reinforced proportional representation', to 173 seats out of 300, a strong majority over all his rivals combined. Armed with this vote of confidence, he addressed himself to the final liquidation of the Cyprus problem. First it was necessary, in order not to appear weak, to reject the British government's plan for 'partnership' in a tri-national administration of Cyprus. Nevertheless the British government declared that it would impose the plan, despite its rejection by the Greeks, and on paper it came into effect on 1 October.

But in the meantime Archbishop Makarios had also seen the writing on the wall. In an unexpected statement to a British Labour M.P. in September, he declared that he would accept independence instead of *énosis* as a solution to the Cyprus problem. Towards the end of the year secret talks on this possibility began in Paris under the auspices of NATO, and the United Nations thankfully washed its hands of the problem by passing unanimously an innocuous compromise resolution.

In January 1959 the Greek and Turkish Foreign Ministers met in Zürich and reached an outline of agreement on independence for Cyprus. In February the discussions were transferred to London, where they were joined by the Greek and Turkish Prime Ministers and by Archbishop Makarios and the leader of the Turkish community in Cyprus, Dr Kütchuk, who later became Vice-President of the island under the Presidency of the Archbishop. Agreement was quickly reached and signed on the creation of a new Republic of Cyprus, which came into existence formally in August 1960 and remained a member of the Commonwealth. The agreement was ratified by the Greek Parliament on 28 February 1959 by 170 votes to 118 after a bitter debate. Among those who sharply criticized the abandonment of the claim to *énosis* was Grivas, who emerged from his hiding place in Cyprus to receive a hero's welcome in Athens. He was awarded high decorations and promoted Lieutenant-General in recognition of what had undoubtedly been a technically remarkable achievement of subversive warfare. But he sharply attacked the government and Archbishop Makarios for signing the Zürich-London Agreements without consulting him, and made repeated threats to enter Greek politics in a revolutionary manner, which few Greeks took seriously. Although it was certain that by no means all Greeks had renounced the ultimate goal of *énosis* for Cyprus, most of them were glad to be relieved of the dispute and the violence which had marred the last five years.

6. THE RETURN TO NORMALITY

The year 1959 marked a return to normality. Normality meant an improvement of Greek relations with Britain, the United States, and even Turkey; and a relative cooling of relations with the Soviet *bloc* and the neutrals. Relations with Yugoslavia continued to be friendly, but when Tito visited Rhodes in March 1959 the communiqué on his conversations with Karamanlis significantly omitted any reference to the Balkan Pact, which was eventually declared to be defunct in June 1960. During the same period there was a notable strengthening of the national economy. Inflation had been brought under control, and the Greeks now had such an unusual degree of confidence in their own currency that they no longer sought to convert their savings as soon as possible into gold sovereigns, and were even willing to invest them in government loans. The conduct of Greek ship-owners was another sign of the times. Having for many years registered their ships under foreign flags of convenience in order to escape Greek taxation, they began to bring them back under the Greek flag, and even to invest their profits in new industrial enterprises in Greece. A new shipyard at Skaramanga, an oil refinery, the beginnings of an iron and steel industry, an aluminium plant, an atomic reactor, were some of the results of the economic resurgence. Tourism also began to develop into a major industry. A five-year development plan was announced in January 1959, and in September an Industrial Development Corporation was established.

The improvement in inter-allied relations was almost immediate upon the signature of the Zürich-London Agreements. It plainly responded to a deeply felt desire on the part of the Greeks. During 1959 the visitors to Athens included the Italian Prime Minister, the British Minister of Defence, the Secretary-General of NATO, and the German Minister of Economic Affairs. The Royal Navy and R.A.F. also paid official visits for the first time in recent years. As a climax, in December the American President, General Eisenhower, arrived in Athens and was received with unexampled enthusiasm. The enthusiasm was further stimulated by the fact that Khrushchev visited Budapest in the same month and spoke warmly there in praise of the Greek Communist Party. The fear of a revival of Communism in Greece made itself felt during the summer when a young Communist, Manolis Glezos, who had distinguished himself in the Resistance, was sentenced to five years' imprisonment for subversive activity. When the Hungarians issued a commemorative stamp bearing Glezos's portrait, the Greeks retorted with a stamp bearing the portrait of Imre Nagy. Relations with the Communist world were in fact back to normal.

There were some unfortunate signs that the conduct of Greek politics might also be reverting to normal. Politicians of the opposition, who had been out of office for an unaccustomedly long period, began to become restless. Kanellopoulos joined the government as Deputy Prime Minister in January 1959, and Papandreou formed a new party in April. The emergence of Grivas as a political figure entailed more speculative possibilities. After quarrelling publicly with Makarios and accusing the government of trying to exterminate him, he consented to a reconciliation with the Archbishop in October, but refused to support his candidature for the Presidency of Cyprus in December—not that that incommoded Makarios, whose election was virtually a foregone conclusion. In July 1960 Grivas announced the formation of a 'new movement', which he expressly said was not a political party, and invited the political leaders to put themselves under his command. Rather surprisingly, 17 Liberal members of Parliament did so. Venizelos, their leader, approved their decision, though he did not follow suit himself. His own contribution to the political ferment was to propose, after a visit to the Soviet Union, that the Communist Party should again be legalized, but the idea fell on deaf ears. Another sign of the restless feeling that it was time for a change was the formation within Parliament of a new group of ten deputies of the Centre.

The stability of the government was unaffected by these manœuvres, but it had other reasons for concern. One was the activity of the Communists: many were put on trial for subversion and espionage during 1960, and the connection of the KKE with the legal left-wing party, EDA, and its newspaper, *Avyi*, became notorious. Another regrettable but transient affair was the publication by a German lawyer, Max Merten, who had been convicted of war crimes in Salonica but amnestied, of allegations about the conduct of certain members of Karamanlis's government and their wives during the occupation. There were acrimonious debates in Parliament on the subject, but no evidence was ever produced. A less important but more genuine scandal led to the resignation of a junior minister in November 1960. All this provoked accusations by the opposition of the 'moral corruption' of the government, accompanied by demands for fresh elections. More disturbing than the activities of the opposition, however, were the renewed signs that all was not well with the national economy.

Greece's economic weakness was brought into prominence by the government's desire to join the European Economic Community, or Common Market, created by the Treaty of Rome in 1957. The chronic deficit on the balance of payments combined with an unbalanced budget, of which nearly one-third was devoted to defence, made it seem unlikely that the national economy could stand the strain of participating in the Common Market on equal terms. Moreover, in 1960 the Organization for European Economic Co-operation reported that Greece's recovery was slowing down. A major difficulty was that whereas imports from the West continued unavoidably to rise, the West did not provide a sufficient market for Greece's agricultural surpluses, particularly tobacco. Attempts were made to remedy the situation by encouraging western countries to establish industries in Greece: the German Federal Republic, for instance, set up a sugar-beet factory in

1960. The Salonica Fair, which was revived and attracted nineteen countries in the same year, also helped to stimulate trade; and in 1961 NATO appointed an economic mission to study the needs of Greece and Turkey. But it was clear enough that it was necessary in any case to trade with countries of the eastern *bloc*, which could help to absorb Greece's agricultural surpluses. Hence economic necessity pulled Greece's foreign policy in a different direction from political sympathy.

New trade agreements were signed during 1960 with Poland and Czechoslovakia, and full diplomatic relations were restored with both countries. The difficult negotiations with the European Economic Community ended early in 1961 in an agreement that Greece should become an 'associate', and a treaty to this effect was signed on 9 July. Although the terms were not easy, the Greeks did not regret having taken a further step in partnership with the western alliance, to which their loyalty never wavered once the trouble over Cyprus was ended. They braved the wrath of the Bulgarian and Soviet governments both in 1959, when Greece signed an agreement with the United States on nuclear weapons, and in 1961, when a conference of the NATO South-Eastern Command and NATO manœuvres were held in Greek and Turkish Thrace. On the latter occasion Khrushchev attacked the Greek government in a speech declaring that his rockets would spare 'neither olive-trees nor the Acropolis', to which Karamanlis made a dignified reply. Despite the difficult economic circumstances and uneasy times, the spirit of the Persian Wars and the campaign of 1940 was not defunct.

That the Greek people generally approved their government was shown for the third successive time by the general election of 1961. Karamanlis resigned on 20 September, and was succeeded by a 'caretaker' government to prepare for the elections. He had taken the risk of passing a new Electoral Law which was relatively favourable to his opponents rather than his own party. Nevertheless the poll on 29 October slightly improved his majority, with almost exactly 50% of the votes cast and 176 seats out of 300. The left-wing coalition, within which the Communists sheltered, lost votes and seats heavily, and the Centre Union, led by Papandreou and Venizelos, with Markezinis's Progressives in alliance, won a little over one-third of the votes and 100 seats. Karamanlis had an overall majority of more than 50. Such a vote of confidence in a Prime Minister who had been in office since 1955 (and indeed under Papagos since 1952) was naturally bitter to the opposition. In consequence there were unusually acrimonious allegations of fraud at the polls, which more than 100 deputies carried to the extreme length of boycotting the opening of Parliament in December. When they finally took their seats in January 1962, it was to denounce the elections as a sham and the government as unconstitutional. In one constituency at Salonica, the Electoral Court upheld the accusations and ordered a new poll; but elsewhere the opposition gained no satisfaction.

Papandreou and Venizelos continued during 1962 to campaign vigorously against the conduct and outcome of the elections. Unfortunately, since the Prime Minister of the 'caretaker' government had been an official of the Royal Court, the King's name became personally involved in the charges. The opposition newspaper, *Eleftheria*, pointedly published a serial on the history of the last great constitutional schism, between King Constantine and the Liberals under Venizelos's father. The opposition also made much play with a remark of King Paul's in addressing army officers at Salonica: 'God has united us; I belong to you and you belong to me.' Papandreou publicly warned the King against pursuing a 'personal policy' like his father. Sharp criticism was also made of the administration of the Royal Welfare Fund, which had been created as an emergency measure during the civil war; and the opposition voted against the dowry accorded to Princess Sophia on her marriage to Don Carlos of Spain. All these pin-pricks were symptoms of a *malaise* such as had not been felt so severely in Greek politics for a generation.

THE RETURN TO NORMALITY

The reluctant involvement of the Crown in politics became more acute in the following year. It came to a head over the acceptance by the King and Queen of an invitation to make a state visit to London. The visit was criticized by left-wing elements in Britain (led, rather inconsequentially, by organizations formed to promote nuclear disarmament), chiefly on the ground that a large number of so-called 'political prisoners' were being wrongfully held in Greek prisons. The prisoners were in fact those sentenced by various courts for crimes against the state during the civil war of 1947–9; and as a constitutional monarch the King had no personal power over their fate in any case. A virulent campaign was nevertheless mounted in London against him, and still more against Queen Frederika, as a 'fascist' monarch. Echoes of the same accusations were heard in Greece also, though the official parliamentary opposition found it difficult to force their criticisms to a vote in the Assembly because they were conscious that most of the so-called 'political prisoners' had been sentenced when they were themselves in office.

To make matters worse, an unfortunate incident involving Queen Frederika occurred while she was on a private visit to London during April 1963. A small crowd of left-wing Greeks, including the British-born wife of a well-known Communist prisoner, Mrs Ambatielos, tried to approach the Queen in a London street, with the result that she had to take refuge in a private flat. There were various accounts of what took place on this occasion; but the certain facts were that the British government officially apologized, their left-wing critics blamed them for doing so, and Greek public opinion was outraged. The desirability of cancelling the proposed royal visit to London, which was planned for July, was widely canvassed. The confused and bitter feelings engendered by the dispute were aggravated by a disastrous incident in Salonica in May, when a left-wing deputy, Grigorios Lambrakis, was killed after speaking at a meeting of the local Peace Committee, and another left-wing deputy was seriously injured. Four senior police officers were later charged with moral responsibility for the tragedy.

In June the government came to the conclusion that in the prevailing circumstances it was desirable to cancel, or at least to postpone, the royal visit to London. The King refused to accept this advice, and Karamanlis accordingly resigned on 11 June, after holding office for the record period of nearly eight years. His resignation provoked a political crisis of a kind once familiar, but now unexpected. Papandreou demanded the appointment of a government under his own leadership, to be charged with the task of holding fresh elections; but neither he nor anyone else seriously expected the King to take such a step. Instead a so-called 'service government' was appointed under Panayiotis Pipinelis, who had previously acted as a constitutional adviser to the Crown; but because he had held office under Karamanlis, the opposition refused to regard his ministry as impartial for the purposes of holding elections. Pipinelis nevertheless received a vote of confidence at the end of the month by 172 votes to 14, the opposition deputies of the Centre Union abstaining. The new government agreed to support the King's decision to carry through the royal visit to London. It took place from 9 to 11 July, and was generally regarded as successful, despite some ugly scenes in London organized by supporters of the extreme left.

The political situation in Athens continued to be both bitter and confused. Even within the opposition there were conflicting views. The Centre Union disliked enjoying the support of the extreme left, represented in parliament by EDA, and was itself divided: Papandreou and Venizelos publicly admitted the impossibility of co-operation between themselves at the end of July, though the prospect of elections soon brought them together again. Pipinelis announced that elections would be held on 3 November, a decision which was confirmed by the King's formal dissolution of parliament in September. A few days later, in deference to the opposition's criticisms of the impartiality of Pipinelis, a new 'service government' was appointed under Stavros Mavromikhalis, the President of the Areopagus or Supreme Court, in his place. It was generally accepted that the appointment of so eminent a judge as Prime Minister was a guarantee of fair elections; and so the event proved.

The general election showed a sharp but not decisive swing towards the Centre Union, which won 42% of the votes cast, against 39% for the National Radical Union (ERE) led by Karamanlis. The distribution of seats was 140 for the Centre Union, 128 for ERE, 30 for EDA, and two for the Progressives; in other words, it was only possible to form a minority or a coalition government. A few days later Papandreou formed a government confined to his own followers, with Venizelos as Deputy Prime Minister. Karamanlis at first declared that he would abandon politics; then withdrew the declaration; then abruptly left Greece, consigning the leadership of his party to Kanellopoulos. Papandreou's minority government won a vote of confidence on Christmas Eve with the support of EDA, but he at once resigned on the ground that he would not be dependent on the Communists. King Paul called upon Kanellopoulos, who was unable to form a government. Parliament was therefore again dissolved, another 'caretaker government' was appointed, and elections were fixed for 16 February 1964. In the meantime a severe crisis had occurred over Cyprus, where Archbishop Makarios, continually frustrated by the virtual right of veto given to the Turkish minority in the constitution, had declared his intention unilaterally to revise it in the direction of absolute independence.

The Cyprus crisis, bursting at a moment of political uncertainty in Athens, had the gravest international consequences during 1964. Atrocities between Turkish Cypriots and Greek Cypriots were of frequent occurrence, and the former, being numerically a minority, found themselves gradually driven into isolated pockets of the island, where the Greeks could sever their communications at will. There was constant danger of conflict between Greece and Turkey, both countries (like Britain) having troops stationed on the island under the 1960 treaty. More than once the two parent nations were on the brink of war, especially after Turkish aircraft attacked Greek

Cypriot positions and harbours in August. Archbishop Makarios, behaving more and more as sole ruler of the island and treating the Turkish minority as rebels, appealed first for the help of British troops, which was given; and then, when their conduct was insufficiently partisan to suit him, to the United Nations, which sent a small international force and a Mediator. As the year went on in increasing tension and confusion, General Grivas emerged from retirement in Athens to lead the Greek Cypriot forces; Makarios made overtures for less disinterested help to both the Soviet and the Egyptian governments; the Finnish mediator died at a critical moment and was replaced by a Latin American successor; and desperate efforts were made, particularly by the U.S. government, to work out a new settlement by negotiation.

It might have seemed, indeed, that the clock had been put back to a state of affairs which would once have been called normal in the most melancholy sense. Yet concurrently in 1964 there unfolded a series of unexpected events which not only seemed to mark the end of an era, but also indicated a new underlying stability in Greek affairs and gave grounds for better hopes in the future.

The general election in February gave Papandreou a clear majority. He won 53% of the votes cast and 174 seats for the Centre Union, against 104 for the ERE and the Progressives, and 22 for EDA. It was the first time in many years in Greece (or indeed anywhere else in Europe outside Britain) that a single strong and coherent party had succeeded another such party in office by a decisive victory at the polls. Papandreou began his term of office with vigour, despite his 75 years. He handled the Cyprus crisis wisely, adopting a conciliatory attitude towards the Turks and his western allies without flouting Greek public opinion; and he was helped by the fact that world opinion was apparently moving round at last to *énosis* (with compensations to Turkey) as the best solution for Cyprus, not least because it might be the only way of neutralizing the turbulent influence of Makarios and Grivas.

THE RETURN TO NORMALITY

The *dramatis personae* underwent other striking changes, too. Karamanlis settled abroad; Venizelos died during the general election; and King Paul, stricken with cancer, lived only long enough to swear-in the new government. He was succeeded by his 23-year-old son, Constantine, bearing a name which always reminds the Greeks of past glories. Constantine II was fortunate in the moment of his accession. He was young and handsome, an Olympic gold-medallist in 1960, and about to be married to the lovely Danish Princess Anne-Marie: altogether a fit subject for Pindar. To say, truthfully, that his political judgment was unformed was to say nothing to the disadvantage of a new monarch. Papandreou, who while out of office had almost renewed with King Paul the quarrel of the elder Venizelos with Constantine I, was unlikely to pursue it as Prime Minister with a King young enough to be his grandson. The general election coming immediately before the death of King Paul had in fact assured the new King of an equally loyal government and opposition (apart from the Communists in EDA), which would not have been the case had he succeeded under a government of the traditional royalists. The opening of his reign was auspicious, despite the international tension over Cyprus. He enjoyed a triumph in his first speech from the Throne (in which he rightly called the Zürich-London agreements on Cyprus unworkable); and again at his wedding on 18 September. There were momentary flurries—for instance, over an abortive project to bestow the title 'Royal' upon the Army, and over the personal future of the Queen Mother, Frederika—to remind public opinion that the monarchy was still not beyond the scope of controversy. But the prevailing atmosphere at the end of 1964 was one of fresh optimism, in which not the least element was the belief that some form of *énosis* for Cyprus could not now be long delayed.

BIBLIOGRAPHICAL NOTE

ANCIENT GREECE

(1) Greek legends preserve the memory of a powerful and wise king (Minos) in Crete and of the heroes of the Trojan War; and the classical Greeks were constantly aware of an earlier age of greatness, the monuments of which, spectacular even in ruins, remained to view at Mycenae and elsewhere. But the modern world tended to discount legend and neglect these remains until the archaeological discoveries of Heinrich Schliemann at Troy, Mycenae and Tiryns (from 1870 onwards), and the work of Sir Arthur Evans in Crete (from 1893 onwards). The great work by Sir Arthur Evans, *The Palace of Minos at Knossus*, 4 vols. (London, 1921-35), not only gives a detailed description of the discoveries at Cnossus but covers the whole field of Minoan civilization, and is particularly rich in illustrations.

Shorter surveys of this early civilization and its archaeological remains are given in the following books:

G. Glotz, *La Civilisation Egéenne* (Paris, 1923), translated by M. R. Dobie and E. M. Riley as *The Aegean Civilization* (London, 1925); revised 1952 by C. Picard and P. Demargne.

H. R. Hall, *The Civilisation of Greece in the Bronze Age* (London, 1928).

J. D. S. Pendlebury, *The Archaeology of Crete: an introduction* (London, 1939). The same author has written an excellent *Handbook to the Palace of Minos* (London, 1933, new edition 1954).

C. H. and H. B. Hawes, *Crete the Fore-runner of Greece* (London, 1909), is short and very readable.

R. W. Hutchinson, *Prehistoric Crete* (Penguin Books, 1962), is authoritative and up to date.

S. Marinatos and M. Hirmer, *Crete and Mycenae* (Thames and Hudson, 1960), with brief text, sumptuously illustrated, covers both Minoan and Mycenaean civilization.

General works in English on the prehistory of mainland Greece are, however, few. In the *Ancient Peoples and Places* series (Thames and Hudson) a volume on *The Mycenaeans* by Lord William Taylor is in preparation.

For a summary outline see A. J. B. Wace and F. H. Stubbings, *A Companion to Homer* (Macmillan, 1962), which also has accounts of the 'Homeric' sites.

On Mycenae itself see:

A. J. B. Wace, *Mycenae, an archaeological history and guide* (Princeton, 1949).

G. E. Mylonas, *Ancient Mycenae* (London, 1957).

Helen Wace, *Mycenae Guide* (1961), an excellent illustrated pamphlet.

(2) The authoritative bibliographies of *The Cambridge Ancient History* (Cambridge, 1923-39 and 1961-) indicate the vast literature that is available about the history of classical Greece.

The most comprehensive of the shorter histories are J. B. Bury, *A History of Greece to the Death of Alexander the Great* (London, 1900, 3rd ed., revised by R. Meiggs, London, 1951), and N. G. L. Hammond, *A History of Greece* (Oxford, 1959). These provide a clear narrative of events, and the latter is more up to date in the section on prehistory.

BIBLIOGRAPHICAL NOTE

An interesting account of the most characteristic political institution of the Greeks is given in G. Glotz, *The Greek City and its Institutions*, translated from the French by N. Mallison (London, 1929).

Another book also by Glotz gives an account of the economic history of Greece up to the Roman Conquest—*Ancient Greece at Work*, translated by M. R. Dobie (London, 1926). This may be supplemented by M. I. Rostovzeff's *A History of the Ancient World* (St Petersburg, 1899), translated from the Russian by J. D. Duff (Oxford, 1926, 2nd ed. 1930).

Finally, one of the most attractive of all books dealing with Ancient Greece is Sir Alfred Zimmern's *The Greek Commonwealth: Politics and Economics in Fifth-century Athens* (Oxford, 1911, 5th ed. 1931). This gives a picture of ancient economic and social history in the light of the geographical conditions of the Greek lands and can be strongly recommended.

(3) Various aspects of Greek civilization form the subject of the following works whose titles are explanatory. All present authoritative summaries of their respective subjects:

G. M. A. Richter, *The Sculpture and Sculptors of the Greeks* (Yale, 3rd ed. 1950).
W. Lamb, *Greek and Roman Bronzes* (London, 1929).
G. M. A. Richter, *A Handbook of Greek Art* (London, 1959).
D. S. Robertson, *Greek and Roman Architecture* (Cambridge, 1929).
L. Robin, *Greek Thought and the Origins of the Scientific Spirit*, translated from the French by M. R. Dobie (London, 1928).
R. M. Cook, *Greek Painted Pottery* (London, 1960).
C. T. Seltman, *Greek Coins: a history of metallic currency and coinage down to the fall of the Hellenistic kingdoms* (London, 1933).

A collection of essays, edited by R. W. Livingstone, provides a summary of many aspects of Greek civilization: *The Legacy of Greece* (Oxford, 1921). A brief and readable survey is H. D. F. Kitto's *The Greeks* (Penguin, 2nd ed. 1958).

MEDIEVAL GREECE

(1) It was at one time the fashion to decry the Byzantine empire, and Gibbon poured contempt upon it. Since then a large number of writers have reassessed the part played by the empire in the history of Europe and the Near East. An authoritative account, complete with exhaustive bibliographies, will be found in *The Cambridge Medieval History*, vol. IV (Cambridge, 1923; a new edition is now in preparation). The volume is entitled *The Eastern Roman Empire* (717–1453), and is devoted entirely to the empire. A short attractive summary of the main features of the Byzantine civilization is given by Norman H. Baynes in *The Byzantine Empire* (London, 1925).

The following two books are particularly useful for a scholarly assessment of the evidence relating to the Slav immigration into Greece: J. B. Bury, *A History of the Later Roman Empire, A.D. 395–800*, 2 vols. (London, 1889); J. B. Bury, *A History of the Eastern Roman Empire, A.D. 802–867* (London, 1912).

Useful books in English on the Byzantine Empire which have appeared since 1945 are: N. H. Baynes and H. St L. B. Moss, *Byzantium: An Introduction to East Roman Civilisation* (Oxford, 1948); J. M. Hussey, *The Byzantine World* (London, 1957); D. M. Nicol, *The Despotate of Epirus* (Oxford, Blackwell, 1957); G. Ostrogorsky, *History of the Byzantine State* (Oxford, Blackwell, 1956: very highly recommended); S. Runciman, *A History of the Crusades* (3 vols., Cambridge, 1951–55).

BIBLIOGRAPHICAL NOTE

(2) Much was done to rehabilitate the history of Byzantine and later Greece by the Scottish scholar George Finlay who spent many years in Greece. His *History of Greece*, published between 1844 and 1862, opened a field that had hitherto been neglected by English writers. A new edition, revised by himself and edited by H. F. Tozer, was later published in 7 vols. (Oxford, 1877).

(3) Not many English scholars have followed in Finlay's footsteps, but an outstanding exception is W. Miller. Like Finlay he lays stress on the fact that 'contemporary Hellas owes as much, or more, to the great figures of the Middle Ages as to the heroes of classical antiquity'. His *The Latins in the Levant* (London, 1908) is a detailed authoritative work covering the period 1204–1566. Another detailed work by the same author is *Essays on the Latin Orient* (Cambridge, 1921). This is a collection of articles and monographs originally published elsewhere. It deals mainly with Frankish Greece, but also has articles on Roman, Byzantine and Turkish Greece. A short and useful summary by the same author is *The Latin Orient* (S.P.C.K. London, 1920).

Another account of Frankish Greece, which summarizes earlier work on the subject, is Rennell Rodd's *The Princes of Achaia and the Chronicles of Morea*, 2 vols. (London, 1907).

(4) An account of Turkish Greece may be found in vol. v of Finlay's *History of Greece* (see above). This may be supplemented by two articles on Turkish and Venetian Greece up to 1718 in W. Miller, *Essays on the Latin Orient* (see above), and by a short summary, *The Turkish Restoration in Greece, 1718–97* (S.P.C.K. London, 1921), also by W. Miller.

An account of the general setting of the history of Turkish Greece can be found in J. A. R. Marriott, *The Eastern Question* (Oxford, 1924). There is also Th. H. Papadopoullos' *Studies and Documents relating to the History of the Greek Church and People under Turkish Domination* (Brussels, 1952).

(5) Of the many travel books written about Greece, two, by W. M. Leake, give an excellent and detailed picture of conditions in Greece between the years 1804–1810: *Travels in the Morea*, 3 vols. (London, 1830); *Travels in Northern Greece*, 4 vols. (London, 1835). These also contain a good deal of material about a number of other topics, e.g. the Slavs in Greece, the Frankish period.

MODERN GREECE

(1) The War of Independence has had many historians, including two Scots who took some part in it: Thomas Gordon, *History of the Greek Revolution* (Edinburgh, 1832); and George Finlay, same title, 2 vols. (London, 1861) or as vols. VI–VII of his *History of Greece* (Oxford, 1877). Useful modern books are: *The Greek War of Independence* (London, 1952) by C. M. Woodhouse (who took part in Greece in the 1940's); *A History of the Greek People, 1821–31* (London, 1922) by W. Miller (long familiar with the Levant and author of other works on it); and *The Question of Greek Independence, 1821–33* (Cambridge, 1930), by C. W. Crawley (mainly on British policy, with a bibliography). See also E. Driault et M. Lhéritier, *Histoire Diplomatique de la Grèce de 1821 à nos jours*, 5 vols. (Paris, 1925–6).

(2) The best short accounts of the history of modern Greece are: W. Miller, *Greece* (London, 1928); J. Mavrocordato, *Modern Greece 1800–1931* (London, 1931); E. S. Forster, *A Short History of Modern Greece, 1821–1956* (3rd ed., London, 1958).

BIBLIOGRAPHICAL NOTE

(3) For the history of the region, and of the part played by Greece in it, see, among others: Sir Charles Eliot, *Turkey in Europe* (London, 1908); Sir John Marriott, *The Eastern Question*, 4th edition (Oxford, 1940); W. Miller, *The Ottoman Empire and its Successors, 1801–1927*, 4th ed. with appendix for 1927–36 (Cambridge, 1936); A. J. Toynbee, *The Western Question in Greece and Turkey* (London, 1922); and various publications of the Royal Institute of International Affairs.

(4) For the period of the second world war, the best sources in English are: Field-Marshal Alexander Papagos, *The Battle of Greece, 1940–1941* (Athens, 1949), for the campaigns against Italy and Germany; Brigadier E. C. W. Myers, *Greek Entanglement* (London, 1955) and C. M. Woodhouse, *Apple of Discord* (London, 1948), for the enemy occupation of Greece; and Sir Reginald Leeper, *When Greek Meets Greek* (London, 1950), for the political background among the Greeks in exile.

(5) The post-war period has been the subject of many books, mainly ephemeral in character. Among the most dependable are: Bickham Sweet-Escott, *Greece— A Political and Economic Survey 1939–1953* (London, 1954), which contains a useful bibliography, and Floyd A. Spencer, *War and Post-war Greece—An Analysis Based on Greek Writings* (Washington, 1952). The contrast of right-wing and left-wing views may be seen in: F. A. Voigt, *The Greek Sedition* (London, 1949), and L. G. Stavrianos, *Greece—American Dilemma and Opportunity* (Chicago, 1952). The most reliable study of the Cyprus dispute is the work of Professor Georges Crouzet, of the University of Lille, not yet published. The best account of the Greek Communist Party (KKE) is *Revolution and Defeat* by Professor George Kousoulas (London, 1965).

INDEX

Abdul Hamid, 107-8
Abraham's Sacrifice, 135
Abyssinia, 133
Acarnania, 65, 66, 79, 97
  rising against Turks (1585), 83
  nationalist rising (1862), 100
Acciajuoli, 60
Achaean League, 28, 31
Achaeans, 4, 13
Achaia, principality of, 53, 61-4, 71
Acropolis,
  lords of, 8
  museum, 12
  Turkish garrison, 97
Actium, battle of, 31
Adrianople, 57, 111, 117
  captured by Turks, 77
  treaty of, 96
Aegean Islands, 78
Aegina, 82
  temple of, 21
Aegospotami, battle of, 19
Aenos, 69
Aeschylus, dramatist, 24
Aetolia, 65, 66, 79
  fortifications, 29
  revolt against Turkey, 83
Aetolian League, 28
Aetolians, guardians of Delphi, 28
Agathias, 73
Ainos, 111
Akkerman, contention of, (1826), 95-6
Albania,
  Albanian colonization of Attica, 61, 63
  dispute over Epirus, 66
  resistance to Turks, 77, 81, 83, 87
  settlement in Aegean islands, 78
  rise of national feeling, 90
  independence established (1804), 90
  remains in Turkish hands, 105
  independence (1912), 111
  granted Epirus (1921), 121
  invaded by Mussolini, 138, 140-2
  Italian interest in, 114, 131, 134
  post-war relations with Greece, 153, 163
  and Balkan pacts, 132, 170

Alexander, King, 115, 119
Alexander I, Tsar, 92, 95
Alexander the Great, 25-6
Alexandria, 36, 137
Alexandroúpolis, 116-17
Alfred, Prince, son of Queen Victoria, 101
Ali Pasha, 90-1
Aliakmon, River, 142-3
Allied Mission for Observing the Greek Elections, 154
Allied Supreme Council, 117
Amalfi, 48, 52
Amalia, Queen of Greece, 99-101
Ambatielos, Mrs, 179
American Mission for Aid to Greece, 155
AMFOGE, 154
Amvrakía, 97
Anaximander, philosopher, 13
Andros, 64
Angerins, 63
Ankara, 120, 164
Anna Comnena, historian, 47
Anne-Marie of Denmark, 183
anti-monarchist groups, 145-8, 150
Antigone, character in drama, 129
Antioch, 36
Apollo, temple of, 21
'Apollo Belvedere', 29
Arcadia, 43
Archipelago, duchy of, 53, 63-4, 67, 83
architecture,
  early Greek, 12-13
  orders, 13-14
  4th and 5th centuries B.C., 21-2
  Hellenistic, 29
  Graeco-Roman, 33
  Byzantine, 75-6
Argolis, 4
Argos, 16, 63, 82
Argyrokastron, 140
Aristophanes, dramatist, 24
Aristotle, philosopher, 25
armatoli, 82
art,
  Minoan, 3
  geometric, 7, 11

INDEX

art *(cont.)*
  in 5th century B.C., 19-21
  Byzantine, 74-5
Arta, 65, 105, 109
  Gulf of, 97
Asia Minor,
  Ionian cities, 11, 15
  epic poetry in, 13
  invaded by Alexander, 26
  Hellenistic building, 29
  Byzantine Empire in, 54-6
  disastrous campaign of, 1920-21, 117-21
  and see Turkey
Aspropotamos, 97
Assembly,
  Athenian, *see* Athenian
  National, *see* National
Athena, statue of, 23
Athenian Assembly, 18
Athenian Empire, 16-19
Athens,
  rise of, 8
  in Persian wars, 15, 18
  confederacy and empire of, 16-19
  privileged under Romans, 31
  sacked by Sulla, 31
  visited by St. Paul, 32
  attacked by Goths, 32
  duchy of, 53, 58-61
  and duchy of Neopatras, 58
  conquered by Turks, 77
  captured by Venetians, 84
  capital of independent Greece, 97
  revolt against Ortho, 100
  growth of population, 101
  seized by League of Officers, 108
  controlled by Allies (1916), 115
  modern literature, 136
  resistance in, 146-7
  post-war riots, 151, 166
  buildings of, 33
  and see National Museum *and* University
Attalus, Portico of, 29
Attica, 7-8
  attacked by Persians, 15
  Albanian colonization, 61, 63
Australians, 143
Austria, 86
Avars, 38-40
Averoff, cruiser, 127

Avyi, 176
Axis Powers, *see* Germany *and* Italy
Ayia Triada, palace of, 3

Baldwin I, Lord of Flanders, 52-3
Baldwin II, 54
Balkan Chamber of Commerce, 132
Balkan Conferences, 132-3
Balkan Entente, 133-4, 138
Balkan Pact, 133, 164, 170, 174
Balkan Wars, 109-13
Balkans,
  Greek inter-war relations, 131-5
  move towards unity, 131-2
Bamberg, 100
barbarian invasions, 37-8
Bassae, temple of, 21
Bavaria, 97
Bavarian Regents, 98-9
beehive tombs, 5
Belgrade, 116, 142, 156
Benedict of Peterborough, chronicler, 49
Benjamin of Tudela, 47, 50
Berlin, Congress of, 105
Bible, 36
Bled, Alliance of, 164
Boeotia, 4, 8, 79
  battle of, 59
Boniface of Montferrat, 58, 61
Bosnia, 80, 108
Boudonitza, marquess of, 68
Brioni, 172
Britain,
  in War of Independence, 93-6
  blockades Piraeus, 99-100
  possible source of new royal family, 101
  cedes Ionian Islands, 101-2
  and Cretan plebiscite, 103
  at Congress of Berlin, 105
  and Cyprus, 105, 123, 165-73
  in World War I, 113-16
  and Greek trade, 129
  guarantees Greek territories, 138-9
  help in World War II, 140-2, 145-6
  Military Mission to Guerillas, 147, 149
  supports king, 146, 148, 150
  keeps troops in Greece, 150-1
  votes against Enosis at U.N., 166
  sends troops to Cyprus, 182

INDEX

British Labour Party, 171
Brusa, 77
Bucharest, Treaty of (1812), 92, 111
Budapest, 175
Bulgaria,
 early invasions by Bulgars, 38, 41, 43–6, 58
 resistance to Turks, 77
 Exarchate, 103, 107
 granted Independence by Sultan (1878), 107–8
 treaty with Serbia, 110, 114
 in World War I, 115–16
 inter-war 'Balkan Conferences', 131–5
 offered free zone in Salonica, 138
 invaded by German troops, 141–2
 annexes Macedonia and Thrace, 143
 condemned by U.N., 158
 post-war relations with Greece, 163, 170, 172
Bury, J. B., 40
Byron, Lord, 88, 94
Byzantine Empire, *see* East Roman Empire
Byzantine Greece,
 economic development of, 48–50
 political condition, 50–1
 western interference, 51–2
 literature, 72–3
 art, 74–5
 architecture, 75–6

Caesar, Julius, 31
Cairo, 148, 149
Calabria, 80
Canning, George, prime minister, 93, 95
Canning, Stratford, British ambassador, 95–6
Capodistrias, president, 92, 93, 94
 assassinated, 96
Carlowitz, Treaty of (1699), 84
Catalan Company, 58
Catalans, 59–60, 83
Catherine the Great, Empress of Russia, 86, 87
Cavafy, Constantine, 136–7
Cazas, 79
Cecaumenos, writer, 46
centralization, Bavarian policy of, 99

Centre Union, 180, 182
Cephalonid, palatinate of, 53, 64–5, 77, 82
Cerigo, 68, 85
Cerigotto, 68, 85
Chaeronea, battle of (338 B.C.), 25
Chalcocondyles, Laonicos, historian, 73
Chamber of Deputies, *see* Deputies
Champlitte, William of, 61
Charles I, King of Naples, 62
Chatalija, 117
China, Communist, 172
Chios, 55
 Genoese settlement of, 69
 taken by Turks (1566), 78, 83
 represented at 4th National Assembly, 97
 centre for revolutionary army (1922), 120, 126
Christianity, 32
 becomes official religion of Roman Empire, 36
 adopted by Bulgars (863), 44
Chronicle of the Morea, 71
Church, Sir Richard, 94
Churchill, Sir Winston, 146, 151
Cithaeron, Mount, 16
city states, 7–9
 rivalry in, 19
 after Macedonian Empire, 27
 leagues of, 27
 under Pax Romana, 31
civilizations,
 Helladic, 2, 4
 Minoan, 2
 Mycenaean, 4
 Hellenic, 11
 Of the 4th and 5th Centuries B.C., 19–25
 Hellenistic, 29–30
 Frankish, 71–2
Claras, Athanasios, 149, 151
Cleisthenese, reforms of, 8
Cnossus, 1, 3, 126
Cochrane, Lord, 94
coins, Greek, 12
colonization, 9–11
 early Greek, 9
 Albanian, 61
 Venetian, 67–8
 Genoese, 68–9

191

INDEX

Cominform, 156, 158
Comnena, Anna, *see* Anna Comnena
Comnenus, Michael Angelus, 65
Commission of Control, 106
'Committee of Union and Progress', 108
Common Market, 176, 177
Communist Party of Greece, *see* KKE
Communists, 128, 145
Conference of Ambassadors (1921), 121
Congress of Berlin, 105
Constantine, Emperor, 35, 36
Constantine, Porphyrogenitus, historian, 41
Constantine I, King of Greece,
  leads Greek army in Balkan wars, 110
  relations with Venizelos, 113, 114, 120
  abdicates (1917), 115
  returns after plebiscite, 119
  abdicates (1922), 120, 124
  newspaper story about, 178
Constantine II, King of Greece,
  accession of, 183
  marriage, 183
Constantinople,
  made capital of East Roman Empire, 35
  Council of (381 A.D.), 36
  raided by Barbarians, 38, 40, 41, 43
  in the Fourth Crusade, 48, 52, 56
  Genoese quarter of, 69
  art in, 74–6
  fall of, 77, 135
  centre of Turkish government, 78
  Russian designs on, 86, 87
  Patriarch executed at, 93
  Treaty of (1913), 111
  proposed as an international city, 117
  see also Istanbul
Constitution, Greek,
  not desired by Russia, 98
  accepted by Otho I, 99
  of 1864, 103
  of 1925, 124
  of 1927, 125
'Constitution of Epidaurus' (1822), 93
'Constitution of Troizen' (1827), 94
Convention of Akkerman, *see* Akkerman
Corfu,
  occupied by Normans, 51
  occupied by Venetians, 65
  special arrangements over (1914), 112
  pact of (1917), 115
  anxieties over (1939), 138
Corinth,
  prehistoric, 1
  Helladic civilization in, 4
  city-state, 16
  in Peloponnesian wars, 19
  Pan Hellenic Congress at (337 B.C.), 25–6
  Roman villa mosaics, 29
  destroyed by Romans, 31
  refounded (44 B.C.), 31
  visited by St Paul, 32
  invaded by Normans, 51
Corinth Canal, 157
Coron, 62–3, 82
Corsica, 84
Cos, 109
Costoboci, 32
Council of Constantinople (381 A.D.), 36
Crete,
  neolithic culture, 1
  Minoan culture, 3–4, 11
  terra-cotta sculpture in, 12
  civil wars in, 16
  raided by Slavs, 40
  centre of slave trade, 49
  conquered by Turks, 78, 83–5
  Cretan War (1645–69), 83–5
  given to Mehemet Ali, 94
  not included in Independent Greece until 1912, 97
  insurrection of 1866, 103
  plebiscite rejected, 103
  armed for war against Turks, 106
  movement to join Greece, 106–9
  attacked by Germans, 143
  German occupation, 144, 152
Crimea,
  Greek emigration to, 87
  Turkish and Russian tension over (1787), 88
Crimean War, 100
Crispi, 64
Crispo, Francesco, 64
Critobulos of Imbros, 73
Croats, 39
Crusade, Fourth, 52, 64, 135

INDEX

Cumans, 38, 43
currency crisis of 1931, 126
Curzon, Lord, 120
Cyclades islands, 63, 72, 87
Cydonia, 16
Cyprus,
  Mycenaean influence, 6, 11
  Knights of St John, 70
  ceded to Britain, 105
  dispute with Britain, 121–4, 153, 163, 165–73
  unofficial plebiscite (1950), 165
  constitutional crisis (1964), 181–2
Cyrenaica, 109
Czechoslovakia,
  trade agreements, 164, 177

Dalmatia, 83
Damascus, Great Mosque of, 74
Damaskinos, Archbishop, 151, 153
Danube, frontier of Roman Empire, 35–9, 43
Daphni, 74, 76
Dardanelles, 6, 113–14, 117
Darius, King of Persia, 15
Dedeagach, *see* Alexandroúpolis
de Gaulle, General, 161
de la Roche, Guy, 59
de la Roche, Othon, 59
Delegeorges, Epaminondas, 100
Deligiannis, premier, 105–6
Delos, 16, 29
Delphi, 9, 21
Demertzig, 128
democracy, Athenian, 16
Demosthenes, orator, 24–5
demotic Greek, 135–6
Denmark, Greek Royal Family from, 101, 183
Deputies, Chamber of (Vouli), 99
Derby, Lord, 103
devaluation of *drachma*, 163
de Villehardouin, Geoffrey, 61–2
de Villehardouin, Isabella, 62
de Villehardouin, William, 62, 71
Digenis Akritas, 73
Dill, General, 141
Diocletian, Emperor, 35–6
Diomedes, Alexander, 158–9
'Discobolus' (Discus-thrower), 23
d'Istria, Capo, *see* Capodistrias

Dodecanese,
  occupied by Italy, 109–12, 114, 121
  declaration by Venizelos, 131
  occupied by Germans, 152
  ceded to Greece (1948), 153, 157
  Leros fortifications dismantled, 170
Don Carlos of Spain, 178
Doria, Andrea, 82
Dorian invasions, 6–7
'Doryphorus' (Athlete with Spear), 23
drama, origin of Attic, 24
Ducas, historian, 73
Durazzo, 51, 113
Dushan, Stephen, 56–7, 66
'Dying Gaul', 30

EAM, 147–51
Eastern Roumelia, 107
Eastern Roman Empire, 35–52
  annexes Thessaly, 58
  breaks up, 61
Echo, Portico of, 29
economy, Greek, 9, 48, 101, 129, 138–9, 152–3, 176–7
EDA, 161–3, 176, 180, 181, 182, 183
Eden, Sir Anthony, 141, 151, 169
EDES, 147–9, 151, 155
Egypt,
  Cretan trade with, 3
  art in, 3
  Ptolemies rule in, 27
  Hellenistic building in, 29
  in the Fourth Crusade, 52
  and War of Independence, 94–6
  government in exile, 143, 145, 148
  claim to Sudan recognized, 161
Eisenhower, General, 175
Eisenhower Doctrine, 171
ELAS, 147–51
Eleftheria, 178
Eleutherae, fortifications at, 21
Elis, 43, 95
Empires,
  Persian, 15
  Athenian, 16–19
  Macedonian, 25–6
  Eastern Roman, 35–52
  Bulgarian, 45, 50
  Turkish, 77–90
Enez, 111
England, *see* Britain

INDEX

énosis, 165, 182, 183
Entente,
  Little, 131–4
  Balkan, 133–4, 138
Enver Bey, 108, 110
EOKA, 168, 169
EPEK, 159, 160, 163
Ephesus, 29, 75
Epic, 13, 23, 30
Epicurus (341–270 B.C.), 30
Epidaurus,
  temple of, 21, 23
  gymnasium of, 21
Epirus,
  attacked by barbarians, 38, 45
  retained in Byzantine Empire, 53, 56
  annexes Salonica (1223), 58
  occupied by Tocco family (1418), 61
  under the Franks, 65–6
  sanjak of, 79
  delegates at Fourth National Assembly, 97
  rising in (1878), 104, 108
  occupied by Italian Troops, 114
'Epirus Northern', 140–1
ERE, 167, 181, 182
Erechtheum, 21
Euripides, dramatist, 24
Erophile, 135
Erotokristos, 135
Euboea, 79, 82, 84, 97
European Economic Community, 176–7
Exarchate, 107
Ezerites, 41

Fabvier, 94
Ferdinand, King of Bulgaria, 108, 116
feudalism, 71
Flamininus, Roman consul, 28
Flemings, the, 62
Florence, 135
Foot, Sir Hugh, 171–2
Fort Roupel, 114
fortifications of ancient Greece, 21
France,
  and War of Independence, 91–6
  and monarchy, 101
  efforts against Mussolini, 138–9

Franco-Italian Agreement (1935), 133
Franks, 65
  influence on countryside, 72
  influence on Byzantine literature, 73
Frederic II, King of Sicily, 59
Frederika, Queen of Greece, 179, 183
freedom, discussed by Socrates, 24
French Revolution (1789), 88–89, 91
frescoes, 74–5
Froissart, 65

Gabalas, Leon, 69
Gallipoli, 113, 117
Garibaldi, 100
Gauls, at Delphi, 28
Geneva, 108
Genoa,
  traders from, 48
  commercial privileges of, 52
  colonization, 68–9
  loss of Chios, 83
geometric art, 11
George I, King of Greece, 101–9
George II, King of Greece,
  High Commissioner of Crete, 107
  suspected of pro-German sympathies, 115
  becomes king, 120
  leaves Greece, 124
  restored, 127–8
  promised fully representative government, 150
  referendum in favour of return, 154–5
  dies, 155
German Federal Republic, 164, 176
Germany, 133–4, 138, 141–3
  occupation of Greece, 143–52
Getae, 38
Gladstone, William, 103
Glezos, Manolis, 175
Gonnaris, 120
Gorgopotamos, 147, 157
Gortyn, 16
Goths, invade Athens, 32, 37
Grabusa, 84
Great War (1914–18), 113–16
Grivas, George, 165, 166, 173, 178, 182,
  forms EOKA, 168

194

INDEX

guerillas in World War II, 144-9
Gyparis, 135

Hadrian, Emperor (117-38), 31, 33
Hainaut, Florent, 62
Halepa, Pact of, 105
Hannibal, 28
haratch, 80
Harding, Field Marshal Sir John, 167, 171
Hastings, 95
Hecataeus, Greek thinker, 13
Herzegovina, 108
Helen of Troy, 6
Helladic Civilization, 4
Helle, 139
Hellenic Civilization, 11
Herodes Atticus, 33
Herodotus, historian, 24, 73
Hesiod, poet, 23
Hetairía, 88, 90, 91-2
Hitler, Adolf, 128, 138-40, 141-2
Hodja, Daut, 140
Holy Alliance, 92
Homer, 13, 23
Honorius III, Pope, 71
Hoover Moratorium, 132
Hosios Loukas, 74-5
Hungary, 141, 164
Huns, 38
Hydra, 91
Hymn to Liberty, 135

Ibrahim, 94-5
Icaria, 55
icons, 74, 75
ideology, differences between Athens and Sparta, 17
Iliad, 13
Imbros, 18, 19, 69, 78, 121
Imperial Army, 40
Independence, Greek War of (1821-32), 92-6
industrial expansion in Greece, 174
Industrial Development Corporation, 174
Ionia, 11, 13, 82, 91
Ionian Islands,
 captured by Turks, 77
 British rule in, 89, 100

returned to Greece, 101-2, 109
 school of poetry, 135-6
 earthquake, 163
Isidore of Seville, 40
Israel, 164
Istanbul, 10, 166
Isthmian games, 28
Istria, 87
Italy
 relations after 1919, 121-3
 pacts with Greece, 131, 134
 invasion of Greece, 140-1
 occupation of Greece, 143-4
 fall of Mussolini, 149
 and the Dodecanese, 151-3, 157
 improved relations with Greece, 161
Itea, 51
Ithaca, 4, 64, 77, 82

Janina, 65, 77, 83, 105, 110
janissaries, 80-1
Japan, 172
Jassy, treaty of, 88, 92
Jerusalem, 36, 52
Jews in Greece, 50
John of Ephesus, chronicler, 39
Justinian, Emperor, 36, 38, 39, 48

Kahriye Djameh, 74, 76
Kalamas, 105
Kalamata, battle of, 83
Kalvos, Andreas, 136
Karamanlis, Constantine, 167-70, 172, 174, 177, 180, 181, 183
Kardelj, 170
Karellopoulos, Parayiotis, 148, 154, 175, 181
Katharévousa, 136
Kathimerimi, 142
Kavalla, 111
Kazantzakis, Nikos, 137
Kemalists, 117
Khrushchev, 165, 175, 177
Khyber Pass, 26
'King of the Hellenes', 103
Kirk-Kilisse, 111
KKE, 147, 149
 attack guerilla forces, 151
 demand withdrawal of British troops, 154

195

INDEX

KKE *(cont.)*
  form rebel government (1947), 156–8
  formation of EDA, 161
  revives (1959), 175–6
Klephts, 82, 91, 107
Knights of St John, 70
Kolettis, 94, 99
Kolokotronis, 94
Kondilis, General, 125–6, 127, 128
Konduriotis, 128
Korais, Adamantios, 89
Korean War, 160
Koritsa, 140, 156
Koryzis, Alexander, 141, 143
Kossovo, battle of (1389), 57, 77
Kutchuk, Dr, 173
Kutschuk Kainardji, treaty of (1774), 87

Lambrakis, Grigorios, 179
language, Greek, 34, 36, 42
  dispute over, 136
Larissa, 51, 58
Lascaris, Theodore, 55
Laurium Silver Mines, 9
Lausanne,
  treaty of (1912), 110
  treaty of (1923), 120, 123
League of Nations, 130
League of Reservists, 115
Lebanon, 172
Lebanon Conference, 150
Leipsos, 109
Lemnos, 18, 19, 69, 77, 121, 130
Leo III, Emperor, 40
Leopold of Saxe-Coburg, Prince, 96–8
Lepanto, 63, 82
Leros, 170
Lesbos, 55, 69, 77
Leukas, 4
Libya, 10
Lie, Trygve, 155
Linear A, 3
Linear B, 3, 5
Literature,
  early Greek, 13
  in the fourth and fifth centuries, 23
  Hellenistic, 30
  Graeco-Roman, 34
  Byzantine, 72–3
  modern Greek, 135–7

Little Entente, 131–2, 133, 134
Lloyd, Selwyn, 172
Lloyd-George, David, 119
Logothetopoulos, 147–8
London Conferences,
  of 1921, 119
  on Eastern Mediterranean, 166
  on Cyprus, 173
London, treaties of,
  1827, 95–6
  1912, 111
  1915, 114
Louis I, King of Bavaria, 97
Lydia, 10, 15
Lysander, Spartan admiral, 19
Lysicrates, monument of, 21
Lysippus, 23

Macedonia,
  emerges as power, 19
  Macedonian Empire, 25–8
  Macedonian Wars, 28
  made Roman province, 28
  invaded by Slavs, 38–9
  colonized, 43, 45
  under Turks, 77, 80
  different nationalities in, 107
Macmillan, Harold, 172
Maina, 56, 62
  revolts against Turks, 83–5
Makarios, Archbishop, 165, 167–8, 170, 181–2
  goes to United Nations, 171
  agrees to independence of Cyprus, 173
  becomes President of Cyprus, 175
Malia, palace of, 3
Marathon, battle of, 15
Marcus Aurelius, 31
Maritza, the, 55
Maritza, battle of (1371), 57
Mark Antony, 31
Markezinis, Spyros, 163
Markos, 158
Marmora, Sea of, 56, 117
Mavrokordato, Alexander, 93, 99
Mavromikhalis, Stavros, 180
Maximos, Dimitrios, 155–6
Mehemet Ali, 90, 94
Melos, 64
Melos, Aphrodite of, 29
Menelaus, King of Sparta, 6

INDEX

Merten, Max, 176
Messenia, 4, 95
Metaxas, General John,
   governs by decree, 128-9
   foreign policy of, 133-4, 139-41
   his régime discredited, 145-6
Metternich, 92-3, 96
Miaoulis, Andreas, 93
Midia, 111
Miletus, 10
Milings, the, 41
Military League of Officers, 108
Miller, W., 41
Minoan civilization, 3-4
Minos, King, 3
Missolonghi, 94
Mistra, fortress of, 56, 62
Modon, 61-3, 82, 94
Moldavia, 90-1
Monemvasia, rock of, 56, 62, 82, 84
Monastir, 115
Montenegro, 110
Montreux Convention, 130
Morea, 79, 82, 84
'Morokampos', 49
Morosini, Francesco, 68, 84
Mosaics, 74-5
Moslems, 37, 49, 80
Mummius, 33
Mussolini,
   promotes Balkan pacts, 131
   invades Albania, 138
   first attacks on Greece, 139-41
Mycenaean civilization, 3, 4-6
Mykonos, 82
Myrivilis, Stratis, 137
Myron, sculptor, 23
Mytilene, 97

Nagy, Imre, 175
Naples, 64
Napoleon, 89, 91-2
Napoleon III, 103
Nasi, Joseph, 64
national anthem, Greek, 135
National Assembly, 93, 95, 101
   fourth, 97
   'Second Revisionary', 108-9
   fifth, 127
national dress, 99
National Museum of Athens, 23

'National Party', 99, 105
nationalism, Greek, 88-90
N.A.T.O., 160-1, 167-8, 170, 173, 177
Nauplia, 63, 82, 98, 100
Navarino, battle of, 96
Navarrese Company, 63
navy, Greek, 130
Naxos, 64, 78
Nero, Emperor, 31, 33
Neuilly, treaty of (1919), 116-17, 135
New Zealanders, 143
Nicaea, 53, 54, 55,
   merged with Constantinople, 56, 58
   conquered Salonica, 65
   helped by Genoese, 68
Nicholas I, Tsar of Russia, 95
Niketas, historian, 50
Nobel prize, 136
Normans, 51

Octavian, 31
Odessa, 90, 91
Odeum, the, 33
Odyssey, 13
Oeniadae, 29
Olympia, 9, 21, 29
Olympic games, 23
orders of architecture, 13
Organic Statute, 103, 105
Orloff brothers, 86
Orsini, Matteo, 64
Orthodox Religion, 42, 99
   relations with Moslems, 79-80
   Russian influence in Greek Orthodoxy, 86-7
Ostrogoths, 38
Otho I, King of Greece, 97-101
Otranto, Straits of, 51

palaces, Mycenaean, 3, 5, 6
Palaeologus, family of, 55
Palamas, Kostes, 136
Pallavicini, 58
Palmerston, 97, 99-100
Pangalos, General, 124, 129
Pan-Hellenic Congress, 25
Pan-Hellenic games, 10
Pan-Slav risings, 104-5

197

INDEX

Papagos, General
  Chief of Staff, 140
  Commander-in-Chief, 158
  misunderstands British, 172–3
  resigns and forms Greek rally, 160–3
  and Cyprus dispute, 165–7
Papanastasion, 124–6, 132
Papandreou, 150–1, 175, 178, 180–3
Paris, 108
Parma, 58
Parthenon, 21–3
'Parties' in the War of Independence, 94
Partsaldis, 158
Patras, 151
  Siege of (807), 41
Patriarch of Constantinople, 99, 103–4
Patzinacs, 38, 43
Paul I, King of Greece, 119, 155, 168, 178
  State visit to London, 179–80
  death of, 182
Paul, the Silentiary, 72
Pausanias, geographer, 32
Pax Romana, 30, 32
PEEA, 150
Peirene Fountain, 33
Peisistratus, 8
Peloponnese,
  in the Byzantine Empire, 56, 57
  Frankish influence in, 61
  under Turks, 63, 75, 79
  and Mehemet Ali, 94, 96
Peloponnesian War, 17–19
Pergamum, 29
Pericles, 16, 18, 129
Perseus, King of Macedonia, 28
Persian Empire, 15, 26
Peter the Great (1689–1725), 86
Phaestus, palace of, 3
Pharsalus, battle of, 31
Phidias, sculptor, 23
Philip of Macedon (359–336 B.C.), 25, 36
Philip V, King of Macedonia, 28
Phocea, 10, 69
Piedmontese, the, 62
Pindar, poet (522–450 B.C.), 23
Pinerolo Division, 149
Piniós, 105
Pipinelis, Panayiotus, 180

piracy, 49, 83
Piraeus, 31, 100–1
Pisa, 52
Pisides, George, 72
Plague, Great (746), 41
Plastiras, Colonel, 120, 126–7, 151, 153, 159
Plataea, battle of, 16
Plato, 25
Plutarch, historian (42–120), 34
poetry,
  modern Greek, 135–7
Poland, 172, 177
political parties in the Republic, 124
Polybius, historian (202–120 B.C.), 16, 30, 34, 73
Polycletus, sculptor, 23
Pompey, 31
population,
  in the 19th century, 101
  exchange of Greek and Turkish, 117, 121
Populist party, 124, 126, 154, 159, 160, 167
Poros, 97
pottery,
  Helladic, 4
  in the Dark Ages, 7
  Athenian, 12
Praxiteles, sculptor, 23
Prevelakis, Pantelis, 137
Preveza, 105
Procopius, historian, 39, 73
Propylaea, 21
prose, modern Greek, 137
Protocol, the (1826), 95,
  (1830), 101
Psaros, Colonel Dimitrios, 148
Psycharis, John,
  My Journey, 136
Ptochoprodromos, 73
Ptolemies, 27
Punic Wars, 28
Pydna, battle of (168 B.C.), 28
Pylus, 3, 6
Pythagoras, Greek thinker, 13

Quadruple Alliance, 92

Radcliffe, Lord, 169
R.A.F., 140
Rallis, John, 148
rally, Greek, 161, 162

INDEX

Ravenna, 74, 75, 76
refugees (1947), 157
Republican Officers League, 124
Republic, Greek, 124-7
resistance movements, 145-7, 148-9, 154
revolution of September 1843, 99, 101
Rhigas, Constantine (1760-98), 88-9
Rhodes, 109, 121
  School of Sculpture, 20
  Knights of, 54, 69-70
Roger of Sicily, 51
Roidis, Emmanuel, 137
Roman Catholic Church, 64, 71
Romania,
  Latin empire of, 54
  overtures to (1912), 110
  and Treaty of Neuilly, 116
  Greek pact with, 131-4
  occupied by Germans, 141
  post-war reconciliation, 164, 170
Rome, 75, 76, 135
  treaty of, 176
Roosevelt, President, 146
Royal Navy, 143
Royal Welfare Fund, 178
Russell, Lord John, 100
Russia,
  influence on Greek affairs, 86-8
  and War of Independence, 91-6
  and monarchy, 98, 101
  Germany attacks, 145
  refuses to join AMFOGE, 154
  trade agreement (1958), 172
Russo-Turkish War (1877-8), 104-5

St Demetrius, 40
St Mark's, 76
St Paul, 32
St Sophia, 74, 76, 79
Sakaria, 120
Salamis, Bay of, 15
Salamvrias, 105
Salonica,
  attacked by barbarians, 40, 43
  annexed by Serbs, 56-7
  under Boniface of Montferrat, 58-9
  new Greek Empire of, 65
  art and architecture in, 74, 75
  under Turks, 77, 79
  headquarters of Committee of Union and Progress, 108

Yugoslavian claims on, 131
  free zone, 138
  riots over Cyprus question, 166
  Pact of, 134
Samos, 10, 55, 97
  Assembly of, 112
Samothrace, 69, 77, 121, 130
San Stephano, Treaty of, 150
Sanjaks, 79
Santa Maura, 65, 77, 84
Sanudo Marino, historian, 71
Saracens, 41
Saraphis, Colonel Stephanos, 148, 150
Schacht, Dr, 133
'Sclavinia', 41
Scobie, General, 150
sculpture,
  early Greek, 12
  in fourth and fifth centuries, 22
  Hellenistic, 29
  Graeco-Roman, 33
  Byzantine, 75
Scutari, 111
Scyros, 18-19
Scythians, 38
Seferis, George, 136
Selevcids, 27
Senate (Yerousía), 99
Serbia, 39, 56, 77, 107
  revolt against Turks, 90
  treaty with Bulgaria, 110
Sèvres, Treaty of, 117, 119, 121
Seychelles, Islands, 168, 170
Shaft Graves, 5
Shepilov, 168
Sicily, 3, 12, 18, 83
Sikelianos, Angelos, 136
Silkworm, 49
Simeon the Great (893-927), 45
Skaramanga, 174
Slavery, 8
Slavs, 38-43
Slovenes, 39
Smyrna, 69, 117, 120, 167
Socrates, 24-5
Sofia, 79, 117
Solomos, Dionysios, 135
Solon, 8
Sophia, Princess, 178
Sophocles, dramatist, 24
Sophoulis, Themistoklis, 153-4, 156-8
Spain, 3, 164

INDEX

Sparta, 15–19
  under Romans, 31
Sperchios, 4
Spezzia, 91
Sphrantzes, historian, 73
Spinalonga, 84
Sporades, 82
'Springtime of Greece', 11
Stalin, 141
Staurakios, General, 41
Stephanopoulos, Stephanos, 167
Strabo, geographer, 31–2
Strategicon, 46
Suda, 84
Sulla, Roman general, 31, 33
Sumeria, 3
Sunium, temple of, 21
Sweden, 147
Synod of Athens, 103
Syracuse, 10
Syria,
  Minoan trade with, 3
  Seleucid rule, 27
  Hellenistic building, 29
  French interest, 123

Taranto, 10
Taygetos, Mount, 41, 62
Tegea, temple of, 21
temple, Greek,
  arrangement of, 13
  zenith of, 21
Tenedos, 121
Tenos, 68, 77, 82, 84, 139
Thales, Greek thinker, 13
Thasos, 69, 77
theatres, in Ancient Greece, 21
Thebes, 16, 59
  silk industry, 49–51
Theocritus, poet, 30
Theotokas, George, 137
Theotokis, Ion, 159
Thermopylae, battle of, 15
Theseum, building of, 21
Thessalonians, Epistle, 32
Thessaly,
  prehistory, 1, 3
  invaded by Slavs, 38
  Wallachian, 56, 58

conquered by Turks (1393), 57, 76, 78–9
movements towards treedom, 97, 100, 103
obtained by Greece (1878), 105, 109
Thiamis, 105
Thrace,
  in Peloponnesian war, 18
  Slav conquest, 39, 43
  Latin rule, 54
  Byzantine rule, 56
  Turkish campaign in, 77
  ceded to Greece (1919), 116–17
  frontier revised, 121
Thucydides, historian, 17, 24, 73
Tigris, river, 35
Tilsit, meeting of Napoleon and Tsar (1807), 92
Tito, 158, 165, 174
Titulescu, M., 134
Tocco, family, 61, 65–6, 77
Torcello, 75
'Tower of the Winds', 29
trade, *see* economy
treasury, Athenian, 16
Trebizond, 53
Trikoupis, 99, 105
Tripoli, 109
Tripolitsa, battle of, 86
Trojan war, 6, 13
Truman, President, 155
Tsaldaris, 125–8
Tsaldaris, Constantine, 154–6, 159–60
Tsolakoglou, General, 143, 147
Tsouderos, Emmanuel, 143, 147–50, 159–60
Turks,
  rise of, 37, 56–7
  arrive in Europe (1354), 57, 77
  conquer Greece, 61, 65, 77–8
  conquer Archipelago (1566), 57, 64, 69–70
  political organization of Greece, 78–82
  resistance of Greeks and Venetians, 82–6
  conflicts with Russia, 86–8, 92
  decline of administration, 89–90
  and War of Independence, 91–6
  fleet destroyed at Navarino, 96
  position at independence settlement, 97

INDEX

Turks *(cont.)*
  declare war on Greece (1897), 106
  Peace Treaty (1919), 117–19
  reconciliation with Greece (1930), 126, 130–4
  escape route in World War II, 145
  'Truman Doctrine', 155
  join NATO, 160
  Balkan Alliance, 164
  Cyprus dispute, 165–73, 181–3
Tuscany, 83

United Arab Republic, 171
United Nations,
  Greece joins, 147
  Commission (1947), 155–8
  and Cyprus, 165–73, 181–2
University of Athens, 31, 36, 100, 129
UNRRA, 151
UNSCOB, 156, 158, 161
U.S.A.,
  in World War II, 146–7, 151
  economic aid, 155–7, 160
  influences Greek politics, 159
  votes against Enosis at U.N., 166, 171
  bases in Greece, 170–1
  agreement with Greece on nuclear weapons, 177
  and Cyprus, 182
U.S.S.R., *see* Russia
Uzes, 43

Valaoritis, Aristoteles, 136
Valerian, Emperor, 32
Valona, 141
Vaphiadis, Markos, 156
Varkiza, 151, 154
Varvaressos, Professor, 153, 163
vase painting, 7, 11–12
Vassilikos, Vassilis, 137
Velegezêtes, 40
Velestino, 58
Velestinon, 40
Veloukhiotis, Aris, *see* Claras
Venezis, Elias, 137
Venice, rise of, 48, 51–3
  possessions (1204–1797), 56, 63–8
  wars with Turkey, 82–6
  extinction of Venetian Republic (1797), 90
  culture, 135
Venizelists, 155–6

Venizelos, Eleutherios, premier,
  Cretan councillor, 107
  Prime Minister (1910–20), 108–10, 113–19, 121
  Prime Minister (1924), 124
  Prime Minister (1928–32), 125–6, 130–2
  death, 127–8
Venizelos, Sophoklis, premier, 150, 154, 159–60, 175, 178, 180–1, 183
Ventris, Michael, 5
Victoria, Queen of England, 101
'Victory', 30
Vienna, 86
  Congress of (1815), 90, 92
Visigoths, 37
Vlachia,
  Great and Little, 46
  see also Wallachia
Vlachs, the, 45–50, 77, 107
Vlakhos, 142
Volos, 166
  Gulf of, 97
Voltaire, 79, 85
Voulgaris, Admiral, 153
Vouli, 99

Wallachia, 47, 90–1
  'Great W.', 58
Wavell, General, 141
Wellington, Duke of, 95–7
William, Prince of Wied, 113
William the Conqueror, 51
Wilson, General, 143
World War I, 113–16
World War II, 139–51

Xanthe, 111
Xenopoulos, Gregorios, 137
Xerxes, King of Persia, 15

Yerousia, 99
'Young Turks', 108–9
Yugoslavia,
  formation of, 115
  Greek inter-war relations with, 131–4
  in World War II, 138, 141–2, 147
  accused of inciting rebellion in Greece, 155, 158
  post-war agreements, 160–1, 164, 170–2, 174

INDEX

Zaccaria, 69
Zaimis, 128
Zakhariadis, Nikos, 158
Zante, 64, 77, 82
Zara, 52
Zeitoun, Gulf of, 97

Zervas, Napoleon, General, 148–151, 155–6
Zeus,
   Olympia, statue of Z., 23
   altar to, 29
Zurich–London agreements, 183